THE
WASHINGTON

REDSKINS

An Illustrated History

RICHARD WHITTINGHAM

SIMON AND SCHUSTER
New York London Toronto Sydney Tokyo Singapore

Simon and Schuster
Simon & Schuster Building
Rockefeller Center
1230 Avenue of the Americas
New York, New York 10020

Copyright © 1990 by Richard Whittingham

All rights reserved
including the right of reproduction
in whole or in part in any form.

SIMON AND SCHUSTER and colophon are registered trademarks
of Simon & Schuster Inc.

Designed by Irving Perkins Associates
Manufactured in the United States of America

1   3   5   7   9   10   8   6   4   2

Library of Congress Cataloging-in-Publication Data

Whittingham, Richard, date.
    The Washington Redskins : an illustrated history/Richard
Whittingham.
        p. cm.
    1. Washington Redskins (Football team)—History.   I. Title.
GV956.W3W47   1990
796.332′64′09753—dc20   90-34205
                                                                                    CIP

ISBN 0-671-66036-5

This book is dedicated to all those stalwart Redskins who have toiled in burgundy and gold from the day in 1932 when the franchise debuted through today, and the legion of dedicated Washington Redskins fans who were always there to share the excitement, entertainment, agonies, and ecstasies, and provide the support that makes it all so worthwhile.

Acknowledgments

The author and publisher would like to extend their deepest appreciation to the Washington Redskins organization for the generous cooperation and assistance they rendered during the course of the research and writing of this book. Special thanks are extended to Redskins Executive Vice President John Kent Cooke and Vice President of Communications Charlie Dayton.

Special thanks are also due to the Pro Football Hall of Fame in Canton, Ohio, especially curator and archivist Joe Horrigan, and National Football League Properties, especially Sharon Kuthe, for their help in many and various aspects of the development of this book.

The author also thanks all those who sat for interviews or otherwise provided information that was essential in terms of accuracy and entertainment in the creation of this history of one of the NFL's noblest franchises.

Contents

1

A Birth in Boston

The year was 1932. The United States was well into the Great Depression, Franklin Delano Roosevelt was out campaigning for the first time for the presidency of the United States while in Germany rabble-rousing Adolph Hitler was coming into power. Amelia Earhart had just become the first woman to fly across the Atlantic solo, famine was sweeping the Soviet Union, and a tall, arrogant, flamboyant laundry tycoon decided to diversify his business interests and launch a professional football team in Boston.

George Preston Marshall, who owned a string of laundries in the Washington, D.C. area, as well as a team in the old National Basketball League, was persuaded by two acquaintances he had made from the basketball circuit, National Football League president Joe Carr and Chicago Bears owner

George Halas, to take on the newly available NFL franchise for Boston.

Marshall lined up three partners: Larry Doyle, a New York stockbroker; Jay O'Brien, a New York investment banker; and Vincent Bendix, an automotive supplier in South Bend, Indiana. The franchise's self-appointed chief executive officer, Marshall, then signed a contract to play the team's games at Braves Field, which was the home of the Boston Braves of baseball's National League. The laundryman promptly dubbed his team the Braves as well.

The Boston Braves were not the first professional football team to appear in Beantown. Back in 1926, in the first American Football League, which had been founded by C.C. "Cash and Carry" Pyle to compete with the NFL, there had been a Boston franchise known as the Bulldogs.

The franchise's first superstar, Cliff "Gip" Battles, was George Preston Marshall's personal pick to lead the Boston Braves into their first season in 1932. A tailback, fullback, and punter, Battles led the Braves/Redskins through the Boston years and earned a place in the Pro Football Hall of Fame. (HOF/NFL Photos)

That league had lasted only a year, however. The Boston Bulldogs were revived in 1929 as an NFL franchise, but after a lackluster season (4–4–0), and a profound failure to attract fans, the team went out of business.

Marshall was told that Boston was a wonderful baseball town; it supported two teams in the major leagues, the Braves and the Red Sox. College football also had a dedicated following at institutions like Harvard, Boston University, Boston College, and nearby schools such as Amherst, Holy Cross, Dartmouth, and Tufts. Marshall was warned, though, that Boston was not a city that waxed warmly to professional football, a game that, in those days, still drew the disdain of college football coaches and the apathy of many otherwise devoted sports fans. After all, it was less than a decade earlier that the legendary coach of the University of Chicago, Amos Alonzo Stagg, had condemned pro football as an insidious force, referring to it as a menace on a par with gambling. And Red Grange's coach at the University of Illinois, Bob Zuppke, had refused to talk to his great running back for several years after the Galloping Ghost signed with the NFL's Chicago Bears in 1925. Many of those same sentiments still lingered in ever-proper Boston, Marshall was informed. But with consummate faith in his entrepreneurial talents and his flair for promotion, the laundry magnate ignored the warning and set about organizing his team.

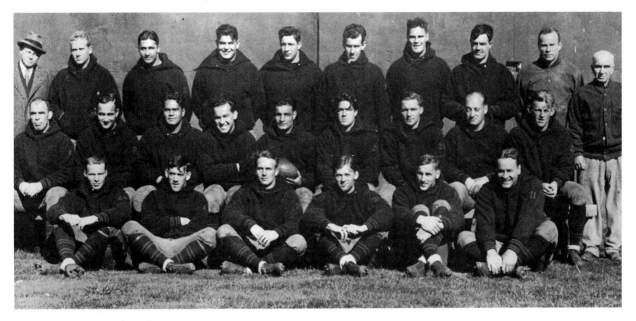

The First Team, The 1932 Boston Braves

Left to right:
Back row: Jack Potter (Mgr.), Reggie Rust, Basil Wilkerson, Turk Edwards, Jim MacMurdo, Dale Waters, Mickey Erickson, Paul Collins, Coach Lud Wray, Johnny Hagan (Trainer)
Middle row: John Spellman, Joe Kresky, Honolulu Hughes, George Hurley, Captain Tony Siano, Jim Musick, Jack Roberts, Paul Schuette, Oran Pape
Front row: Cliff Battles, George Kenneally, Lee Woodruff, Algy Clark, Nip Felber, Erny Pinckert (HOF/NFL Photos)

The National Football League in 1932 was a world away from the NFL of today. There were only eight teams, no divisions or conferences, no playoffs or formal championship game. Of the eight teams, only five franchises besides Mr. Marshall's would survive into the modern NFL: the Chicago Bears, the Green Bay Packers, the New York Giants, the Chicago (later St. Louis and still later Phoenix) Cardinals, and the Portsmouth (Ohio) Spartans, who would eventually relocate in Detroit and change their name to the Lions.

There was no uniformity of schedule in those early years of the league either. The Bears, for example, played 14 games in 1932, the Spartans 12, and Marshall's Braves just 10.

The NFL was still very young. Only 12 years had elapsed since Ralph Hay of the Canton Bulldogs, George Halas of the Decatur Staleys (soon-to-be Chicago Bears), and several other pro football owners had gotten together at the now-famous meeting in Hay's Hupmobile showroom in Canton on September 17, 1920, to organize what would become the National Football League. And it was only seven years since pro football had been put on the proverbial sports map by the game's most dazzling and most publicized running back, Red Grange. After joining the Chicago Bears in 1925, Grange was sent with them on a whirlwind barnstorming tour that took pro football from the Midwest to the East Coast, down to Florida, across the country to California, and up to the State of Washington. (During the first part of the junket the Bears played

The first two touchdowns the Braves scored in the Boston area are recorded for posterity. Above, halfback Tony Plansky runs 18 yards for the Braves' first touchdown. Below, fullback Jim Musick takes a lateral in for the second touchdown of the day.

an incredible eight games in 11 days in eight different cities.) When it was over, professional football had stepped out of its infancy with a following that had not been there before. No longer would teams perform on Sunday afternoons to crowds as small as two or three thousand, nor would game results and league standings be relegated to some inconspicuous slot inside the various newspapers' sports pages. It was, however, still a long way from the filled stadiums and front-page headlines, which would not come until after World War II.

By 1932 the league had had to withstand a variety of perils. Besides fan indifference during its first five years, there had also been the competition from a new league, the first AFL, to which Grange and a number of other important NFL players defected in 1926. There was also, of course, the onslaught of the worst economic depression in the nation's history.

None of this fazed George Preston Marshall. A supreme optimist—with an ego to match—in any venture, he looked with relish on the challenge of endearing professional football to the citizens of Boston, Massachusetts.

After securing a place to play, Marshall hired Lud Wray as head coach and gave him full responsibility for recruiting a team. Wray, who had played for the Buffalo All-Americans and Rochester Jeffersons in the NFL in the early 1920s, and had coached at his alma mater, the University of Pennsylvania, set about the task with enthusiasm.

"How do you go about assembling a brand-new football team?" James J. Haggerty asked in his book *Hail to the Redskins* in 1964. "In 1932, it wasn't all that difficult. The college draft had not yet been invented, so the entire collegiate pool was available and there were only eight NFL teams bidding. In addition, the folding of three teams

14

THE FIRST STARTING LINEUP, 1932
BOSTON BRAVES

		Hgt.	Wgt.	College
E	Paul Collins	6'1"	195	Pittsburgh
E	George Kenneally	6'	190	St. Bonaventure
T	Turk Edwards	6'2"	230	Washington State
T	Jim MacMurdo	6'1"	205	Pittsburgh
G	Joe Kresky	6'	210	Wisconsin
G	George Hurley	6'	200	Washington State
C	Mickey Erickson	6'2"	210	Northwestern
QB	Honolulu Hughes	5'10"	195	Oregon State
HB	Cliff Battles	6'1"	190	West Virginia Wesleyan
HB	Erny Pinckert	6'	200	Southern California
FB	Jim Musick	5'11"	205	Southern California

Coach Lud Wray

after the previous season had sent some 60 experienced pros scurrying for another chance.

"Wray signed up 40 players another 30 or more willing to pay their own expenses to Boston for a tryout came in over the transom. To save travel money, Marshall rented a bus on the West Coast. Albert Glen "Turk" Edwards, a very large tackle from Washington State, drove the bus cross-country, picking up the signees at various stops."

The biggest find was Marshall's, however, and it was one of pure serendipity. The youngster was Cliff "Gip" Battles from the obscure college of West Virginia Wesleyan.

Glen "Turk" Edwards, a bruising 260-pound tackle, was on hand from the very beginning, playing from 1932 through the move to Washington, where he retired after the 1940 season. An All-Pro four times, he was inducted into the Pro Football Hall of Fame in 1969. (HOF/NFL Photos)

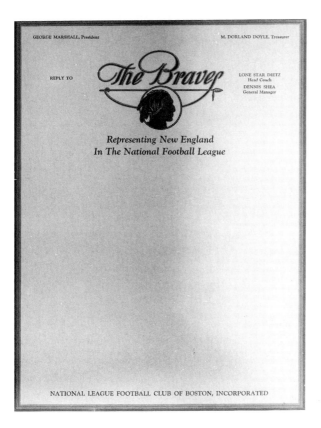

A fleet halfback who could also pass and kick, Battles had starred in a game the year before in Washington against Georgetown, which Marshall had just happened to attend. Now that he had a team, Marshall wanted Gip Battles on it and, as it was soon to become evident, George Preston usually got what he wanted. He sent a scout down to West Virginia to sign him. The scout allegedly asked, "What if he won't sign?" "Then just keep on going," Marshall is said to have told him. Battles was signed by Boston; it helped, of course, that the other NFL teams had not heard of him down at tiny West Virginia Wesleyan.

Other major acquisitions besides Battles and Turk Edwards, both of whom would eventually represent the Redskins in the Pro Football Hall of Fame, were two gifted backs from Southern Cal, Erny Pinckert, an exceptional blocking back, and Jim Musick, a punishing fullback.

The class of the league, however, was spread among three teams. The Green Bay Packers, coached by Curly Lambeau, had won three straight NFL titles. They had a balanced offense that featured the speed and pass-catching abilities of halfback Johnny "Blood" McNally; the league's top passer, tailback Arnie Herber; and the bruising power of fullback Clarke Hinkle. In addition, they boasted a pair of linemen destined for the Hall of Fame, tackle Cal Hubbard and guard Iron Mike Michalske.

There was also Green Bay's stalwart rival, the Chicago Bears, whose backfield show-

Fullback Ace Gutowsky of the Portsmouth Spartans is upended by Redskins defensive back Ike Frankiah in this 1933 game at Fenway Park. Number 57 is the helmetless Father Lumpkin, another well-known Portsmouth back. (HOF/NFL Photos)

MARSHALL'S CODE OF CONDUCT

In the 1930s, George Preston Marshall, as fastidious as he was stubborn, published a Code of Conduct for his players and distributed it.

You will be expected to conduct yourselves in such a manner as to always be a credit to the game and your club.

Violation of publicly accepted and traditional training rules for athletes—

rowdiness, boisterousness and ungentlemanly conduct of any and every sort will not be tolerated.

In hotel lobbies, dining rooms and restaurants, and at all public functions where the team appears as a unit, shirts, ties and coats are to be worn unless otherwise instructed.

Night clubs, bars, cocktail lounges and gambling spots are definitely out of bounds.

---

cased a pair of football legends, halfback Red Grange and fullback Bronko Nagurski. The Portsmouth Spartans were indeed a factor, too, guided on the field by All-Pro tailback Dutch Clark and augmented by two other exceptional backs, Ace Gutowsky and Father Lumpkin.

So it was in the autumn of 1932 that George Preston Marshall brought his brand-new Braves to confront the Depression, the Packers, the Bears, the Spartans, and the whims of Boston sports fans.

The Braves made their Massachusetts debut not in Boston, but in nearby Quincy, in an exhibition game against the semipro Quincy Trojans at a place called Fore River Field. About 3,000 fans turned out for the game that late September Sunday afternoon. Boston, which according to a local sportswriter of the day, Arthur Sampson, was "displaying its All-America-studded cast of former intercollegiate stars," had little trouble dispatching the Quincy gridmen, winning 25–0. Fullback Jim Musick contributed two touchdowns and Tony Plansky and Reggie Rust accounted for the other two. But it was hardly

a lesson in slick-smooth football; according to Arthur Sampson in his game wrap-up: "Frequent penalties, sloppy handling of the ball, indecisive blocking, and missed assignments cropped out often enough to prevent either team from many sustained marches."

The Braves opened the 1932 regular season at their own ballpark before a crowd of about 6,000 on Sunday, October 2, playing host to the Brooklyn Dodgers. The Dodgers were led by one of the game's best passing quarterbacks, Benny Friedman, although passing was still only a minor part of each team's offensive game plan. Friedman and an impenetrable Brooklyn defense managed to blank the Braves in their premiere performance in Boston, 14–0. George Preston Marshall made his presence known, not only by his sartorial splendor as he sat in his box, but also on the sideline from time to time as he passed on a variety of opinions regarding strategy, substitutions, and other such tips to coach Lud Wray.

The following Sunday, Marshall's Braves posted their first regular-season victory. It was also staged at Braves Field and it involved another New York team, Tim Mara's

Giants, who were captained and coached by tackle Steve Owen. The Giants also featured such future Hall of Famers as center Mel Hein and ends Ray Flaherty and Red Badgro, as well as a pair of electrifying backs, Chris Cagle and Shipwreck Kelly. But behind the tailbacking of Cliff Battles, and an impressive 55-yard return of an intercepted lateral by defensive back Algy Clark for a touchdown, the Braves prevailed, 14–6.

The rest of the season seesawed. The Braves found they could not beat the Bears, Packers, or Spartans, but they handled themselves respectably against all the other teams in the league. At season's end, the Braves, with a record of 4–4–2, were in fourth place in the NFL behind, unsurprisingly, the Bears, Packers, and Spartans.

Cliff Battles had the honor of leading the league in rushing, with 576 yards on 148 carries, gaining more yards than such illustrious backs as the Bears' Bronko Nagurski, the Stapletons' Ken Strong, Green Bay's Clarke Hinkle, and Portsmouth's Dutch Clark.

Although the Braves played some good football and showcased some exciting players, Bostonians for the most part interested themselves in other Sunday activities, and the team ended the season with a loss of about $46,000. It was enough to induce Marshall's three partners to look for a safer investment, but the laundryman was hooked on pro football, and announced he was in it to stay and was gearing all his efforts to making it "not only a treat for the people of Boston but also a profitable venture, without stinting on hiring the best players that money can buy."

There were to be major changes, however. Lud Wray had felt Marshall's dissatisfaction. At the same time, the coach had begun to harbor similar sentiments toward his meddling boss, who had spent a major part of the season personally delivering or sending messages to Wray on the sideline or in the locker room—most of which the coach had ignored. Before Marshall could fire Wray, however, he quit to coach the Philadelphia Eagles, who had just joined the NFL.

Wray was replaced by William "Lone Star" Dietz, a full-blooded Indian who had played alongside the legendary Jim Thorpe at Carlisle and had coached the Indian team at Haskell Institute. Dietz was an appropriate selection, because Marshall, who had just changed the team's name to the Redskins, had decided that he would exploit to the fullest the "Indian motif," as he called it. To set the tone, he now had his Redskins players pose with Indian war paint on their faces and wearing feathers. Their new coach was also known to appear from time to time in full Indian headdress.

FIRST YEAR, 1932: 4–4–2

Braves	0	Brooklyn Dodgers	14	Home
Braves	14	New York Giants	6	Home
Braves	0	Chicago Cardinals	9	Home
Braves	0	New York Giants	0	Away
Braves	7	Chicago Bears	7	Home
Braves	19	Staten Island Stapletons	6	Home
Braves	0	Green Bay Packers	21	Home
Braves	0	Portsmouth Spartans	10	Away
Braves	8	Chicago Cardinals	6	Away
Braves	7	Brooklyn Dodgers	0	Away

William "Lone Star" Dietz was hired by George Preston Marshall to coach the Redskins in 1933. During his two years with the Redskins he compiled a record of 11–11–2.

TRICK PLAYS

Lone Star Dietz was a colorful coach in many ways, from his Indian outfits to his trick plays—which, incidentally, never worked. Cliff Battles described the plays in an interview with Bob Curran, for his book *Pro Football's Rag Days*.

"He had a fondness for trick plays. One of these was the Fake Fumble. On the Fake Fumble play the tailback would get the pass from center and then fake a fumble. At this the defense was supposed to relax. Then the tailback would either leap into the air and throw a pass or he would run with the ball.

"Then there was the Broken Shoelace play. One of our players would pretend he had a broken shoelace and we would all pretend we had taken a time-out. When the defense relaxed, we would do almost anything.

"We didn't like these plays. I didn't especially because I always ended up getting pounded harder than usual by the other team. Lone Star used to take our quarterbacks aside and bribe them. He'd give them money out of his own pocket if they would call these special trick plays.

"When I found out about the bribes, I told him that he was going to give me special compensation for the pounding I took on those plays. Nothing came of that, of course."

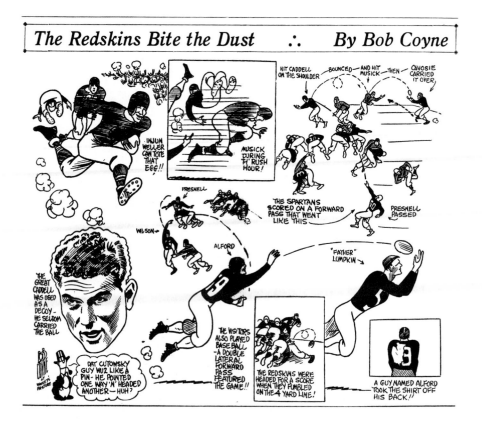

Marshall then moved the team from Braves Field to Fenway Park, home of the Boston Red Sox.

Pro football itself had also undergone some changes when the Redskins took the field in 1933. Some of the changes were the result of the efforts of George Preston Marshall. He was a veritable novice in the league compared to George Halas of the Chicago Bears, Curly Lambeau of the Green Bay Packers, and Tim Mara of the New York Giants, but Marshall, with the backing of those stalwarts, persuaded the other owners to restructure the league into two divisions, with a championship game between the division winners at the season's end. There was also a slew of new rules pushed through by Marshall and Halas to make the game more offense-oriented and thus higher-scoring. Forward passing was now permitted from anywhere behind the line of scrimmage (previously it had only been allowed from five yards or more behind the line), lateral passes could be made anywhere on the field. The ball was brought 10 yards in from the sideline on plays that ended out of bounds or near the sideline for the next play, the goalposts were moved from the end line to the goal line, and a new, slimmer football, which was more advantageous for passing, was introduced.

The Redskins were slotted in the NFL East along with the New York Giants, Brooklyn Dodgers, Philadelphia Eagles, and Pittsburgh Pirates. Both the Eagles, founded by Bert Bell, and the Pirates (later to become the Steelers), launched by Art Rooney, were newcomers to the NFL. The year before, the Redskins had finished higher in the league standings than the other three teams now in the NFL East. If a favorite to win the division had been picked before the season, it would have been Marshall's Redskins. But it was not to be. Losses to the Bears and the Portsmouth Spartans and a tie with Green Bay in their first five games effectively kept the Redskins out of the running. The rejuvenated New York Giants, who had added triple-threat, All-Pro Ken Strong to their backfield, marched through the division to an 11–3–0 season.

Despite the best running attack in the entire NFL, the Redskins of 1933 were still unable to break the .500 barrier, winning five, losing five, and tying two—a finish that

was only good enough for third place in the NFL East. The Redskins did have the two top rushers in the league, however, with Jim Musick grinding out 809 yards on 173 carries and Cliff Battles sprinting for 737 on 146 carries. Both Battles and tackle Turk Edwards were named to the NFL's All-Pro team.

The move to Fenway Park, however, didn't entice more fans than Braves Field had the year before. The team was again in the red at the end of the year, and money was so tight that during home games, the story has often been told, when a ball was kicked into the stands Marshall would per-

Erny Pinckert closes in to intercept a pass from Chicago Cardinals quarterback Joe Lillard in a 1933 game the Redskins won by a score of 10–0.

sonally go in after it and demand that it be returned.

The Redskins added several impressive rookies in 1934, most notably a 6'4" end from Texas A&M, Charley Malone, and halfback Pug Rentner from Northwestern University. On the downside, however, Marshall could not come to terms with league-leading rusher Jim Musick, and the fullback decided to sit out the season.

Once again the Redskins struggled in the first part of the season. Losses to the Dodgers, Giants, and Detroit Lions (formerly the Portsmouth Spartans) in the first five games of the '34 season almost prevented them from attaining a second-place finish and moving a step closer to the division-winning Giants (8–5–0). The Redskins lost both their encounters with the Giants.

Cliff Battles gained 511 yards rushing, but was omitted from that season's All-Pro squad—it was the year that the Bears' Beattie Feathers, behind the blocking of Bronko Nagurski, became the first NFL rusher to gain more than 1,000 yards (1,004, a 9.4-yard average). Rookie Charley Malone made his presence felt by leading the team in pass receptions with 11 for 121 yards—the fourth most in the NFL that year, illustrating how run-oriented the game was in the 1930s.

Unable to produce a winning season in two tries, Lone Star Dietz was expelled from the tribe, and Marshall replaced him with a hometown favorite, Eddie Casey. For the four previous years Casey had been the head coach at neighboring Harvard, and back in 1919 he had won All-America honors as a halfback at that institution. Casey was well-known around Boston and respected for his football leadership, and George Preston Marshall felt he had landed both a winning coach and a local hero sure to attract additional fans to Fenway Park, to watch his Redskins.

The Redskins acquired a fine pair of rookies in 1935: Bill Shepherd, an all-around back from Western Maryland, and Jim Barber, a tackle out of San Francisco University. Shepherd led the team in rushing and passing in 1935, but did not complete the season in Boston. He was sent to Detroit in a trade because he could not get along with coach Casey.

Marshall, it would seem, liked Casey a lot; he sat on the bench next to him at almost every game, offering plays, strategies, and other bits of football advice. He liked him, at least, through the season opener. After two preseason romps over semipro teams, the Redskins outbattled the Brooklyn Dodgers, 7–3, to open the 1935 season on a winning note. Unfortunately, it was the only victory they would post until the next to last game of the year. With a record of 2–8–1 and a fourth-place finish, Casey lost his seat next to Marshall on the sideline.

The new coach for 1936, the Redskins' fourth in their five-year history, was Ray Flaherty, an often-honored All-Pro end who had retired from the Giants at the end of the 1935 season. Flaherty had a keen eye for football talent, and in that first year of the collegiate draft he focused it well. In the first round, the Redskins selected All-America tailback Riley Smith of Alabama, known to be a fine passer, something Marshall's team had lacked in its first four years. To give Smith a top-notch receiver to throw to, Boston acquired All-America end Wayne Millner from Notre Dame in the eighth round. A fine receiver, but also an exceptional blocker and defensive player, Millner in six seasons with the Redskins would perform well enough to earn entry into the Pro Football Hall of Fame. Two other acquisitions for the backfield were Eddie Britt of Holy Cross and Ed Justice of Gonzaga.

In his first year, Flaherty not only added a plethora of talent to the Redskins team, he

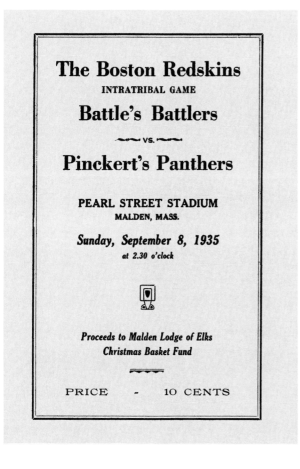

The Boston Redskins
INTRATRIBAL GAME
Battle's Battlers
~ vs. ~
Pinckert's Panthers

PEARL STREET STADIUM
MALDEN, MASS.

Sunday, September 8, 1935
at 2.30 o'clock

Proceeds to Malden Lodge of Elks
Christmas Basket Fund

PRICE - 10 CENTS

SALARIES, 1936

George Preston Marshall was never known for throwing nickels around with abandon during his three decades of running the Redskins. He set the standard, so to speak, from the very beginning. These are the salaries of the highest-paid members of the Boston Redskins the year they reached their first NFL championship game.

		Salary per game
HB	Cliff Battles	$210
QB	Riley Smith	$200
HB	Erny Pinckert	$165
T	Turk Edwards	$165
E	Wayne Millner	$165
FB	Jim Musick	$165

Most of the other players earned about $100 a game. Head coach Ray Flaherty received $450 a game, more than twice his highest-paid player.

		Salary per game
FB	Pug Rentner	$150
HB	Eddie Britt	$140
C	Larry Siemering	$140
HB	Ed Justice	$135
HB	Ed Smith	$135

Total expenses for the Redskins, according to the organization's accounting sheets, for 26 players, two coaches, one trainer, and the office staff, were less than $45,000 for the eastern divisional champions that year.

also did what no other Boston coach had been able to do. He got Marshall off the sideline and into the grandstands. Flaherty demanded autonomy in running the team, and Marshall, perhaps still feeling the awful pain of a 2–8–1 season, conceded it to him.

With full field control, Flaherty sailed into the 1936 season with what the Boston sports press considered a leaky ship patched with new but still unproven timbers. Coach Flaherty, however, ignored the preseason prognostications. He continued to ignore them even after the Skins were shut out in the opener at Pittsburgh, 10–0, by a team that had posted a paltry 4–8–0 record the year before.

Cliff Battles reversed the momentum the

League Standing (Nov. 26)

	Eastern Division					Western Division			
	Won	Lost	Tied	Per.		Won	Lost	Tied	Per.
New York	7	4	0	.636	Chicago Bears	11	0	0	1.000
BOSTON	5	6	0	.454	Detroit	10	1	0	.909
Brooklyn	4	5	0	.444	Green Bay	6	5	0	.545
Philadelphia	3	7	0	.300	Chicago Cards	4	6	0	.400
Pittsburgh	2	10	0	.166	St. Louis	1	9	0	.100

CAPTAIN ERNY PINCKERT with the faithful "Snooks," Mascot

☞ ORDER YOUR 1935 SEASON TICKETS IN ADVANCE

scheduling). And those were the two teams Flaherty's contenders had to face.

Pittsburgh came to Fenway Park for the Redskins' last home game of 1936, hoping to wrest first place from Boston with a victory. But the Skins were ready and destroyed any lingering hope Pittsburgh had for a divisional title with a 30–0 triumph, then the second-highest margin of victory in Redskins history (they had defeated the Pirates 39–0 in 1934).

George Preston Marshall was enthralled with the overwhelming performance of his team that Sunday, but he was appalled at the

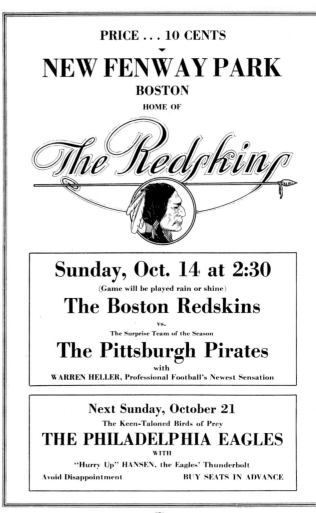

PRICE . . . 10 CENTS

NEW FENWAY PARK
BOSTON
HOME OF

The Redskins

Sunday, Oct. 14 at 2:30
(Game will be played rain or shine)
The Boston Redskins
vs.
The Surprise Team of the Season
The Pittsburgh Pirates
with
WARREN HELLER, Professional Football's Newest Sensation

Next Sunday, October 21
The Keen-Taloned Birds of Prey
THE PHILADELPHIA EAGLES
WITH
"Hurry Up" HANSEN, the Eagles' Thunderbolt
Avoid Disappointment   BUY SEATS IN ADVANCE

Washington Press, Inc.   242 Dover Street, Boston

following week, however, when he once again asserted his team leadership on the field and led the Redskins to a 26–3 victory over the Philadelphia Eagles. The following week he contributed a 65-yard touchdown run to another win, this time by 14–3 over the Brooklyn Dodgers.

From that point on, the Redskins joined a season-long title battle with the divisional champion Giants and the Pittsburgh Pirates.

With just two games remaining in their regular season, the Redskins were essentially tied for first place, with a record of 5–5–0. The Giants and Pirates were also in the running, with respective records of 4–5–1 and 6–5–0 (the Pirates had only one game remaining in those days of convenience

sparsely filled stadium—only a few more than 4,800 had turned out to see the crucial contest. One reason many stayed away, however, was the fact that Marshall had suddenly raised ticket prices on the day of the game. More than a few disgruntled fans had turned their backs on the box office and sought Sunday entertainment elsewhere.

Marshall's disenchantment with the lack of paying customers and the indifference of the city's sports scribes exceeded his threshold of patience. After the game, he announced that he was through with the city. "I'm licked, so far as Boston is concerned," he said. "Fans in paying quantities don't seem to want us. Maybe they don't want me. Whatever it is, five years of trying and $100,000 (his estimated losses over that period) in money is enough to spend in one place when you can't get anywhere. We'll stay in the game, but it will be somewhere else."

With that in mind, Marshall and Flaherty took the Redskins down to New York to face the Giants at the Polo Grounds in a game that would decide that year's NFL East title. The Redskins were 6–5–0 and the Giants, who had defeated the Dodgers while Boston was mauling the Pirates, had a record of 5–5–1 (the Pirates had ended their season with a record of 6–6–0 and were mathematically eliminated from the race).

A heavy rain earlier in the day had made the field a mud hole, and an intermittent cold drizzle throughout the game did not make for the best of conditions. Still, more than 18,000 stalwart fans passed through the turnstiles at the Polo Grounds, a fact that did not go unnoticed by Marshall.

The Redskins managed to march to the New York one-yard line after Cliff Battles snagged a short pass and ran 20 yards with it. From there fullback Don Irwin, who had just been acquired the week before, bulled in for a touchdown. In the second half, the fleet Cliff Battles, seemingly unfazed by the semi-swamp in which he was playing, darted and dodged, slipped and slid 75 yards for another touchdown. It was all the scoring that would take place that rain-swept afternoon, giving the Redskins a 14–0 triumph and their first divisional crown.

The NFL East winner was scheduled to host the 1936 championship game. So it was to Boston that Curly Lambeau's Green Bay Packers, triumphant in the NFL West, were scheduled to come to do battle for the NFL title. But Marshall, who felt that Boston had abandoned him and his team, decided to abandon Boston. Remembering the 18,000 who had braved the rain and cold in New York to watch a football game and the 4,800 who had showed up in Boston, he announced that the 1936 title game would be played at the Polo Grounds in New York.

The divisional champs met on that neutral site on December 13, 1936. There the now-orphaned Redskins fell to a favored Green Bay Packer team, 21–7.

A week after the game, George Preston Marshall announced that in 1937 the Boston Redskins would be known as the Washington Redskins, and would play their games at Griffith Stadium, home of baseball's Washington Senators, in the nation's capital and at the hub of his laundry empire.

The First Championship Game, 1936

George Preston Marshall, snubbing Boston for its lack of support of his team, took the Redskins to the Polo Grounds in New York for their first NFL championship game. Having won the NFL East from the New York Giants on the last game of the regular season, the 7–5–0 Redskins had to face the Green Bay Packers (10–1–1), who were a heavy favorite. Besides losing only one game

Somewhere in this pile of mud-splattered Redskins and Giants is Boston fullback Don Irwin who has just oozed his way into the end zone at the Polo Grounds in New York. The touchdown helped the Redskins to a 14–0 win over New York and their first NFL divisional title in the last game of the 1936 season. (HOF/NFL Photos)

all year, the oddsmakers figured, the Packers had defeated the Redskins twice during the regular season, by scores of 31–2 at Green Bay and 7–3 in Boston.

Curly Lambeau, the Hall of Fame-bound coach of the Pack, had opened up his offense by frequently passing the football, a tactic disdained by most teams in the league. Lambeau had a fine passing quarterback in Arnie Herber and two superb Hall of Famers as receivers, end Don Hutson and halfback Johnny Blood McNally. To augment the passing attack, Packers relied on the powerful running of fullback Clarke Hinkle, an-

LINEUPS		
Boston Redskins		**Green Bay Packers**
Wayne Millner	E	Don Hutson
Charley Malone	E	Milt Gantenbein
Turk Edwards	T	Ernie Smith
Jim Barber	T	Lou Gordon
Les Ollson	G	Tiny Engebretsen
Jim Karcher	G	Lon Evans
Frank Bausch	C	George Svendsen
Riley Smith	QB	Arnie Herber
Cliff Battles	HB	George Sauer
Ed Justice	HB	Johnny Blood McNally
Don Irwin	FB	Clarke Hinkle
Ray Flaherty	coach	Curly Lambeau

other player bound for football immortality in the Hall of Fame at Canton, Ohio.

It was a sunny, relatively mild Sunday afternoon when the two teams squared off. The Redskins' chances faded quickly when, early in the first quarter, star back Cliff Battles lateraled to Riley Smith, who fumbled it away to Green Bay. On top of that, Battles was hurt on the play and had to leave the field for the rest of the game.

The Packers took advantage of the turnover when shortly thereafter Herber and Hutson hooked up on a 43-yard touchdown pass. The Redskins came back in the next period of play, mounting a 78-yard drive, culminating in a one-yard touchdown plunge by fullback Pug Rentner. But Riley Smith, in one of his less memorable games of that season, missed the extra point and the Redskins trailed 7–6 at the half.

In the third quarter, Herber destroyed the Redskins when he teamed with Johnny Blood McNally on a 52-yard pass play, then followed that with an eight-yard touchdown toss to end Milt Gantenbein.

In the fourth quarter, with the Skins trailing 14–6, Riley Smith was back to punt deep in his own territory, but did not get it off in time. Clarke Hinkle blocked it and recovered the ball on the Redskins' three-yard line. Moments later Green Bay halfback Bob Monett carried it in for the last touchdown of the game. The Packers prevailed at the whistle, 21–6.

Watching the coin toss before the 1936 NFL championship game are Redskins captain Turk Edwards (17) and Green Bay Packer captain Milt Gantenbein (22) along with NFL commissioner Joe Carr (right). The Packers took the crown by a score of 21–6. (HOF/NFL Photos)

GEORGE PRESTON MARSHALL

Shirley Povich, in an article for *The Washington Post,* once accurately and insightfully described the Redskins' founding father in a single sentence. "The supreme authority of the Washington Redskins was George Preston Marshall, as dashing a figure as ever strode the American sports scene, and sometimes as notorious and unloved as he was famous and admired for his innovations."

He was known as The Big Chief, and no one ever doubted that he ruled the tribe like a true autocrat from its inception in 1932 until poor health forced him to step down in 1962. He made all the business decisions, as well as many of those regarding football strategy; he hired and discarded coaches as if they came from a temporary-help agency; and he was an outspoken and highly active leader in league affairs. Always the showman, the personification of pizzazz, he also introduced to the National Football League the marching band and halftime entertainments, appropriately billed as extravaganzas. In his hometown of Washington he became a legend of sorts. As Jack Walsh of *The Washington Post* observed, "Whether having a shampoo in the Statler-Hilton barber shop, dining at Duke Zeibert's, or holding court on the Shoreham (hotel) terrace, Marshall considered it a lost opportunity were he not the center of attention."

To the chagrin of his parade of coaches, Marshall was notorious for giving his opinions on everything from game plans to player personnel, not to mention specific plays during the course of a game. He telephoned instructions from his private box to the bandstand to dictate songs and the specifics of halftime entertainments by his beloved band. One Washington reporter even noted, "He [Marshall] never obtained a license to drive an auto, but he always sat beside his chauffeur giving directions and instructions."

His contributions to the National Football League and the football fans of Washington, however, were profound, enough to gain for him charter membership in the Pro Football Hall of Fame. His inno-

The dapper laundryman turned sportsman, George Preston Marshall. (HOF/NFL Photos)

28

The Big Chief fully committed himself to the Indian motif. Here, before one of his legendary parades, Marshall has his own personal headdress properly fitted by his wife, former film star Corinne Griffith. (HOF/NFL Photos)

vations on and off the field, from rule changes to a team fight song, were instrumental in forming the professional football league we know today and in popularizing the sport.

In 1932, Marshall, with three partners, purchased the franchise designated for Boston and named his team the Boston Braves. It was reported that he put up only $1,500 for the franchise and posted another $1,500 as a guarantee. Later he claimed he never paid a single penny for the franchise itself. After a dismal year at the box office and a mediocre one on the field (4–4–2) and a net loss of $46,000, Marshall lost his three partners but hung on to the team.

In 1933, his second year in the NFL, Marshall and his friend and archrival George Halas of the Chicago Bears were the guiding forces behind a league reorganization and the adoption of a variety of new rules. Generally regarded as the dawn of the "modern NFL," these Marshall/Halas innovations included: forming two separate divisions with a championship game between the winners of each, allowing forward passes from anywhere behind the line of scrimmage, instituting hash marks, and moving the goalposts from the end line to the goal line. The result was a more open, high-scoring game, and a much more dramatic season finale.

Show business had always been part of Marshall's life. After graduating from Randolph-Macon College in Virginia, he aspired to be an actor. He landed a few small parts in shows in Washington and New York but finally admitted, "I wasn't much of an actor." Then he quickly added, to counter the negative, "I once brought the house down delivering just a single line. It was at the Walker Theater in Winnipeg, Canada, in 1917. The stage manager asked me to go out at intermission and make an announcement. I stepped out in front of the curtain and said: 'The United States has just declared war on Germany.' And those Canadians went crazy."

Marshall had inherited the Palace Laundry in Washington, D.C., from his father back in 1918, and over the next three decades he built it into a booming business that eventually had 57 outlets

George Preston Marshall is presented the Helms Hall of Fame award for his contributions to professional football by U.S. Vice President Richard Nixon, an unabashed and notorious Redskins fan. (HOF/NFL Photos)

(thus the nickname "Wet Wash King" Marshall by which he was known in certain corners of the NFL). It was Marshall's flair for promotion that turned an otherwise run-down laundry shop into an extremely profitable business.

In the later 1920s, he sponsored a semipro basketball team and named them the Palace Big Five. It was through that organization that he met then-NFL president Joe Carr and Chicago Bears owner/coach George Halas, both of whom were associated with the basketball league in football's off-season. It was at their urging that he took on the NFL's Boston franchise in 1932.

The city of Boston and George Preston Marshall, however, did not exactly embrace each other with fervor. As Shirley Povich once observed in *The Washington Post*, "Certain habits of Boston people had outraged Marshall. First it was their custom of not attending his team's games in great numbers. Second, it was the low priority given his team in the sports pages, with the city's sports editors allotting more importance to traditional Boston favorites such as Harvard and Boston College football and its two big league baseball teams, the Red Sox and Braves. Marshall's pique peaked on one game day when Boston's leading newspaper gave more prominence to the Radcliffe girls hockey team than to his precious football lads."

When he raised ticket prices during the 1936 season, even more fans otherwise occupied themselves on Sunday afternoons; the newspapers finally gave him some attention, but it was to berate him for the ticket-price increase.

So Marshall gathered up all the players, shoulder pads, helmets, uniforms, and other assorted paraphernalia, and left town, and he did it in true Marshall fashion. His team had won the NFL Eastern Division title in 1936, earning them the right to face the Green Bay Packers for the league championship. Marshall talked the league into staging the contest for the crown, scheduled to be played in Boston, in New York City instead. And after the game, he kept right on going south until he reached the nation's capital and the hub of his laundry business.

Marshall engaged the Washington football fans immediately, first by bringing them rookie superstar Sammy Baugh and second by giving them an NFL championship his first year in town. The love affair that developed that 1937 season between the city and the Redskins never wilted, despite frustrating times and an unholy 25-year drought between two championship eras.

With an excellent team and Marshall-designed theatrics, he filled the 29,000 seats of Griffith Stadium, then added 6,000 more to accommodate the crowds, which were much more enthusiastic than those encountered in Boston. Tickets ranged from $4.40 down to $3.60, and they were hard to obtain.

Awash in the popularity of his team, Marshall extended it by setting up a radio network that broadcast the Redskins games throughout the mid-Atlantic and southern states. As a result, the team became the NFL's first to build a large following outside its own metropolitan area.

Marshall was also the first NFL owner to publicly announce that he wanted to attract women to his ballgames. "For the women, football alone is not enough," he said during the early Washington years. "I always try to present halftime entertain-

The Big Chief's enshrinement in the Pro Football Hall of Fame. He was inducted as one of the seventeen charter members in 1963. (HOF/NFL Photos)

ment to give them something to look forward to—a little music, dancing, color, something they can understand and enjoy." He also added that if he got women to come out to the games, he would get that many more men to come out.

Those he did not encourage to come were blacks, at least in the uniform of his team. The Redskins, under Marshall, were the last team in the NFL to add a black player to their roster. And they did not do it until 1962, long after the other teams had easily (and very effectively) integrated their squads. When criticized for his nonemployment of blacks, Marshall responded, "I'll start using negroes when the Harlem Globetrotters start using white basketball players." But in 1961, Secretary of the Interior Stewart Udall threatened to oust the team from the new and metropolitan-controlled D.C. Stadium if it did not begin hiring blacks.

So, in 1962, Marshall finally integrated the team by signing Bobby Mitchell, who would prove to be one of the finest receivers in the history of the NFL and who would merit enshrinement in the Pro Football Hall of Fame, as well as three other blacks.

It was the same year that failing health forced the 65-year-old Marshall to give up managerial control of the team and the marching band he loved so well.

George Preston Marshall died in 1969, bequeathing not only the Redskins to the world of professional football, but a long list of innovations and unique contributions to the sport.

A VIEW FROM BALTIMORE

In eulogy, John F. Steadman, then sports editor of the *Baltimore News-American,* captured the essence of the flamboyant and complex founder of the Washington Redskins.

"George Preston Marshall was involved in every facet of the game, which meant improving the product.

"He was also a strong-willed, unbending, non-compromising man with the strength of his convictions in all matters, be it in the area of politics, sports, religion or racial relations.

"We heard him express himself on the question of integration and watched as he fought against hiring a Negro player for his Washington Redskins—a team that so much reflected the Marshall personality because of the way he operated it.

"Suffice to say that George Preston Marshall was not a hypocrite. Whether you liked him or found him repulsive, you knew the stand he had taken because he let the world know it.

"Marshall rarely backed away. He would arrive at a position and there was no changing him. Logic and reasoning and even the facts weren't going to influence Marshall's opinion on anything.

"He was dictatorial in how he lived and tried to make others live. Marshall never allowed any of his employees with the Redskins to wish him a happy birthday because he wasn't cognizant of age and, in his world, he was going to live forever. . . .

"It was Marshall's unfortunate belief he was infallible. Equipped with this kind of a personality meant that he made enemies at almost every turn. But he cared not, or at least it appeared that way.

"Marshall would take an unpopular position and hold it—regardless of how much fire he had to face. If ever a man was his own man it was this tall, articulate, flamboyant figure who dominated the football scene for almost three decades. . . .

"George Preston Marshall died at age 72 after a lingering, painful illness. He was proud and he was vain. Maybe now he might possibly admit that death is going to come to us all since he found out that even George Preston Marshall wasn't to be excluded."

2

The Great Runners

Over the years, the Redskins have had a number of certifiably great runners carrying the ball for them. The first was Hall of Famer Cliff Battles, who debuted in their initial season in 1932, when the Redskins were the Braves and their hometown was Boston and not Washington. Next came another Hall of Fame honoree, Bullet Bill Dudley, who joined the Skins in 1950. In 1969, Larry Brown came aboard and made his presence felt throughout the defenses of the NFC. Mike Thomas arrived in 1975. The following year the raucous John Riggins began his career in Washington. And in 1985 Heisman Trophy winner George Rogers came from New Orleans to give the Skins a much-needed running game.

The most productive rusher ever in burgundy and gold was John Riggins. In his nine years with the Redskins, Riggins gained 7,472 yards, almost 1,600 yards more than Larry Brown, who ate up 5,875 yards during his eight years in Washington.

Riggins also had the two top totals for the most yards in a season rushing, gaining 1,347 yards in 1983 and 1,239 the following year. Only four Redskins have gained more than 1,000 yards in a single season: Riggins (four times), Larry Brown and George Rogers (twice), and Mike Thomas (Brown and Thomas did it in 14-game seasons).

The mark for most yards gained in a single game was set back in 1933 when Cliff Battles gained 215 yards on 16 carries, an average of more than 13 yards per carry, in a game against the Giants. It was not until 1985 that another Redskins runner broke the 200-yard mark—George Rogers, when

34

he gained 206 against the St. Louis Cardinals. The only other Washington rusher to top 200 yards in a game is Timmy Smith, who dazzled the football world with 204 at Super Bowl XXII in January 1988.

The longest runs from scrimmage belong exclusively to early ballplayers. Billy Wells scampered for 88 yards for a touchdown against the Chicago Cardinals in 1954. Rob Goode accounted for the next longest run in 1950, when he raced 80 yards for a score in a game with the Packers. And both Cliff Battles and Wilbur Moore have 75-yard touchdown runs to their credit, the former against the Giants in 1937 and the latter through the Chicago Cardinal defense of 1944.

Larry Jones holds the record for the longest kickoff return, 102 yards for a touchdown against the Eagles in 1974. The longest punt return was logged by Bill Dudley in 1950, 96 yards, resulting in another touchdown, in a game with the Steelers.

There have been other fine ball-carriers over the almost six decades of Redskins football, less renowned perhaps than those mentioned above, but certainly worthy of note. In the late 1930s and '40s there were Jim Musick, Pug Rentner, Andy Farkas, and Dick Todd. The best of the 1950s included Rob Goode and Don Bosseler, and there was some brief but outstanding running from Charlie "Choo Choo" Justice, Billy Wells, and Vic Janowicz. The 1960s, a much leaner decade in terms of rushing yardage, had some memorable days provided by Dick James, Charley Taylor, and A.D. Whitfield. In the 1970s, an era dominated by the greats Brown, Thomas, and Riggins, Washington also got considerable yardage from Charley Harraway. And in the 1980s, there have been memorable performances from Joe Washington, Kelvin Bryant, and Timmy Smith.

From these fine runners have come some of the most exciting moments in Washington Redskins history, from dazzling breakaway runs to 200-yard rushing days to game-winning touchdowns.

Cliff Battles

Cliff "Gip" Battles was a 6'1", 190-pound tailback from West Virginia Wesleyan. George Preston Marshall discovered Battles himself—at least that's the way The Big Chief liked to tell the story. Marshall had seen him play in Washington in a game in 1931 against Georgetown and had been duly impressed.

Marshall was not alone in his judgment of Battles. The New York Giants and the Portsmouth Spartans were also aware of him and offered contracts, but Battles chose to go with the Boston Braves in 1932 because they were the only team to actually send someone to personally see him in West Virginia. And so he joined the fledgling Braves in their very first season in the National Football League.

Battles was the highest-paid player on Marshall's new ball club, signed for a reported salary of $175 a game, with the stipulation that he would not be required to play more than two games in any one week. Almost all the other players of that maiden team were paid $100 a game or less. As Battles wryly observed later, "Our game checks were so small we were able to cash them on the bus after the game."

The Gip, as he was called, had been a magnificent runner in college—in one game against Salem, Battles gained 378 yards rushing and another 85 on punt returns. Had he played for a larger college he surely would have won All-America honors.

Battles proved his worth from the very start. The Braves were a mediocre team in 1932, winning four games, losing four, and tying the other two. But Battles gained 576

Cliff Battles, who played for the Braves and the Redskins from 1932 through 1937, was both a fleet and punishing runner. His five years of pro ball with the Redskins earned him an induction into the Pro Football Hall of Fame. (HOF/NFL Photos)

yards rushing, the most in the league that year—more than Red Grange, Bronko Nagurski, Johnny Blood McNally, Dutch Clark, Ken Strong, and Clarke Hinkle, among others.

The following year, working out of a new double-wing formation installed by new coach Lone Star Dietz for the newly named Redskins, Battles gained 737 yards, second only in the NFL to his fullback, Jim Musick, a rookie who ground out 809 for the Redskins. As he had the year before, Battles won All-Pro honors.

Battles was the star attraction through the next two seasons, but they were unexciting ones (6–6–0, 2–8–1). In 1936, however, he was able to lead the Skins to their first NFL

divisional title. Leading the team in rushing yardage with 614 yards, and in scoring, with 42 points, he was again named All-Pro.

In 1937, Battles moved with the Redskins to Washington and became one prong of the best two-pronged offense up to that time in NFL history. Marshall had signed Slingin' Sammy Baugh to pass for the Redskins while Battles, now a 201-pound fullback, would run the ball for them. The tandem did their jobs so well that each led the league that year—Baugh with 81 completions and 1,127 yards passing and Battles with 874 yards rushing (at the time the second most in NFL history). They also brought Washington its first NFL championship.

To get to the championship game that

year, however, the Redskins had to win their last game of the season against the always difficult Giants in the always hostile Polo Grounds. They did it on the legs of Cliff Battles, who turned in one of the finest single-game performances of his illustrious football career. He scored two touchdowns and set up two more with a 75-yard run from scrimmage and a 76-yard interception return. When the afternoon was over, Battles had gained 170 yards rushing (an average of seven yards per carry) and the Redskins were on top of a 49–14 score.

In the championship game against the Chicago Bears, which would prove to be the last pro football game of Cliff Battles's career, he gained 51 yards rushing and another 82 catching Baugh passes to help lead the Redskins to a 28–21 triumph.

A Phi Beta Kappa scholar in college, Battles was also an astute businessman. When George Preston Marshall refused to raise his yearly salary above $3,000 after his electrifying All-Pro season of '37, the 28-year-old Battles quit and took a job coaching at Columbia University for $4,000 a year.

When he left, Battles had gained more yards rushing than any player in NFL history, 3,622 yards. An All-Pro in three of his six years in the NFL, Cliff Battles was inducted into the Pro Football Hall of Fame in 1968.

Bill Dudley

"Bullet" Bill Dudley came to the Redskins in 1950 as an established star, having shone for six years on the fields of the Pittsburgh

One of the more memorable backs to don a Redskins uniform was "Bullet" Bill Dudley (35). Dudley played for the Redskins in 1950, 1951, and 1953; he was enshrined in the Pro Football Hall of Fame in 1966. (HOF/NFL Photos)

Bill Dudley
1950–1953 (Washington Redskins)

Steelers and Detroit Lions. A true triple-threat back, although just a mere 5'10" and 175 pounds, he had been an All-America halfback at the University of Virginia and an All-Pro in the National Football League.

The nickname "Bullet" was not altogether appropriate, because he was never known for great speed. But he was renowned for his elusiveness when carrying the ball, which enabled him to provide some spectacular runs. He was an accomplished passer, but he threw the ball sidearm. He had the most unorthodox place-kicking style in the game (he never used an approach step), but he was consistent and effective. Dudley was also one of pro football's most feared punt-return specialists.

Dudley was, as they say, in the autumn of his career when he came to Washington. He had been traded to the Redskins by the Detroit Lions, but when he sat down to discuss his contract with Washington coach Herman Ball they could not come to terms. Afterwards, Dudley recalled, "George Preston Marshall . . . called me and asked me to meet him for lunch at this Greek restaurant. [He] came in wearing this very expensive suit. He was impeccable, very impressive. He said, 'Bill, you're going to be playing for the first time for a football team that knows what it's doing.' " After some haggling and Marshall's discovery that Dudley was as intractable in negotiation as he was elusive on the football field, the laundryman "hit the table with his fist and said, 'All right, go tell Herman to give it to you.' " The "it" was a one-year salary of $12,500.

To show his appreciation, Dudley gave Marshall what The Big Chief later said was "one of the most exciting things I've ever seen on a football field." The Bullet fielded a punt in a 1950 game against the Pittsburgh Steelers at his own four-yard line and wove his way back 96 yards for a touchdown. At the time it was the second-longest punt return in NFL history.

Dudley played for the Redskins in 1950 and 1951, left for a year to coach the backfield at Yale, and then returned to Washington for his last season in 1953. For the Skins, Dudley carried the ball, passed it, caught passes, kicked field goals and extra points, punted, and played defensive halfback.

Dudley's days in Washington were only one segment of a pro football career rich enough to gain admittance to the Hall of Fame, an honor that was bestowed on him in 1966. During those years in the early 1950s, he brought many people out to Griffith Stadium to watch his wily runs and flat-footed kicking style.

When the collective statistics were compiled for his nine-year NFL career, Bullet Bill Dudley had rushed for 3,057 yards (an average of four yards per carry), caught 123 passes for 1,383 yards, scored 19 touchdowns on runs and 18 on pass receptions, kicked 33 field goals and 121 extra points, gained 1,743 yards returning kickoffs and another 1,515 bringing back punts, intercepted 23 passes (returning two for touchdowns), and scored a total of 484 points.

Larry Brown

Vince Lombardi, in his first and only year as head coach of the Redskins, knew his team desperately needed to develop a running game if it was to be a contender in the NFL East. He found his solution in the eighth round of the 1969 draft: 21-year-old running back Larry Brown from Kansas State. The legendary Lombardi saw Brown as the perfect counterpart in the Redskins backfield to the Hall of Fame passing combination of Sonny Jurgensen and Charley Taylor.

Lombardi not only fused the 5'11", 204-pound rookie into his starting backfield, but in the preseason took care of a hearing problem that was making it difficult for Brown to hear signals when he lined up to the left of the quarterback. "I picked up my helmet one day and there it was," Brown said, "a hearing aid attached inside."

Larry Brown dives for a few extra yards. Brown is the second leading rusher in Redskins history with 5,875 yards. (Washington Redskins)

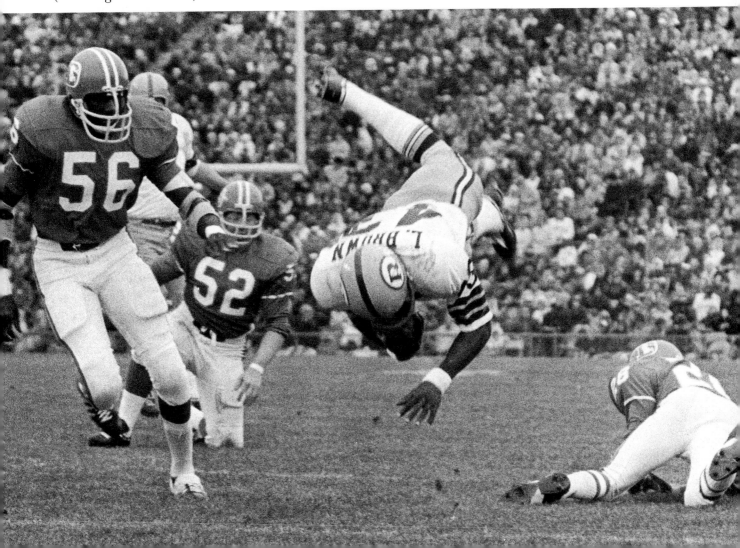

Larry Brown
1969–76 (Washington Redskins)

Brown responded by gaining 888 yards rushing that first season, then the second most in club annals (Rob Goode had ground out 951 in 1951). It was the fourth-highest rushing total that year in the NFL, behind Gale Sayers of the Bears, Calvin Hill of the Cowboys, and Tom Matte of the Colts. He added another 302 yards on pass receptions, earned an invitation to the Pro Bowl, and

was runner-up to Calvin Hill for NFL Rookie of the Year.

The following year Brown became the first Washington running back to gain more than 1,000 yards in a season. The 1,125 yards he churned out, with an average of 4.7 per carry, was the most in the NFL, and he was named All-Pro for his performance. He also rushed for more than 100 yards in six games, which remains the all-time Redskins mark, a record he would tie in 1972.

His finest year was 1972. In the first 11 games of that season, Brown scored 12 touchdowns, including an electrifying 88-yard run after a one-yard pass from Billy Kilmer in a game against the New York Jets. In a game against the New York Giants, he ran for 191 yards, a team record, eclipsing the 190 rushing yards Johnny Olszewski logged against the Cleveland Browns in 1959. The 1,216 yards Brown gained in the 14-game 1972 season, another club standard (which stood until John Riggins broke it in 16 games in 1983), was the most in the NFC and only 35 yards fewer than league-leader O.J. Simpson of the Buffalo Bills. In the playoffs that year, Brown helped the Skins to wins over the Packers and Cowboys by rushing for 101 and 88 yards, respectively. After the Redskins eliminated the Cowboys from the 1972 playoffs, Dallas coach Tom Landry shook his head and said, "Larry Brown is the catalyst of the Redskins. He's what makes them go."

After five years with Washington, Brown had gained 5,467 yards rushing. He was only the third player in NFL history to average over 1,000 yards a season for five consecutive years, joining the illustrious company of Jim Brown of the Browns and Jim Taylor of the Packers.

When Larry Brown called it a career after the 1976 season, he stood as the Redskins' all-time leading rusher, with a total of 5,875 yards and a then-record 19 100-yard games.

He had earned another 2,485 yards on pass receptions. His total of 330 points scored came from 35 rushing touchdowns and 20 on pass plays. The four trips he made to the Pro Bowl are the most of any running back in Redskins history.

Mike Thomas

By pro football standards, Mike Thomas, at 5′11″ and 190 pounds, could be described as diminutive. He was also not the fastest of backs, admitting himself, "I have always survived not because of speed but because of my quickness." He more than survived for four fine years with the Redskins and proved to be a worthy successor to Larry Brown as the ball-carrier of the Washington offensive game plan.

George Allen had the highest regard for Thomas going into the 1975 draft, but had to hope that the feisty halfback, who had gained more than 3,000 yards and scored 40 touchdowns at the University of Nevada at Las Vegas, would last into the fifth round. Under the Allen philosophy of "The future is now," the first four Washington draft picks had already been traded.

He was there and Allen grabbed him, to the surprise of many, since the Redskins already had a veteran backfield that included Larry Brown, Duane Thomas, Moses Denson, and Bob Brunet. Allen had so much faith in the rookie, something alien to the coach's veteran-loving nature, that he shifted Brown to fullback and slotted Thomas as halfback.

Mike Thomas not only earned a starting role in the Redskins backfield as a rookie, but ended up leading the team in rushing with 919 yards, then the fifth most in Redskins history. Thomas was known for gaining yards the hard way. As former Redskins great and then Washington scouting direc-tor Bobby Mitchell noted, "He really runs better inside than outside, and there's a reason for that. He runs with a quick shuffle of the feet, so he can change direction very fast. When he goes inside, it doesn't take much for him to change directions and spurt." His first 100-yard performance came in the fourth game of the regular season against the St. Louis Cardinals, and it was actually a "100-yard half," because he had sat out the entire first half of the game. Thomas also gained 483 yards on 40 receptions that year, which was enough for him to win the NFL's Offensive Rookie of the Year award for 1975.

The following year Thomas became only the second rusher in Washington history to gain more than 1,000 yards in a season,

Mike Thomas
1975–1979 (Washington Redskins)

joining Larry Brown as the only Redskin with that distinction. His 1,101 yards gained was fifth best in the NFC. His most memorable performance that year, and also his career best, came when he gained 195 yards rushing, a club record, in a game against the St. Louis Cardinals.

The tenure of Mike Thomas came to an end in Washington after the 1978 season, when he was traded to the San Diego Chargers. Upon his departure, only Larry Brown had gained more yards rushing for the Redskins than Thomas's 3,360. He caught 131 passes for 1,405 yards and scored 15 touchdowns rushing and 11 on pass receptions.

John Riggins

John Riggins can lay claim to two Washington Redskins titles: He was the most productive, and certainly the most flamboyant,

Washington running back Mike Thomas (22), after taking a handoff from Billy Kilmer (17), plunges for a first down in a 1975 game against the St. Louis Cardinals. A rookie that year, Thomas led the Skins in rushing with 919 yards. Thomas wore the burgundy and gold from 1975 through 1979. (Washington Redskins)

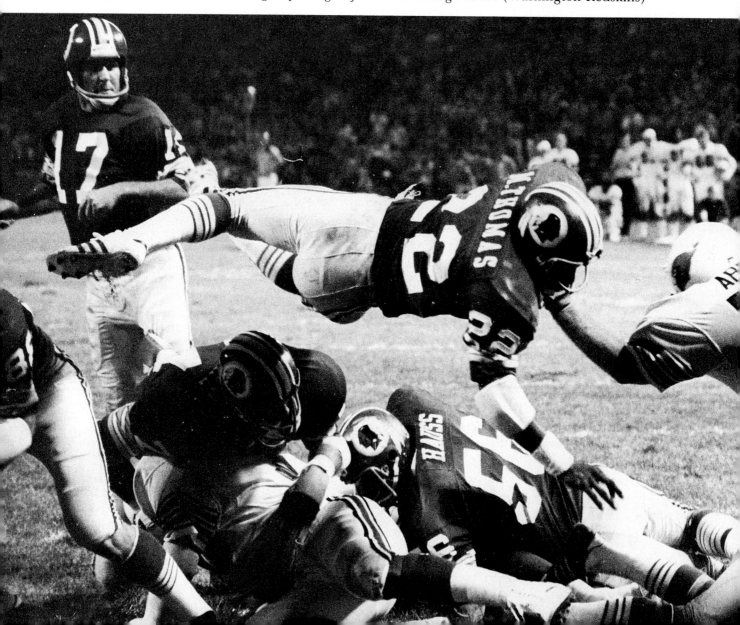

John Riggins
1976–79, 1981–85 (Washington Redskins)

running back in team history. He carried the ball more often, gained more yards, scored more touchdowns rushing, and toted up more 100-yard games than any Redskins running back ever. He also once sported a Mohawk haircut, painted his toenails green, attended a contract signing stripped to the waist and wearing a derby with a feather stuck in it, and made camouflage clothes the fashion in Washington.

The tempestuous and talented John Riggins, out of the University of Kansas, was a first-round draft choice of the New York Jets in 1971. After a fine five years in the backfield there, the 6′2″, 240-pound fullback signed with the Redskins as a free agent in 1976. At first Riggins was not happy there. He was the up back in George

Allen's I formation and was used mainly to block for Mike Thomas. He later expressed his disenchantment in public: "George Allen's idea of offense was, 'Don't lose the game with it and the defense will win for you.' It was a joke, my being there, a waste of my time and their money."

It was not until 1978, under new head coach Jack Pardee, that Riggins was properly appreciated in the Redskins backfield. That year he became the third Washington running back in history to churn out more than 1,000 yards in a season (1,014). The next year he became the first Skin to post back-to-back 1,000-yard seasons when he gained 1,153 yards. It was in the last game of that season that he ripped off the longest run of his career, a 66-yard jaunt for a touchdown against Dallas.

The following year the irrepressible Riggins asked for a new contract and a raise to $500,000 a year. He did not get it, and sat out the year back in Lawrence, Kansas. But in 1981, the then 32-year-old Big John was back in the Washington camp and ready to show the Redskins' new coach, Joe Gibbs, that he was still a force to be reckoned with. His only comment to the press was, "I'm bored, I'm broke, and I'm back."

He was indeed back, setting a club record by rushing for 13 touchdowns. In 1982, he became football's Reggie Jackson, illuminating the postseason for the Redskins and carrying his team to its first Super Bowl championship. In the wild-card game against the Lions, Riggins romped for 119 yards. A week later, in the playoff game against the Vikings, he gained 185 yards rushing, still a Redskins playoff standard. Then, in the 1982 NFC title battle with the Cowboys, he chalked up another 140 yards and two touchdowns. And, finally, in Super Bowl XVII, he rushed for 166 yards, including a 43-yard run for the touchdown that put the Skins ahead of the Miami Dolphins

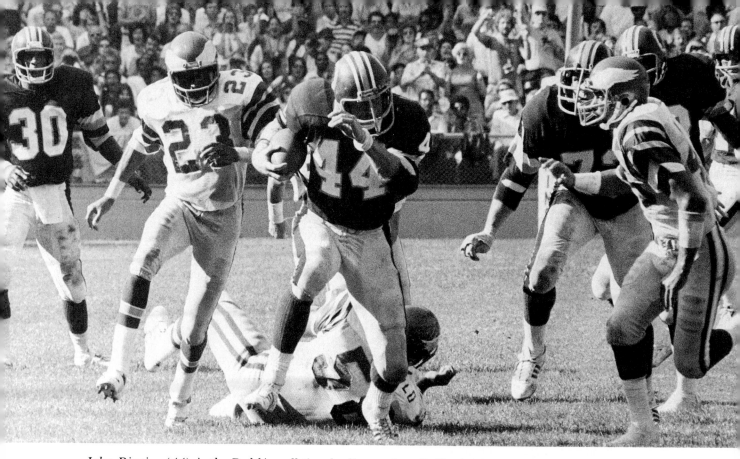

John Riggins (44) is the Redskins all-time leading rusher. Fullback Riggins gained 7,472 yards from 1976 through 1985, and holds practically every Washington record. His 24 rushing touchdowns in 1983 are an NFL record, as is his streak of 13 consecutive games with a rushing touchdown. (Washington Redskins)

for good. As reward, Riggins was named the game's Most Valuable Player.

Riggins added 1,000-yard seasons in 1983 and 1984, the 1,347 yards he gained in '83 remaining the team's all-time high. It was also in 1983 that Big John scored 24 touchdowns rushing, an NFL record, and was the recipient of the Bert Bell Award as NFL Player of the Year.

After the 1985 season, Riggins retired. Of his 13 years in the NFL, he spent eight of them in Washington and became one of the town's most recognizable celebrities. His iconoclastic behavior off the field was as well known as his sterling performances on it. Riggo, as he came to be known around the nation's capital, left football with practically every team rushing record: most yards gained (7,472), most in a season (1,347 in 1983), most carries (1,988), most carries in a season (375 in 1983), most carries in a game

(38 against the Dolphins in Super Bowl XVII), most 100-yard games (25), most touchdowns rushing (79), and most touchdowns rushing in a season (24).

Besides holding the NFL record for most rushing TDs in a season (24), John Riggins is the fifth-leading rusher in NFL history, his total of 11,352 yards behind only Walter Payton, Jim Brown, Franco Harris, and Tony Dorsett. He ranks second behind Hall of Famer Jim Brown in total touchdowns scored (116) and touchdowns rushing (104).

And, he was an honorary member of the Hogs, the only non-lineman to be so slopped.

George Rogers

George Rogers had gained more than 5,000 yards in five years with the New Orleans Saints before being traded to the Redskins

George Rogers
1985–87 (Washington Redskins)

Washington's premier ball carrier, but he labored through much of the 1985 season. Before Game 14 he had gained just 642 yards, noticeably below his output in New Orleans. The press did not quite believe him when he announced before that game, "I know I can still get a thousand." They should have. He went out that afternoon and ran for 150 yards. The following week it was 95, including a game-winning touchdown run of 34 yards against the Cincinnati Bengals. Then, in the last game of the season, Rogers raced for 206 yards against the St. Louis Cardinals, the most ever in a single game by a Redskins runner. At season's end, he had finished with 1,093 rushing yards.

The next year, George Rogers became only the second Redskins back to post consecutive 1,000-yard seasons (John Riggins had done it twice) when he rumbled for 1,203. He also turned in five 100-yard games that year, the second most in team history, and scored a league-high 18 touchdowns rushing (only John Riggins's 24 in 1983 are more in Redskins annals).

Bothered by a toe injury early in the 1987 season, Rogers was unable to gain his previous form and his yardage was limited to 613. With the promise shown by rookie running back Timmy Smith, the Redskins decided to release Rogers after the '87 season. In his three years with the Redskins, George Rogers gained enough yards to become the team's fifth all-time rusher (2,909). Only John Riggins and Larry Brown turned in more 100-yard games than Rogers's 12, and only those two scored more touchdowns rushing than his 31. When he left the Redskins, George Rogers ranked 15th among all-time rushers in the NFL, with a total of 7,176 yards.

in 1985. Washington had to give up a first-round draft choice for him, but Joe Gibbs knew he needed a top-flight back to fuel the running game, since John Riggins, at 36, had slowed perceptibly.

The 1980 Heisman Trophy winner from South Carolina, Rogers quickly became

3

A Championship for Washington

The move to Washington was a smooth one for the Redskins. The Big Chief, George Preston Marshall, had easily secured league approval for the relocation, and skillfully negotiated a beneficial deal for playing home games in Griffith Stadium on Florida Avenue. Clark Griffith, owner of the ballpark and the Washington Senators, agreed to add removable steel seats that would accommodate an additional 10,000 spectators, and installed a new, modern lighting system, a new public-address system, and a tarpaulin that would cover the entire playing field and keep it dry.

To insure that the Redskins would get the press coverage that had been nearly nonexistent in Boston, which meant so much to showman Marshall, the Redskins hired George Washington University's publicity agent, Jack Espey, and gave him the title of general manager.

Marshall also lined up a brass marching band, which soon was expanded to 150 pieces, to entertain before games and at halftime. And he adopted a fight song, the music written by Barnet "Barnee" Breeskin, then the bandleader of the Shoreham Hotel orchestra in Washington. Marshall's wife, silent-film star Corinne Griffith, was given the assignment of writing the lyrics after other professional lyricists had turned down the challenge. She wrote them, and soon the song "Hail to the Redskins" became as much a part of the team as its offense and defense.

What would prove to be the organization's most important addition, however, was the lanky cowboy from Texas who had starred at Texas Christian, Slingin' Sammy Baugh,

the Redskins' first-round draft choice for 1937. Sports columnist Grantland Rice had touted Baugh to Marshall, suggesting that he was the best passer and punter in the college game. Marshall knew that a passing attack would surely complement the fine running game the Redskins boasted, with such ball-carriers as Cliff Battles, Don Irwin, and Erny Pinckert; it would also enliven the game that The Big Chief wanted to dish up to his newfound fans.

Signing Baugh was a different matter. Marshall, whose highest-paid player the year before, Cliff Battles, earned $2,100 for the season (plus about $180 for playing in the NFL title game), kept his offer a well-guarded secret. It was said to have been $5,000, which Baugh turned down. It was not until after a lot of haggling and Baugh's threat to devote all his time to baseball—he had signed a contract with the St. Louis Cardinals—and forget about professional football altogether that Marshall cringingly upped his offer to $8,000. Baugh accepted.

Marshall, ever the consummate promoter, arranged to have Baugh brought to Washington to be formally introduced to the city's press and radio corps. The story has often been told that Marshall orchestrated the entire event with his own unique brand of showmanship. But it really never happened the way it was later hyped. As Sammy Baugh

Opening night, September 16, 1937, at Griffith Stadium. Reconstruction Finance Chief, Jesse Jones, throws out the ceremonial first ball. He is flanked by team captains Turk Edwards (17) of the Redskins and Mel Hein (7) of the New York Giants. (HOF/NFL Photos)

himself explains, "Some writer wrote how George Preston Marshall, the owner of the club, called me up down in Texas and asked me if I had cowboy boots and a 10-gallon hat and that I said no. He was supposed to have told me then to go out and buy the things and that he'd pay me back in Washington. . . . Well, hell, that's just a made-up story. . . . I normally wore that kind of stuff. I didn't need him to tell me to wear it and I sure didn't need to go out and buy it. . . . Some writer just made it up and everybody picked it up. Writers like to embellish things

like that. After it was written, though, Mr. Marshall got a big kick out of it."

A signed and sealed Baugh was, however, late showing up for training camp, because he was in Chicago practicing with the College All-Stars, who were slated to take on the NFL champion Green Bay Packers to start the 1937 preseason. At that spectacle Baugh gave the first hint of what he was about to bring to the National Football League and the Washington Redskins: his penchant for defeating pro football teams. His 47-yard touchdown pass to Gaynell Tinsley of Lou-

48

isiana State provided the winning touchdown as the collegians beat the Pack, 6–0.

When tailback Baugh did link up with the Redskins at their training camp in Anacostia, Maryland, that summer, he was quickly assimilated into a single-wing backfield that also featured halfback Cliff Battles, fullback Don Irwin, and quarterback Riley Smith.

Before Baugh had arrived the Redskins had honed their skills by crushing the American Legion All-Stars at Frederick, Virginia, 50–0. It was an age when preseason schedules were a good deal less defined than they are today.

Baugh was ready for the Redskins' debut in Washington. In town, to launch the 1937 football season and the city's new entry in the NFL, were the New York Giants. The game was set for Thursday night, September 16. Marshall had hopes for a crowd of about 25,000, but he had to settle for a paid attendance of 19,941. He had also hoped to have President Franklin Delano Roosevelt throw out the first football, but he had to settle instead for Jesse Jones, head of the Reconstruction Finance Corporation.

If The Big Chief did not get exactly what he wanted in the grandstands of Griffith Stadium that opening night, he at least did on the playing field. The Giants were a highly regarded team, picked by many to win the NFL's Eastern Division that year. They showcased one of the best rushers in the game in fullback Tuffy Leemans, who was also very popular in Washington, because he had starred there in the backfield for George Washington University just two years earlier. But Baugh, passing to ends Charley Malone and Wayne Millner, drove the Redskins into range for two Riley Smith field goals. The Washington defense, spearheaded by monstrous tackle Turk Edwards (6'2", 260 pounds) and defensive back Riley Smith, who picked off a Giants pass and ran it back 60 yards for a touchdown, held New

York to just a single field goal all evening. At game's end, the Redskins were on top of a 13–3 score, and in possession of the first regular-season victory in their new hometown.

The following week the Redskins played on a Friday night at Griffith Stadium, but this time were the unproud possessors of their first defeat in Washington. It was a surprise doled out by the mediocre Chicago Cardinals, 21–17.

Wayne Millner of Notre Dame was the Redskins eighth-round choice in the NFL's initial college draft in 1936. He proved to be one of the finest all-around ends in the game of pro football, a dangerous receiver, formidable blocker, and superb defensive player. Millner starred for the Redskins through the 1941 season, then returned for one more in 1945 after three years of military service. He was elected to the Pro Football Hall of Fame in 1968. (HOF/NFL Photos)

It was, however, only one of three losses the Redskins would suffer all year. On their way to a climactic showdown with the Giants in the last game of the regular season, they would fall to the Philadelphia Eagles and the Pittsburgh Pirates, as the Steelers were known in those days, but would prevail in games with the Brooklyn Dodgers twice, the Cleveland Rams, the Green Bay Packers, who were the defending NFL champions, as well as the Eagles and Pirates.

By December, the Redskins were the toast of Washington. With a record of 7–3–0, they barely trailed the Giants, who led the NFL East at 6–2–2. Rookie Sammy Baugh, leading the entire league in passing, and Cliff Battles, the top NFL rusher of 1937, were certified local heroes. They would have to go up to New York, however, to face the Giants, who the oddsmakers favored despite the fact that the Redskins had beaten them in the season opener, to determine the divisional title on December 5.

Washington's support of the Redskins had enthralled Marshall, and it reached a crescendo in The Big Chief's heart when approximately 10,000 fans boarded 15 special trains in Washington's Union Station the day of the game to trek to New York and cheer on their team. Marshall chipped in by bringing along his 150-piece band, replete with full, white-feathered Indian headdresses. Marshall also provided a burgundy feather for each of the hats of the loyal 10,000.

George Preston Marshall and wife Corinne Griffith were on hand to greet the loyalists at Penn Station in New York. As the band and the fans spilled off the trains, he announced, "The Indians have come to reclaim Manhattan Island." Then, with The Big Chief himself in the lead and impeccably attired in a flowing raccoon coat, the throng paraded up Seventh Avenue to the lilting airs of "Hail to the Redskins."

If Marshall had the fans enthusiastic, coach Ray Flaherty had his players fully inspired. They stormed onto the field at the Polo Grounds and mercilessly destroyed the Giants that Sunday afternoon, 49–14. With Sammy Baugh's pinpoint passing to ends Charley Malone and Wayne Millner and a bevy of backs, plus the running of Cliff Battles (he raced 75 yards from scrimmage on one play and returned an interception 76 yards for a touchdown), there was never a doubt.

An ebullient, exhilarated Marshall led his team, band, and fervent fans back to Washington with the NFL East crown.

When all the stats were in for the regular season, Sammy Baugh had led the league in pass completions (81) and yards gained passing (1,127) and Cliff Battles had rushed for the most yards in the NFL (874) and scored the most touchdowns rushing (five). In addition, Charley Malone was the league's third-ranked receiver, catching 28 passes for 419 yards. Baugh, Battles, and tackle Turk Edwards were named All-Pro.

Now all they had to do was face the Chicago Bears, victors in the NFL West, to determine which team would wear the NFL crown for 1937.

Championship Game, 1937

George Halas's Chicago Bears, with a record of 9–1–1, had brutally mauled just about every opponent they faced in the NFL West in 1937. The Bears were a running team, like most others in the NFL during that era. They had the indomitable Bronko Nagurski at fullback, as well as such yardage-gobbling runners as Ray Nolting, Gene Ronzani, Beattie Feathers, and Jack Manders, who was also the top field goal kicker in the league that year. Blocking for them were three future Hall of Famers: tackle Joe

The Redskins band and 10,000 loyal fans march on Manhattan before the game between the Redskins and Giants to decide the NFL east title for 1937. Later that day, they were rewarded with a 49–14 Washington triumph. (Washington Redskins)

LINEUPS

Washington Redskins		Chicago Bears
Wayne Millner	LE	Eggs Manske
Turk Edwards	LT	Joe Stydahar
Les Olsson	LG	Danny Fortmann
Ed Kawal	C	Frank Bausch
Jim Karcher	RG	George Musso
Jim Barber	RT	Del Bjork
Charley Malone	RE	George Wilson
Riley Smith	QB	Bernie Masterson
Sammy Baugh	LH	Ray Nolting
Erny Pinckert	RH	Jack Manders
Cliff Battles	FB	Bronko Nagurski
Ray Flaherty	coach	George Halas

Stydahar and guards Danny Fortmann and George Musso.

The Bears themselves loomed as one obviously measurable obstacle, and so did the weather in Chicago, where the game was to be played at Wrigley Field, home to the Chicago Cubs. A bitter cold front had moved into Chicago the week before the game, which was not a big surprise in the Windy City in December, and by game day the playing field was frozen solid. Advertisements in the Chicago newspapers announced that there were still 25,000 seats available for the NFL title game.

On Sunday, December 12, at game time, the temperature was 15 degrees above zero and the wind blew at about 12 miles per hour, creating a wind-chill factor of about six below zero. It was enough to keep many of those 25,000 seats at Wrigley Field unoccupied, and only 15,878 well-bundled and hardy fans observed firsthand the combat for the NFL title (about 3,000 of them were Redskins fans who had made the junket from Washington by train). But those who made the sacrifice bore witness to one of the most exciting NFL championship games ever.

The field not only had the solidity of an iceberg, it was also as slippery as one. Both teams, therefore, donned sneakers, having apparently learned from the New York Giants' use of them on a similar ice-coated field in the NFL championship game of 1934. At halftime of that game, the New Yorkers had switched to sneakers and turned a 10–3 deficit into a 30–13 victory over the Bears.

Turk Edwards kicked off for the Redskins and the Ice Bowl, as some called it, was under way. Bronko Nagurski returned it to the 33. It was not until midway through the first period that a scoring drive was mounted. And directing it was Sammy Baugh. Two passes to Riley Smith and another to Erny Pinckert moved the Redskins to the Chicago 10-yard line. Then it was Cliff Battles's turn. He gained three yards, and on third down burst through for the remaining seven and a touchdown.

The Bears, however, came right back. Expecting Chicago's patented running attack, the Redskins were stunned by a 51-

yard pass play from Bernie Masterson to Eggs Manske. Moments later Jack Manders carried it in, and the score was tied at 7–7.

It appeared the oddsmakers were correct when George Wilson intercepted a Baugh pass a few plays later and the Bears offense again exploded. This time, Masterson threw a 12-yard pass to Manders at the Washington 25-yard line and the Bears' back shook off a tackler and raced in for another score.

That was the last of the scoring in the first half, but the game was far from over. Sammy Baugh, who had missed most of the second quarter after being shaken up, came back, and with him returned the Redskins' offense. On their first possession of the second half, Baugh connected with Wayne Millner on a 55-yard touchdown pass, and the score was tied at 14 apiece.

The Bears then reverted to their running game, and Nagurski, Nolting, and Manders ground out the yardage, moving the ball all the way to the Washington four-yard line. There, with fourth down and goal to go, Masterson faked a handoff and then lobbed a jump pass to Manders in the end zone, and the Bears had the lead again.

Baugh responded with quick and deadly vengeance. After the kickoff, he went to Millner again. Dropping back from the line of scrimmage at the Washington 22, he threw a perfect strike at the 50 to Millner, who then outran all defenders for a 78-yard touchdown play.

With the score tied at 21–21, the Redskins defense tightened. When the team got the ball again, Baugh put on another aerial display to thrill the fans who had accompa-

One of the mightier forces the Redskins had to contend with in the 1937 title game was fullback Bronko Nagurski. Identifiable Redskins are tackle Turk Edwards (17), guard Les Olsson (21), and tackle Jim Barber (15). (HOF/NFL Photos)

nied the Redskins to Chicago. Passes to Charley Malone and Millner and finally a 35-yard touchdown toss to Ed Justice put Washington in the lead, 28–21.

In the fourth quarter the ball changed hands with metronomic regularity. But no one scored. At the final whistle, the Redskins remained on top.

George Preston Marshall had not only brought professional football to Washington in 1937, he had given the city an NFL championship as well.

TRIVIUM

The gross gate receipts for the 1937 NFL championship game were less than a single player's winning share of the Super Bowl in the late 1980s. The total take of $32,198 is almost $4,000 less than the $36,000 earned by each triumphant Super Bowl player. Each winning Redskin in 1937 received $225.90 for toiling in that title game, and each losing Bear earned $127.78

IN THE HEAT OF THE BATTLE

Protecting Sammy Baugh was the name of the game in the 1937 battle for the NFL championship. Coach Ray Flaherty reminded his team before the game that a healthy Baugh would be a major factor that day and it behooved all conerned to see that he stayed that way on the field of play.

The reminder was felt necessary because the George Halas-coached Chicago Bears, with certified monsters such as Bronko Nagurski, George Musso, and Joe Stydahar, among others, had a deserved reputation of being tough, nasty, and downright dangerous.

Tackle Turk Edwards took it sincerely to heart and was heard more than once warning opposing defensive linemen that they had better not try any rough stuff with Slingin' Sam or horrendous retribution would be paid. In one overzealous moment, Edwards was so intent on protecting his passer that in his eagerness to block for Baugh he backed over him, causing a 15-yard loss.

Later in the game, Chicago end Dick Plasman took special offense at something defensive back Baugh did on a pass play in which they had become entangled, and he threw a punch at Sammy. Unfortunately for Plasman, it was a short five yards from the Washington bench and, as Shirley Povich later described in *The Washington Post,* "Coach Flaherty was the first to leap to his feet and the first to rush to the battle scene. He tackled Plasman high—high around the mouth—with a set of knuckles and put an end to the battle."

Baugh finished the game in good health, and the Redskins, of course, were triumphant.

Ray Flaherty (right), new head coach of the Redskins in 1936 poses with his boss George Preston Marshall. Strong willed and confident in his own abilities, Flaherty made it clear from the outset that he would not permit Marshall to meddle in the coaching of the Redskins. (HOF/NFL Photos)

THE SONG

What is *the* song? "Hail to the Redskins," of course. It was not the first fight song penned for a pro football team, as George Preston Marshall often claimed—the Chicago Bears and the Frankford Yellow Jackets had adopted their own inspirational music and lyrics in the 1920s—but it is arguably the most famous.

As Morris Siegel wrote in an article about the song in a 1983 edition of *Game-Day* magazine: "It was sung badly, if enthusiastically, on the White House lawn by Secretary of State George Shultz.

"It was performed nightly for a week in the Kennedy Center for the Performing Arts by the National Symphony Orchestra under the direction of Russian-born conductor Mstislav Rostropovich.

"It was proposed as the official song of the nation's capital, which now is identified as much as the headquarters of the Super Bowl XVII champions (the Washington Redskins naturally) as the seat of the federal government.

"It was extolled by a unanimously adopted resolution of the Maryland State Senate, a display of bipartisanship at its highest level.

"In Washington, it continues to be number one on the people's charts regardless of which Top 40 show they listen to. It remains a unifying battle cry at restaurants and bars on Capitol Hill. . . .

"However poorly it is sung or played, 'Hail to the Redskins' immediately brings Washingtonians to attention."

How did this paean to George Preston Marshall's noble Redskins come about? Let Corinne Griffith, The Big Chief's wife

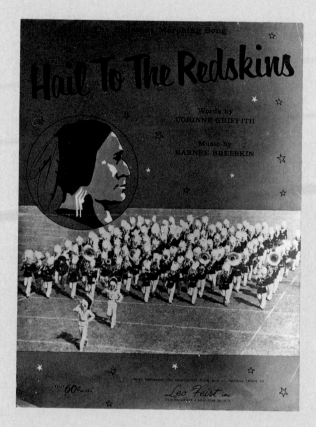

and the fight song's lyricist, tell the story, as she did in her book *My Life with the Redskins* (A.S. Barnes, 1947).

We returned to the Shoreham Hotel in Washington after leaving Dallas early in the summer of 1937. Things were *fairly* quiet one morning, when the telephone rang. It was Barnee [Breeskin], leader of the Shoreham orchestra. Since the Redskins were going to be in Washington, he said, he thought they should have a song and he had written one which he wanted us to hear. He was calling it "Hail to the Redskins."

I turned from the telephone, held my hand over the receiver and asked George

HAIL TO THE REDSKINS

Words by
CORINNE GRIFFITH

Music by
BARNEE BREESKIN

The Band—in Griffith Stadium. (Washington Redskins)

The Band Silenced

The Redskins band, at least according to recorded history, was silenced only once. And it was the night of one of the team's most glorious victories.

For the last game of the 1937 regular season at the Polo Grounds, one that would decide the NFL East title that year, Marshall brought his marching band along with the team to New York. The band, all wearing white headdresses and appropriate Indian costumes, marched down Seventh Avenue in Manhattan with The Big Chief at the head of it. Inside the Polo Grounds its rendition of "Hail to the Redskins" so inspired the team that they decimated the Giants 49–14, thus earning the right to play in the NFL title game against the Bears.

After the game, the band, the team, and Marshall and his entourage boarded the last train back to Washington. At Union Station in Washington at about 11 o'clock that night, some 10,000 fans were waiting to welcome home the victors. Marshall thought it only proper for his beloved band to lead a little march up Pennsylvania Avenue.

The Washington police, less musically inclined than Marshall, especially just before midnight, told him that he could not stage his victory march without an official city license. Marshall argued vehemently with them. The police stood firm: "No license, no parade."

Marshall left angrily, but not in defeat. He marshaled as many members of the band as he could find and guided them up the avenue, out of sight of the police—at least so he thought. There they would march a single block to the tune of "Hail to the Redskins."

As the first few bars of that famous fight song lilted into the balmy Washington night air, the police reappeared. The music stopped and the police threatened to arrest the entire band. But, having only one patrol wagon with them, they settled for merely collaring the drum major.

A deprived, frustrated Marshall grumped that hostile New York had allowed his band to march on *its* streets while his own hometown was denying him and his triumphal team that very same, simple honor. But to no avail. He followed the paddy wagon down to 1st Precinct headquarters and came up with the $25 to bail his drum major out of jail.

4

Between Titles

After the Redskins won their first NFL title in 1937, they remained in hot contention in each of the ensuing eight years. Four times they reached the title game (1940, 1942, 1943, and 1945), and in the other four seasons they were always close in the NFL East divisional race, usually edged out by their nemesis of that era, the New York Giants.

Washington had lost its star running back, Cliff Battles, before the start of the 1938 season. Despite his All-Pro season the year before, his request for a $1,000 raise was turned down by George Preston Marshall. Battles surprised everyone, especially The Big Chief himself, when he then quit to take an assistant coaching job under Lou Little at Columbia University (that was when Columbia had Sid Luckman, the future great T-formation quarterback for the Chicago

Bears, at tailback and won most of its games, as opposed to the Columbia of modern times). Marshall tried to get Battles back into a Redskins uniform, but the exceptional running back refused to reconsider his decision.

Sammy Baugh was also embroiled in a brief contract dispute with Marshall, but The Big Chief was not about to let his prize tailback leave the tribe. Slingin' Sam was signed in time to play in the preseason opener, the College All-Star Game in Chicago, in which the Skins were embarrassed by the collegians, 28–0.

In 1938, the Redskins had made two important additions, halfback Andy Farkas from Detroit University and tackle Wee Willie Wilkin of St. Mary's College in California. Despite the retirement of Battles and the loss of Sammy Baugh for most of the

first half of the year because of a shoulder separation suffered in the first game of the regular season, the Redskins managed to compete for the divisional crown all the way to the last game of the year. With a record of 6–2–2, all they needed was to defeat the New York Giants, who were 7–2–1, to cop the title. Washington had fallen to the Giants earlier in the season, 10–7, at Griffith Stadium, but hopes were high as the Redskins, their marching band, and 12,000 of their fans entrained for Manhattan for the decider. The fervent fans repeated their now-famous march on Manhattan, this time up Broadway, but it did little to inspire the Redskins of '38. The New Yorkers, on a blustery December Sunday, blew them away, 36–0, to avenge the 49–14 humiliation

Washington had dealt them in the deciding game of the 1937 season.

The Redskins' record of 6–3–2 secured only second place in the NFL East for 1938. Sammy Baugh had had a good year, completing 63 passes for 853 yards. His chief receivers remained Charley Malone, with 24 catches for 257 yards, and Wayne Millner, who grabbed 18 for 232 yards. Tops among rushers was Andy Farkas, who gained 315 yards with a 4.2-yard average and had a league-high six rushing touchdowns.

The most strategic acquisition for the 1939 season was tailback Frank Filchock, whom Marshall acquired on waivers from the Pittsburgh Pirates. Coach Ray Flaherty promptly decided to spare Sammy Baugh some of the punishment he had been endur-

THE NATIONAL FOOTBALL LEAGUE
UNIFORM PLAYER'S CONTRACT

The PRO-FOOTBALL, INC. .... herein called the Club,
and .... SAM BAUGH ...., of .... SWEETWATER, TEXAS
herein called the Player.

    The Club is a member of **The National Football League.** As such, and jointly with the other members of the League, it is obligated to insure to the public wholesome and high-class professional football by defining the relations between Club and Player, and between Club and Club.

    In view of the facts above recited the parties agree as follows:

    1. The Club will pay the Player a salary for his skilled services during the playing season of 19..40., at the rate of ..$1.00 ---------------.... dollars for each regularly scheduled League game played. For all other games the Player shall be paid such salary as shall be agreed upon between the Player and the Club. As to games scheduled but not played, the Player shall receive no compensation from the Club other than actual expenses.

.... Plus transportation to and from training camp. If team wins championship player .....
      agrees to play one game as directed as per terms of this contract. Player is not
.... to receive compensation for exhibition games other than herein stipulated ....

    2. The salary above provided for shall be paid by the Club as follows:

    Seventy-five per cent (75%) after each game and the remaining twenty-five per cent (25%) at the close of the season or upon release of the Player by the Club.

    3. The Player agrees that during said season he will faithfully serve the Club, and pledges himself to the American public to conform to high standards of fair play and good sportsmanship.

    4. The Player will not play football during 19...40 otherwise than for the Club, except in case the Club shall have released said Player, and said release has been approved by the officials of **The National Football League.**

    5. The Player will not participate in an exhibition game after the completion of the schedule of the Club and prior to August 1 of the following season, without the permission of the President of the League.

    6. The Player accepts as part of this contract such reasonable regulations as the Club may announce from time to time.

    7. This contract may be terminated at any time by the club giving notice in writing to the player within forty-eight (48) hours after the day of the last game in which he is to participate with his club.

    8. The Player submits himself to the discipline of **The National Football League** and agrees to accept its decisions pursuant to its Constitution and By-Laws.

    9. Any time prior to August 1st, 19..41., by written notice to the Player, the Club may renew this contract for the term of that year, except that the salary rate shall be such as the parties may then agree upon, or in default of agreement, such as the Club may fix.

    10. The Player may be fined or suspended for violation of this contract, but in all cases the Player shall have the right of appeal to the President of **The National Football League.**

    11. In default of agreement, the Player will accept the salary rate thus fixed or else will not play during said year otherwise than for the Club, unless the Club shall release the Player.

    12. The reservation of the Club of the valuable right to fix the salary rate for the succeeding year, and the promise of the Player not to play during said year otherwise than with the Club, have been taken into consideration in determining the salary specified herein and the undertaking by the Club to pay said salary is the consideration for both the reservation and the promise.

    13. In case of dispute between the Player and the Club the same shall be referred to the President of **The National Football League,** and his decision shall be accepted by all parties as final.

    14. Verbal contracts between Club and Player will not be considered by this League, in the event of a dispute.

Signed this............. day of .... September ....A. D. 19.....40

Witnesses:

                                         PRO-FOOTBALL, INC.

-------------------------------------   (Club)

                          By *Ray Flaherty* (Coach)

-------------------------------------   *Sam Baugh*

                                         (Player)

Original copy to be held by Club Management

Sammy Baugh's contract for 1940. Note the "$1.00" per game. Even then the dollars and cents were kept secret. (HOF/NFL Photos)

ing as tailback/defensive back for the preceding two seasons, by invoking what is considered the first platooning of tailbacks in NFL history, with Baugh usually handling the first and third quarters and Filchock the second and fourth.

The Redskins and Giants met at Griffith Stadium in the second week of the regular season that year and found, to both teams' dismay, that their volatile offenses of the past two years were totally lacking. They played to a scoreless tie. But it set the stage for what was considered a toss-up title match again on the last Sunday of the regular season. Going into that game, which was staged, as it had been in 1937 and 1938, at the Polo Grounds, both teams had records of 8–1–1.

Once again trainloads of Washingtonians converged on New York City, marching, chanting "Hail to the Redskins," and otherwise disturbing the peace of the Polo Grounds. And, as they had been earlier in the season, the offenses were overwhelmed by the defenses—although there was some scoring in this encounter. The Giants worked their way into field goal range three times; Ken Strong booted one three-pointer and Ward Cuff two others.

The Redskins were unable to make a mark on the scoreboard during the first three quarters of play, but in the fourth period, with the Giants deep in their own territory, the mammoth Wee Willie Wilkin burst through and blocked a punt by Hank Soar, a fine Giant back who would later become better known as a major league baseball umpire. It was recovered by Washington guard Clyde Shugart. On second down Frank Filchock dropped back and rifled the ball to Bob Masterson for a touchdown. Bo Russell kicked the extra point and the Redskins trailed by just two points, 9–7.

The Redskins got the ball back and, with less than a minute left in the game, had moved it to the New York 10-yard line. On fourth down coach Flaherty sent his field goal kicker, Bo Russell, onto the field. Frank Filchock took the snap and Russell applied his toe to the ball. It appeared, at least to the Redskins and their legion of fans, that the kick was good. They were leaping in jubilation at the seemingly game-winning, title-clinching field goal.

Yet, there was referee Bill Halloran, not with his arms extended into the air, but slashing them back and forth in front of him, signaling that the kick was *not* good. Flaherty was the first onto the field to scream at the stone-faced referee, and had to be forcibly restrained. Redskins players raged at Halloran. Fans clambered out of the stands and the New York police swiftly moved out onto the field to protect the suddenly and surely threatened Halloran. But the call stood, the field was cleared, and the game ended with New York on top, 9–7, and the possessor of the NFL East crown for the second year in a row.

After the game Flaherty said: "If that guy [Halloran] has got a conscience, he'll never have another good night's sleep as long as he lives." No one knows how many good nights' sleep he subsequently had, but it is known that he never refereed another NFL game, thanks to the persuasiveness of George Preston Marshall at the owners' meetings prior to the 1940 season.

So again impresario Marshall, coach Flaherty, and the Skins had to settle for a second-place finish to the Giants. Their record of 8–2–1 was impressive, but not enough to extend the football year. Fullback Andy Farkas had the distinction of scoring more points than anyone else in the NFL that year, a total of 68, which he amassed with five rushing touchdowns, five TD receptions, a scoring interception return, and two extra points. He was also the team's leading rusher, with 547 yards. The freshly arrived Filchock proved to be the most productive passer, his 55 completions for

THE FIELD GOAL THAT WASN'T

Referee Bill Halloran, who made the controversial call on Bo Russell's attempted field goal in the waning moments of the game that decided the 1939 NFL East title, had no harsher critic than author Morris A. Bealle, who let his feelings fly in his book *The Redskins, 1937–1958*. As he described the gloomy event:

> Eight thousand Redskin fans journeyed to New York by special trains. They saw their team beat the Giants 10–9 for the Eastern title; they saw a Providence [RI] politician named Halloran, who was refereeing the game, beat the Redskins 9–7. . . .
>
> Your author was in the upper stands. He followed the ball and saw it hit squarely between the two clocks under the Elevated Railroad platform. He looked down expecting to see Halloran's arms upright, signalling the field goal.
>
> Halloran was still cogitating. He [Bealle] looked at the ball again and saw the crowd scrambling for it—exactly between the two clocks. He looked down again and Halloran was waving his arms horizontally, indicating he had at last decided to disallow the 3 points. . . .
>
> Next day your author went out to the Polo Grounds with a steel tape and drew up [this] sketch, which proved conclusively that only a blind man or a crook could have disallowed Russell's field goal. Motion pictures of the kick, displayed in Keith's Theater next day, showed the ball between the uprights.

Measurements taken at the east end of the Polo Grounds the day after Bo Russell kicked a winning field goal which was disallowed by the referee. This shows it was impossible to have been called anything but a field goal by anyone but the most calloused official.

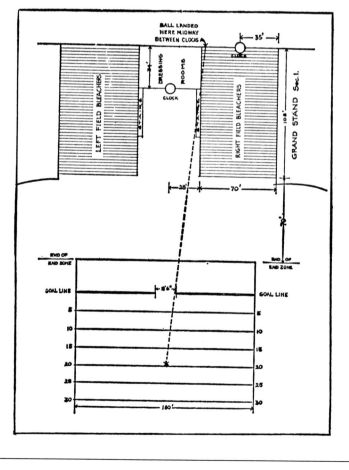

66

1,094 yards edging out Sammy Baugh, who completed 53 for 518 yards. Their favorite receivers were again Wayne Millner (19 for 294 yards) and Charley Malone (18 for 274 yards), plus halfback Dick Todd, who grabbed 19 for 230 yards.

The Redskins did make it to the NFL championship match in 1940. But after *that* truly horrific game, many Washington fans retrospectively wished that referee Bill Halloran had been around to deprive them of the NFL East title as he had the year before, to prevent them from falling victim to the most brutal massacre since Custer decided to camp out at Little Big Horn.

The Redskins of 1940 were little different than those of 1939. Sammy Baugh was actually in better physical shape than he had been. And Andy Farkas was coming off a year in which he led the NFL in scoring with 68 points (11 touchdowns and two extra points). The defense of 1939, which had allowed only a little over seven and a half points per game, was back in full force.

There was, however, the usual salary turmoil before the preseason—precipitated, according to the players, by The Big Chief's niggardliness and, according to Marshall, by the avarice of the players. Whichever, Wayne Millner was holding out and Frank Filchock and Wee Willie Wilkin turned down the contracts offered by Marshall. Sammy Baugh, who was under contract but not apparently with overwhelming satisfaction, announced that he was planning to retire at the end of the season to go into coaching on the college level.

However, by the time they were ready to board the Liberty Limited in August for training camp in Spokane, Washington, all had been signed.

George Preston Marshall announced that seating had been increased, so that Griffith Stadium could now accommodate 40,000

spectators. He also added that the $1.65 tickets were to be increased to $2.20 and the $2.20 seats upped to $3.20.

The Redskins got off to a beautiful start in 1940, leading the season off with a 24–17 win over a very good Brooklyn Dodgers team, led by future Hall of Fame tailback Ace Parker. The next week they sank the usually spoilsport Giants, 21–7. In fact, Washington won their first seven games of the regular season.

It was not until they traveled to Ebbets Field to face the Dodgers again that they evinced any vulnerability. That day they could not contain the versatile Parker and lost a squeaker, 16–14. In that game, Slingin' Sammy Baugh slung his way to an NFL record of 23 completions in a single game (two were for Washington's only touchdowns).

The following week presented perhaps the biggest challenge of the season. The Chicago Bears were coming to town, leading the NFL West and from the very start of the year an odds-on favorite to win the NFL title. Bert Bell, then owner of the Philadelphia Eagles, said in the preseason, "No one's going to beat the Bears this year. They're the greatest team ever assembled."

They were imposing, with six future Hall of Famers in the starting lineup: quarterback Sid Luckman, halfback George McAfee, center Bulldog Turner, tackle Joe Stydahar, and guards Danny Fortmann and George Musso. They also had All-Pros in fullback Bill Osmanski, end Ken Kavanaugh, and tackle Lee Artoe. But Bert Bell was wrong: They could be beaten. Washington proved that on a mid-November afternoon in Griffith Stadium.

The Bears scored first on a field goal by "Automatic" Jack Manders, but had great difficulty with the Washington defense throughout the rest of the first half. In the second quarter, Frank Filchock moved the

Redskin Big Chiefs Hold Powwow (Associated Press Wirefoto)

Among Redskins gathered in the Nation's Capital to bring downfall to Chicago's Bears in pro football's "World Series" tomorrow are the potent warriors above. Left to right, Sammy Baugh, Dick Todd, Frank Filchock and Andy Farkas. A sellout is expected at Griffith Stadium which seats some 36,000.

Redskins to inside the Bears' 20-yard line, then pitched out to halfback Dick Todd, who wove his way through the Chicago defense for a touchdown.

The second half was a defensive battle all the way to the last possession of the game. With the score still standing at 7–3, Washington, George McAfee, a scatback for the Bears who could be devastating in the open field, broke loose and made it all the way to the Redskins' one-yard line. The Washington defense held fast, and in fact pushed the Bears back to the six-yard line. Then, on the last play of the game, Luckman rolled out and threw to Bill Osmanski in the end zone. Redskins defender Frank Filchock went up and separated receiver and ball, and the final gun sounded. The Bears screamed foul. Coach George Halas rushed onto the field claiming Osmanski had been interfered with by Filchock. But there was no flag on the field. The final score remained: Redskins 7, Bears 3.

After the game, however, George Preston Marshall—in a state of exultation and always anxious to give it to his friend and football archrival George Halas—made a statement to the press that he would come to rue. The Big Chief said: "The Bears are front-runners, quitters. They're not a second-half team, just a bunch of crybabies! They fold up when the going gets tough."

Halas read it, then saved all the newspapers in which it appeared.

The Redskins lost to the Giants the following week, 21–7, but this year it did not spoil their title pursuit. Washington, leading the division with a record of 8–1–0 going into the Giants' game, had already outdistanced the 5–3–1 New Yorkers. All they had to do now was defeat the Philadelphia Eagles in the last game of the season, because the second-place Brooklyn Dodgers had lost three games. And at Griffith Stadium they did just what was required of them, beating Philadelphia, 13–7.

The Redskins, with a record of 9–2–0, the most games they had won thus far in their history, were the NFL East champs for the second time since moving to Washington in 1937. Sammy Baugh had reasserted himself as the team's premier passer, completing 111 for league highs of 1,367 yards and 12 touchdowns. Filchock added another 460 yards passing. With Andy Farkas out for the season with a knee injury, Dick Todd led the team in rushing in '40, picking up 408 yards, with a 5.4-yard average. He also gained more yards on pass receptions (402) than any other Redskin. Baugh made All-Pro for the second time in his now four-year Redskins career.

Meanwhile, over in the NFL West, the Bears had apparently dried their tears and defeated the Cleveland Rams, 47–25, and the Chicago Cardinals, 31–23, to clinch their division title.

The NFL championship game of 1940 was scheduled for the home stadium of the NFL East titleholder. So the Redskins and Bears would meet in the same arena where they had battled so defensively a few weeks earlier. Despite the fact that Washington had won that encounter, the bookmakers favored the Bears; so did most of the sportswriters. Bob Considine of the *New York Times-Herald* suggested 9–5 odds; Shirley Povich of *The Washington Post* was a bit more conservative—he thought 7–5 was more appropriate.

Neither Marshall nor Halas agreed with the oddsmakers. According to Corinne Griffith, Marshall remarked at the breakfast

THE LONGEST PASS

Frank Filchock and Andy Farkas teamed up to set an NFL record in 1939 for the longest pass play in NFL history. Against the Pittsburgh Steelers, and with the ball on the Washington one-yard line, Filchock threw a little two-yard pass to Farkas, who raced 97 more yards with it for a touchdown.

Since then, only four other 99-yard pass plays have joined it in the record book, and two of them were carried off by the Redskins. In 1963, George Izo tossed a 45-yard pass to Bobby Mitchell, who raced an additional 54 yards for a score in a game against the Cleveland Browns. Five years later, Sonny Jurgensen unloaded *another* 45-yard pass, which was caught by Jerry Allen, who sprinted the remaining 54 yards for a touchdown against the Chicago Bears.

table in his Washington home the day of the game: "The so-called experts make us a slight underdog today...that's ridiculous....We already beat them....Why, we only lost two games this year. The bookmakers must be crazy." Halas, adopting a different psychological strategy, said: "Those guys [the oddsmakers] must be crazy. This game is an even-money game or nothing at all. Sure, we've got power, but look at the Redskins—they have Sammy Baugh and Dick Todd, a combination we have to stop if we're going to win this championship."

Whatever the odds, it was pegged by all to be a battle royal. Robert Ruark, a sportswriter in those days before he discovered Africa, described it this way: "It says right here in the paper that 35,000 tickets have been sold for the football game Sunday between the Bears and the Redskins and

Dick Todd (41), a Redskins halfback from 1939 through 1942 and, after military service, from 1945 to 1948, skirts the right end in this 1940 game against the Bears. (HOF/NFL Photos)

that there isn't a spare pew in Pa Griffith's ballpark. You know what all those people are paying to see? Not a football game. A fist-fight."

Coach George Halas was the first Bear in the locker room that December Sunday at Griffith Stadium. Still in his psychological mode, he had with him the newspaper clippings of Marshall's remarks after the Redskins defeated the Bears earlier that season. He taped them all over the locker room. Later, as the Bears donned their uniforms, they had ample time to reflect on Marshall's description of them. Then, just before they were to take the field, Halas confronted them, and, pointing at the clippings, said: "Gentlemen, this is what George Preston Marshall thinks of you. *I* think you're a great football team, the greatest ever assembled. Go out on the field and prove it."

Halas proved that crisp, sunny Sunday

Odds Surprise Favored Bears

The 'Arms' Question -:- -:- **By Burris Jenkins, Jr.**

Sammy Baugh

Sid Luckman

30,000 to
See Irish

Chicagoans Believe 9-5 Price Too High

By Garry Schumacher

WASHINGTON, Dec. 7.—Reading the morning papers over their breakfast ham-and-eggs, the Chicago Bears learned upon arrival in Washington today that they have been installed as the favorites for tomorrow's National League championship play-off in the Griffith Stadium.

New York has made them the 9 to 5 choice, and even local enthusiasm has not been able to take **Speculate**

afternoon that he was the psychological equal to Sigmund Freud, and the Bears provided irrefutable evidence that they were the battlefield equivalent of Caesar's legions.

Washington fans prefer not to dwell on the cataclysm. But for the sake of historical reference, here is what happened. With the game only 55 seconds old, Bears fullback Bill Osmanski broke out around left end and ran 68 yards for a touchdown. Later in the first quarter, Sid Luckman quarterback-sneaked in for another Chicago touchdown. Then halfback Joe Maniaci eluded all Washington defenders on a 42-yard scamper for another score. In the second period Luckman connected with end Ken Kavanaugh for still another Bears touchdown. The score

at intermission: Chicago 28, Washington 0.

In the second half, Bear defender Hampton Pool picked off a Sammy Baugh pass and ran it 15 yards for a touchdown. Then halfback Ray Nolting ran 23 for another score. Redskins tailback Roy Zimmerman threw, unfortunately, to Bear defender George McAfee, who carried it back 35 yards for a touchdown. Minutes later it was linebacker Bulldog Turner's turn; he grabbed another Zimmerman pass and toted it 20 yards for a touchdown. Halfback Harry Clark, on a double reverse, then ran 44 yards for a score. Fullback Gary Famiglietti followed with a two-yard plunge. And lastly, if not mercilessly, Harry Clark bucked in from the one-yard line.

71

The Bears were everywhere in the contest for the 1940 NFL crown as Jimmy Johnston (31) of the Redskins could duly testify. The Washington fullback, in the arms of Sid Luckman, is about to be ushered out of bounds. (HOF/NFL Photos)

The score was 73–0, Bears, when the final gun sounded, the piercing report of which prompted one press box wag to observe to the sportswriter sitting next to him: "Marshall just shot himself."

George Preston Marshall was neither dead nor speechless after the slaughter. "What can I say," he said. "We needed a 50-man line against their power. We had the greatest crowd in Washington's history and we played our poorest game. I am mortified to think what we did to that crowd."

Sammy Baugh was a little more subdued. "We weren't quite as high as we should have been. They were higher than hell."

To bear testament that Redskins fans were true in their hearts and that even something like a 73–0 catastrophe right before their very eyes in normally friendly Griffith Stadium could not daunt them, they approached the 1941 season with hope. A news item announced that seven weeks before the season opener the Redskins had advance season ticket sales surpassing

THE MORNING AFTER

Some thoughts and comments after the carnage, better known as the NFL championship game of 1940:

Sammy Baugh, when asked if the outcome might have been different had Charley Malone caught what appeared to be a touchdown pass in the first quarter with the score a mere 7–0, Bears: "Hell, yes, the score would have been 73–6."

Bob Considine, in his column "On the Line": "The Chicago Bears massacred the Washington Redskins 73–0 yesterday. . . . The unluckiest guy in the crowd was the five-buck bettor who took the Redskins and 70 points."

Shirley Povich, in his column "This Morning" for *The Washington Post*: "If you're wanting to know what happened to the Redskins yesterday, maybe this will explain it: The Bears happened to 'em. . . . It reminds us of our first breathless visit to the Grand Canyon. All we could say is: 'There she is, and ain't she a beaut.' When they hung up that final score at Griffith Stadium yesterday, all

we could utter was: 'There it is, and wasn't it awful.'"

Bill Stern, famous sports broadcaster: "It got so bad that, toward the end, the Bears had to give up place-kicking the extra points and try passes instead because all the footballs booted into the stands were being kept by the spectators as souvenirs. And they were down to their last football."

Red Smith, in his column "Sports of the Times" for *The New York Times*: "George Preston Marshall, the mettlesome laundryman who owned the Redskins, looked on from the stands—except when he turned his back to charge up the aisle and throw a punch at a dissatisfied customer—and when his ordeal was over, every hair in his raccoon coat had turned white."

George Preston Marshall: "We were awful and you don't need to ask me if we are going to clean house. Some of the boys are going to be embarrassed when the time comes to make contracts for next year."

THE LINEUPS

Chicago Bears		Washington Redskins
Bob Nowaskey	LE	Bob Masterson
Joe Stydahar	LT	Wee Willie Wilkin
Danny Fortmann	LG	Dick Farman
Bulldog Turner	C	Bob Tichenal
George Musso	RG	Steve Slivinski
Lee Artoe	RT	Jim Barber
George Wilson	RE	Charley Malone
Sid Luckman	QB	Max Krause
Ray Nolting	LH	Sammy Baugh
George McAfee	RH	Ed Justice
Bill Osmanski	FB	Jimmy Johnston
George Halas	coach	Ray Flaherty

$100,000, a new record for preseason orders. Total season ticket sales were more than 13,500.

Coach Flaherty obtained a fine center in Ki Aldrich in a trade with the Chicago Cardinals, and Andy Farkas had recovered from his knee injury. There were also some promising rookies: end Ed Cifers (Tennessee), tackle Fred Davis (Alabama), end and kicker Joe Aguirre (St. Mary's of California), and blocking back Cecil Hare (Gonzaga).

The Skins were unsteady in the opener in Washington and were defeated by the Giants, 17–10. They won their next five games, but the only notable team they beat was the Brooklyn Dodgers. Then, with a disheartening turnabout, they dropped the next four in a row, to the Dodgers, Bears, Giants, and Packers. A win over the Eagles in the last game of the season made no difference in the standings. The Redskins, with a record of 6–5–0, were in third place behind the Giants and Dodgers in the NFL East.

That last game of the 1941 regular season was, however, a memorable one. It was played in Washington on December 7, 1941, before a crowd of just more than 27,000 that included an array of government dignitaries who had no idea of what was going on halfway around the world at Pearl Harbor.

During the game, the public address suddenly came alive. "Admiral W.H.P. Bland [U.S. Navy Chief of Ordnance] is asked to report to his office at once." Then: "Secretary Stimson [of War] please telephone the White House immediately." And: "Secretary Knox [of the Navy] contact the White House." And on and on the public-address calls continued, summoning military and FBI men, newspaper editors, and a host of others. In the press box, the wags learned from a telegraph message that Japan had attacked the U.S. base at Pearl Harbor. In the stands, rumors spread like a brushfire. On the field, the game went on, although there was little response, even to Sammy Baugh's game-winning touchdown pass to Joe Aguirre. The fans left Griffith Stadium that solemn Sunday thinking much more about what was in store for them and the

Leader and Unit Leaders of Redskins Band 1941

JOHN D. D'ANDELET................Director
FRED A. FETTER, JR................Assistant Director
GEORGE J. WEISNER................Librarian

HERBERT THOMPSON................President
BILLY DAY................Drum Major
C. R. TRANTER................Drum Major

Backbone of the Washington Redskins' 112-piece marching band are the unit leaders and section leaders shown above. Reading from left to right, front row, are Ed Hindman, Altos; G. S. Berthe, Clarinets; J. A. Govan, Head of Brass Section; John D. D'Andelet, Director of Band; Fred Fetter, Reeds; John Thompson, Snare Drums; L. J. Laughton, Tubas. Second row, Guy Gaston, Saxophones; R. V. Gill, Trumpets; R. H. Thrasher, Baritones; E. C. Hutchins, Saxophones; C. S. Keller, Trumpets; George Clampitt, Trombones, and Ray Gicker, Bass Drum.

REDSKINS BAND ROSTER 1941 SEASON

TROMBONES—George Clampitt, J. L. Ankers, J. Hanna, G. O'Connor, W. J. Payne, Jr., C. E. Palmer, H. Hinker, D. G. Chase, F. Stoddard, B. Williams.

TUBAS—L. J. Laughton, W. J. Hanson, E. F. Cole, B. Tallent, J. H. Robinson, Dan Miller, George Durham, W. H. Kilmer, Joseph Farren, R. L. Sheaffer.

BARITONES—R. Thrasher, C. Danton, J. R. Marcus, L. Horowitz, P. Stottlemeyer, M. R. Hood.

TENOR SAXOPHONES—C. Brown, D. Kearney, Guy Gaston, S. G. Utterback.

BELLS—G. W. Mason.

HORNS—Ed. Hindman, W. R. Percival, H. F. Moore, V. Moreland, S. J. Borowsky, H. L. Copenhaver, R. H. Thrasher,

Jr., H. C. Keesling, L. Anderson, E. W. Hawk.

TRUMPETS—J. A. Govan, R. V. Gill, A. DiBartlo, C. H. Davis, R. Fickinger, A. M. Smith, R. W. Fuller, Alex. Rohan, Art. Rohan, C. S. Keller, J. A. Smith, H. S. Loos, W. A. Toothacher, H. E. Strong, F. W. Peter, W. E. Eden, Ed. Eagleston, H. L. Wait, Earl Webb, Jr., E. Brown.

TOM TOMS—B. Gralton, H. Berman, Jr., S. Davenport, M. Baxter, H. Harrison, H. Berman, Sr.

CYMBALS—C. E. D'Andelet, C. F. Kettner.

BASS DRUMS—Ray Gicker, I. H. Silverberg.

SNARE DRUMS—John Thompson, W.

W. Jones, H. C. Cook, D. A. Wills, C. W. Golbreath, G. A. Bell, J. R. Chew, Wm. McWilliamson, A. H. Walschmidt.

SOPRANO SAXOPHONE—F. A. Fetter.

ALTO SAXOPHONES—R. Athey, W. L. Rothgeb, John Cherry, Elmer Odell, J. D. Babcock, William Boyle.

BARITONE SAXOPHONE — E. C. Hutchins.

CLARINETS—W. F. Hortman, W. Warmkessel, J. C. Williams, J. Irwin, J. Kezer, J. Hermanson, Carl Baum, D. G. Fabel, G. Underwood, W. Livchak, G. S. Berthe, E. M. Bachman, L. Lowery, L. B. Olmstead, L. Tylenda, B. Isenberg, W. Mitchell, R. Hodgdon, E. Klavans, G. J. Weisner.

GLEE CLUB ROSTER 1941

FIRST TENORS—Hugh Buckingham, Joe Moss, Don Rush, R. C. Swanson, Carrol Hefner.

SECOND TENORS—Karl Benson, Jesse Nussear, Everett Rightsell, Herbert Blank, Willis Fisk.

BARITONES—Jean Boardman, John Metz, Howard Hefner, Wilson Reeves, Raymond Fordyce.

BASS—Dale Hamilton, Lysle Winders, William Stevens, Jack Dorsey, Willard Smith.

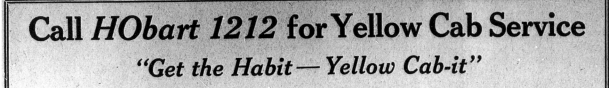

Call *HObart 1212* for Yellow Cab Service

"Get the Habit — Yellow Cab-it"

sive back. "I actually liked to play defense," Baugh once said. "Hell, when I'd punt a ball I'd be about the third or fourth man down the field to make the tackle. You see, they couldn't touch the punter, so I could just kick the ball and get the hell down the field while all the others were blocking each other." An example of his great versatility was a feat in 1943 that will never be matched in this age of football specialization. That year Baugh led the NFL in passing (149 completions for 1,953 yards and 24 touchdowns), punting (45.9-yard average), and interceptions by a defender (11).

He was also an unquestioned team leader. There was a common belief among most of his teammates that the more nervous Baugh got before a game, the better he was going to be and consequently the better they would fare that day. "The tip-off was the number of times he went to the john during the time he was getting suited up," said former teammate and fullback Jim Castiglia. "If he went more than three times, we knew we were going to have a helluva day. You can book it."

As great a year as Baugh had in 1937, Washington came close to losing him to major league baseball. After college he had signed a contract to play for the St. Louis Cardinals, beginning in the spring of 1938. Following the Redskins' championship season, however, Baugh injured his breastbone in a postseason exhibition game. It had not properly healed by the time he reported to the Cardinals for spring training. In camp, he was shifted from third base to shortstop, but his performance was hampered by the injury and he made a less than auspicious debut. The Cardinals gave him an ultimatum; they wanted him to give up football completely and concentrate solely on baseball. Baugh gave it a good deal of thought.

"I always loved baseball more than anything I had ever done," Baugh later related,

"but I knew I had a better future in football. So I gave up baseball and never regretted it one bit. I had trouble hitting the change-up pitch and the curve and, besides, Marty Marion was also in the farm system. I knew he was going to be the shortstop at St. Louis pretty soon, not me."

So Slingin' Sammy stayed with football, determined to stay healthy and leave his mark on the game. "One thing I especially remember from when I first started with the pros was that there wasn't a lot of protection for the passer," Baugh said. I did all our passing and I know it sure was hell. Passers took a terrible beating. That's one rule Mr. Marshall finally got changed. I remember he called me in and asked me if it would help if he could get a rule through that would protect passers. I said, 'Heck, yes, it would probably let me play 10 years longer.' " Marshall did get the rule passed, and Baugh went on to set the record for number of seasons played in the NFL.

Sammy Baugh used the forward pass as a potent weapon. Never the possessor of great speed, he made up for it with an uncanny knack for evading oncoming defenders, a consistent ability to find open receivers, and one of the quickest releases in the history of the game.

"The way to make a passer is to let him make every mistake in the book," Baugh later explained, "and find out for himself how to correct them. If I went out to quarterback a team now, I doubt I'd do things much different than I did before. My theory, the way I was taught by Dutch Meyer (his coach) at TCU, was you try to beat a defense. They're going to let you have a weak spot, so you find it and pick on it. You keep going to a weakness until they adjust to cover it. Then they leave themselves open somewhere else and you go to that."

Another deadly weapon Baugh used from his position at tailback was the quick kick.

Eddie LeBaron (14) confers with his predecessor Sammy Baugh on the sideline in 1952, the year he took over the quarterbacking duties in Washington. Miniature by NFL size standards, LeBaron played for the Skins for seven years. (HOF/NFL Photos)

Many opponents thinking pass on third down were surprised and embarrassed to see a thundering Baugh punt soar over their heads and bounce unattended downfield until a Redskin downed it.

In 1944, however, Baugh moved to a new position. In that year, the Redskins adopted the T formation, which George Halas and his converted tailback-to-quarterback Sid Luckman had been using so successfully for the Chicago Bears.

"When I switched from a single-wing tailback to a T-formation quarterback in '44, it was the most difficult thing I'd ever had to

do in my football career," Baugh admitted. By 1947, he had the position mastered better than anyone who had ever played it before. That season he had the best passing year of his career, setting two NFL records by completing 210 passes for 2,938 yards, both of which would remain league standards until the 1960s.

"Actually, the T was good for me," Baugh said. "I'd played ten or eleven years of single-wing ball, counting college, and I figured I only could go maybe another year or two as tailback. Hell, I was getting beat up and hurt all the time and my shoulders and knees were getting pretty bad by that time. But with the T formation I didn't take such a beating and that enabled me to play another seven or eight years."

When Sammy Baugh, at age 38, retired from professional football after the 1952 season, he had thrown more passes (2,995), completed more of them (1,693), gained more yardage passing (21,886, or approximately 13 miles), and passed for more touchdowns (187) than any previous passer in NFL history. He led the league in passing six times and in number of pass completions five times, two league records that still stand today.

His passing, punting, defensive skills, and team leadership combined to earn for him the honor of being one of the 17 charter members enshrined in the Pro Football Hall of Fame.

Eddie LeBaron

He was called "The Little General," and the press release announcing that Eddie Le-Baron was joining the Redskins in 1950 referred to him as "a pint-size package of dynamite." The reason was that coming out of the College of the Pacific that year he stood at 5′9″ and weighed somewhere in the vicinity of 160 pounds, which afforded him the distinction of being the smallest quarterback in Redskins history.

LeBaron, Washington's 10th-round draft choice that year, played in only two pre-season games before joining the Marines to serve in the Korean conflict, where, incidentally, he was wounded twice. He returned in 1952 to take up the quarterbacking chores that were being abandoned by Sammy Baugh in the last year of his pro career. He proved an able replacement, passing for 1,420 yards and 14 touchdowns. In one game against the Giants, he threw four touchdown passes. He was subsequently named the NFL Rookie of the Year.

After another year in Washington, The Little General, who did not get along with his defense-emphasizing coach, Curly Lambeau, defected to the Canadian Football League, but he returned to the Skins in 1955 when Joe Kuharich took over from Lambeau. LeBaron led the team on the field for the next five years, although only for part of the season in 1956, when he was benched with an injury.

The most memorable game of LeBaron's

Eddie LeBaron
1952–53, 1955–59 (HOF/NFL Photos)

career in Washington was the opener of his first season back from Canada. The Skins went to Cleveland to take on the Browns, a team they had never beaten in nine previous encounters, and had been annihilated the year before by a score of 62–3, which remains today their worst regular-season defeat. As Eddie tells it, "It was exciting going into Cleveland that day. It wasn't hard for me to get pumped up with the anticipation of playing against a guy like [Otto] Graham. And they were also the NFL defending champs." The Little General turned the tide on the Browns that day, throwing passes for two touchdowns and running 20 yards for another to lead the Skins to a 27–17 victory. "It got the momentum going and we went on to have our best season while I was in Washington [8–4–0]."

LeBaron's own best season was in 1957, when he completed 99 passes for 1,508 yards and received a quarterback rating of 88.6. His most impressive individual performance, although not the most personally memorable, was the day in 1958 when he tossed five touchdown passes in a 45–31 triumph over the Chicago Cardinals.

In 1960, after announcing his retirement, he decided to return to the game when Tom Landry of the newly enfranchised Dallas Cowboys selected him in the expansion draft, and Eddie played another four years. He ranks fifth in pass completions in the Redskins' books, behind only Joe Theismann, Sonny Jurgensen, Sammy Baugh, and Billy Kilmer. In his overall pro career of 11 years, The Little General gained 13,399 yards with his passing, to rank 66th in that category in NFL annals.

Norm Snead

Norm Snead could legitimately say that he surfaced in the wrong place at the wrong time when he signed with the Redskins in

1961 after a notable college career at Wake Forest. He had been Washington's first-round draft choice that year, but it was a team that had won only one game the season before, had ended up in last place in the NFL East, and was sorely in need of a quarterback.

At 6'4" and 215 pounds, Snead was a gargantuan replacement for the diminutive Eddie LeBaron and the unproductive Ralph Guglielmi, who had called the signals for the Skins the year before. The rookie had little trouble landing the starting job, which he quickly learned was definitely hazardous to his health. Besieged by seemingly undeterred pass rushers from the first game of '61, which Washington lost to the San Francisco 49ers, 35–3, until the last game of the season, Snead went a long time without the sweet smell of victory. In one game, against the Giants, he was tackled in the end zone twice for safeties, contributing four points to New York's 53–0 win. Snead's calm appraisal of it all: "That first year I really learned to throw under pressure."

Finally, however, in the last game of the season, things changed. With the Skins' record at 0–12–1, most of the fans came out to D.C. Stadium, according to one sportswriter, "to watch the wing-ding Christmas show that Marshall traditionally stages during the intermission of the final game." They and Norm Snead were surprised, however, to find that suddenly the quarterback had some time to throw the ball, and the result was that he not only moved the Redskins, but they defeated the Dallas Cowboys, 34–24. (It was their first win since they beat the Cowboys 25 games earlier [26–14 in Washington, October 9, 1960].)

When the stats were in, Snead had completed 172 passes for 2,337 yards and 11 touchdowns, all three records for a rookie in the NFL—not bad for a quarterback who had spent most of the season scrambling for

Norm Snead (16), called the signals for the Redskins from 1961 through 1963. Snead ranks fifth in Redskins lore for total passing yardage (8,306). (HOF/NFL Photos)

won only three of their 14 games that year, but Snead set a club record by gaining 3,043 yards passing, the first NFL quarterback ever to broach the 3,000-yard mark.

After the season, however, Snead was traded to the Eagles for their quarterback, the rather rotund but well-seasoned Sonny Jurgensen. Snead played 10 more years in the NFL, with Philadelphia, the Vikings, and the Giants, turning in career totals of 2,049 completions for 28,238 yards and 182 touchdowns. He ranks fifth in all-time passing yardage for the Skins, his 8,306 topped only by Joe Theismann, Sonny Jurgensen, Sammy Baugh, and Billy Kilmer.

Sonny Jurgensen

Ron Reid, writing for *Sports Illustrated,* summed up Sonny Jurgensen delicately but well: "A free spirit for whom training rules have, at times, been just too vexing." He also noted, however, that the sometimes-stout quarterback was "without peer in the art of throwing a football."

Born Christian Adolph Jurgensen III in Wilmington, North Carolina, Sonny played quarterback at Duke, where he threw only six passes in three years before matriculating to the pros. A fourth-round draft choice of the Philadelphia Eagles in 1957, he was then a relatively solid 5'11", 200-pound would-be quarterback who was slated to be a backup to the aging Bobby Thomason. The next year he played the subordinate role to veteran Norm Van Brocklin, who had been brought in to replace the retiring Thomason.

It was not until 1961 that Jurgensen got his chance to show what he could do tossing a football. Van Brocklin, after 12 memorable seasons in the NFL, retired, and Sonny was given the job. He took to it like Mozart to music. In that first full season, Jurgensen set three NFL passing records when he

his life. After the season, his coach, Bill McPeak, said, "It'll take about three years, but Snead is going to be a great one."

The Redskins were definitely better the following year (5–7–2), and so were Snead's stats. He was helped enormously by the addition of Washington's first black player, a remarkable flanker named Bobby Mitchell who would lead the league that year in pass receptions and receiving yardage. Snead completed 184 passes for 2,926 yards (only 12 yards shy of the club record set by Sammy Baugh in 1947) and 22 touchdowns.

In 1963, Snead continued to demonstrate his propensity for throwing the football—especially to Bobby Mitchell. The Redskins completed 235 passes for 3,723 yards and 32 touchdowns, and he easily earned All-Pro honors.

From the start, Jurgensen was defined as a pocket passer, and after that first year more than one observer noted that he had the quickest release in pro football. "I never thought it necessary," he once said, "to run around or hang around too long in one's own backfield." He also built an off-field reputation for roistering that would make him acceptable company for the likes of Johnny Blood McNally, Shipwreck Kelly, Bobby Layne, Art Donovan, Paul Hornung, and Doug Atkins, among other notorious NFL souls. As *SI's* Ron Reid pegged him, "The guy whose identifying mark was a six-pack gut . . . rumor has it, paid enough fines to meet the taxi squad's payroll and sneaked out of camp so often that his room

The memorable Sonny Jurgensen, elected to the Pro Football Hall of Fame in 1983, had fine careers with both the Eagles (1957–63) and the Redskins (1964–74). Possessed with one of the finest passing arms in the NFL, he completed 2,433 passes for 32,224 yards and 255 touchdowns during his 18-year career. (HOF/NFL Photos)

6

A Second NFL Title

Five years had elapsed since the Redskins had taken home their first NFL trophy. The Great Depression was over and World War II was under way. They had not been uneventful years for the Redskins and their fans either, with Washington getting to the championship game once and battling the New York Giants down to the wire for the eastern divisional title three other years.

In their first five years in Washington, the Redskins had yet to experience a losing season in the nation's capital, having finished first in the NFL East twice, second place twice, and third once. Coach Ray Flaherty had posted an impressive regular season record of 37–15–3 for Washington's faithful fans.

Now it was time for another championship season.

There were not a lot of players left over from the 1937 title winners. Sammy Baugh was still tailbacking at All-Pro level and Ed Justice occasionally carried the ball, but that was about all, the others gone to either retirement or military service. Ray Flaherty still ruled from the sideline, but announced that he would be leaving for the U.S. Navy at the end of the season.

Fullback Andy Farkas, who had come to the Redskins from the University of Detroit in 1938, had been the most productive rusher of the previous few years, but the Redskins had Dick Todd, Ray Hare, Bob Seymour, and Dick Poillon as well. Ends Bob Masterson and Ed Cifers and halfback Todd were Baugh's favorite receivers. The line was powerful and the defense would prove to be the best in the league that year, keyed around a behemoth tackle with the inappropriate name of Wee Willie Wilkin (6'4", 265 pounds). Other impressive linemen included center/linebacker Ki Aldrich and guards Steve Slivinski and Dick Farman.

The Redskins held training camp in San Diego, California, for the 1942 season, their workouts and scrimmages often providing entertainment for scores of navy men and marines who came over from the nearby San Diego Naval Base. Near the end of camp the Redskins went up to Los Angeles to stage an exhibition game with the Army All-Stars, a team made up of college and pro stars turned soldiers. The military men were guided by Maj. Wallace Wade, who had made an institution of himself coaching at Alabama in the 1920s and at Duke in the 1930s. In Southern California, which would not entertain professional football on a regular basis until the Rams moved out there in 1946, the game attracted a fine crowd. Among the 60,000 in attendance were Hollywood celebrities Pat O'Brien, Linda Darnell, George Raft, Ann Sheridan, George Brent, and King Vidor. Washington, on the strength of Sammy Baugh's passing, won the contest easily, 26–7, and headed back east.

The Redskins were coming off their poorest season yet in the nation's capital, a 6–5–0 third-place finish in the NFL East in 1941. The reigning divisional champions, the New York Giants, were favored again, but the Pittsburgh Steelers were also formidable, a fact the Redskins learned in their home opener. Pitt had drafted an exceptional multiple-threat back in Bullet Bill Dudley out of the University of Virginia, a player who George Preston Marshall coveted, but had been unable to obtain. The Redskins got by the Steelers that opening Sunday in 1942, 28–14, but it was the defense that did it. Contributions included a blocked field

goal by Ki Aldrich, who snatched the ball from the ground and ran it back 93 yards for a touchdown.

The next week Washington hosted the hated Giants, who had destroyed their dreams so often in the past few years. New York still had future Hall of Famers Tuffy Leemans in the backfield and Mel Hein in the middle of the line. The Redskins defense proved faultless that day, however, except on one play when Leemans tossed a 30-yard touchdown pass to end Will Walls. The defense was so good, in fact, that it did not give up *one* first down the entire game. But Leemans's TD toss and the interception of a Dick Poillon flat pass that was returned for another score by Neal Adams were enough to give the New Yorkers a 14–7 triumph.

The Redskins are in hot pursuit of Cleveland Rams tailback Parker Hall (32) in a 1942 encounter at Griffith Stadium. The Washington defenders are Fred Davis (17), Ray Hare (42), Dick Poillon (25), and Bob Tichenal (18). (HOF/NFL Photos)

The Redskins, with a 1–1 record and an offense that had yet to shake the governor from its engine, hardly appeared to be *the* team of '42, as George Preston Marshall had referred to them in the preseason.

But they were. The next nine regular-season games laid the first paving of proof for Marshall's prognostication. One after the other, the Redskins dispatched the Eagles, Rams, Dodgers, Steelers, Eagles, Cardinals, Giants, Dodgers, and Lions. The defense was overwhelming, limiting the opponents in those nine games to 74 points, an average of just a little over eight points a game, while Washington, its offense finally accelerating, tallied 192 points.

The team's record of 10–1–0 is today the best won-lost ratio in its history, and it remained the most wins in a single season until George Allen's Super Bowl-bound Redskins of 1972 won 11 of their 14 regular-season games. Second-place Pittsburgh (7–4–0) was clearly outdistanced, and the Giants had collapsed (5–5–1) after five consecutive winning seasons.

Sammy Baugh, still working from tailback in the single wing, had the best completion percentage of any passer in the league (59%), gaining 1,524 yards on 132 completions, and led the NFL in punting with an average of 46.6 yards per punt. His leading receivers were again Dick Todd (23 for 328 yards) and Bob Masterson (22 for 308 yards). Handy Andy Farkas gained the most yards for the Redskins carrying the ball, 468 on 125 jaunts. The Redskins landed only two players on the All-Pro squad that year, however: end Masterson and tackle Wee Willie Wilkin.

Championship Game, 1942

Just as they had in their two previous visits to the championship classic, the Redskins were to face the abominable Bears, who had wreaked such havoc on them two years earlier in that ignominious 73–0 rout of 1940. Its grimy cloud still hovered over Washington, unfettered even by the mem-

LINEUPS

Chicago Bears		**Washington Redskins**
Bob Nowaskey	LE	Bob Masterson
Ed Kolman	LT	Wee Willie Wilkin
Danny Fortmann	LG	Dick Farman
Bulldog Turner	C	Ki Aldrich
Ray Bray	RG	Steve Slivinski
Lee Artoe	RT	Bill Young
George Wilson	RE	Ed Cifers
Sid Luckman	QB	Ray Hare
Ray Nolting	LH	Sammy Baugh
Hugh Gallarneau	RH	Ed Justice
Gary Famiglietti	FB	Andy Farkas
Hunk Anderson	coaches	Ray Flaherty
Paddy Driscoll		
Luke Johnsos		

ory of the Redskins' triumph over the Bears in their first championship appearance in '37 and their blitzkrieg of a season in '42.

There was another ominous overtone for the Redskins besides the awful memory of the last visit to Griffith Stadium by George Halas's Monsters of the Midway. The Bears had virtually rocketed through the 1942 season in the NFL West, easily winning all 11 of their games by a collective score of 376–84. They had held their opponents to 18 points *less* than the vaunted Redskins defense, while outscoring Washington 376 to 227.

Besides that perfect season, the Bears now had won 24 consecutive games, including preseason and postseason contests, and had in fact won 39 of their last 40 games.

Still working out of the T formation be-

hind All-Pro quarterback Sid Luckman, the Bears were truly an intimidating entity. Their line now had four future Hall of Famers tending the trenches—center Bulldog Turner, tackle Joe Stydahar, and guards Danny Fortmann and George Musso—as well as tackle Lee Artoe, who had earned All-Pro honors that year. Bruising fullback Gary Famiglietti was their leading ground gainer with 503 yards on 118 carries, and the Bears were well stocked with halfbacks, alternating Hugh Gallarneau, Ray Nolting, Frank Maznicki, Harry Clark, and Scooter McLean. McLean was also the team's top receiver; his 571 yards gained on pass receptions was second only to Green Bay's great Don Hutson in the league that year.

The only loss the Bears had suffered was that of their coach and owner George Halas, who was called to active duty in the U.S. Navy midway through the season of '42.

The point spread favored the Bears by an overwhelming 22 points. But ever the optimist, Big Chief Marshall could talk only about revenge. Before the game, he entered his team's locker room, without a word walked to the blackboard, chalked on it in large numerals

73–0

and then left his players and coach Flaherty to dwell on its grisly significance.

The Washington fans must have shared Marshall's emotions. Despite the war and bitterly cold weather, 36,006 spectators filled Griffith Stadium, the largest crowd to attend a sporting event there since the 1933 major league World Series. Among the stalwarts in attendance were singer Al Jolson; figure skater Sonja Henie and her husband, Dan Topping, who owned Brooklyn's football Dodgers and would later own the New York Yankees baseball team; NFL Commissioner Elmer Layden and coaches Greasy Neale of the Eagles, Curly Lambeau of the

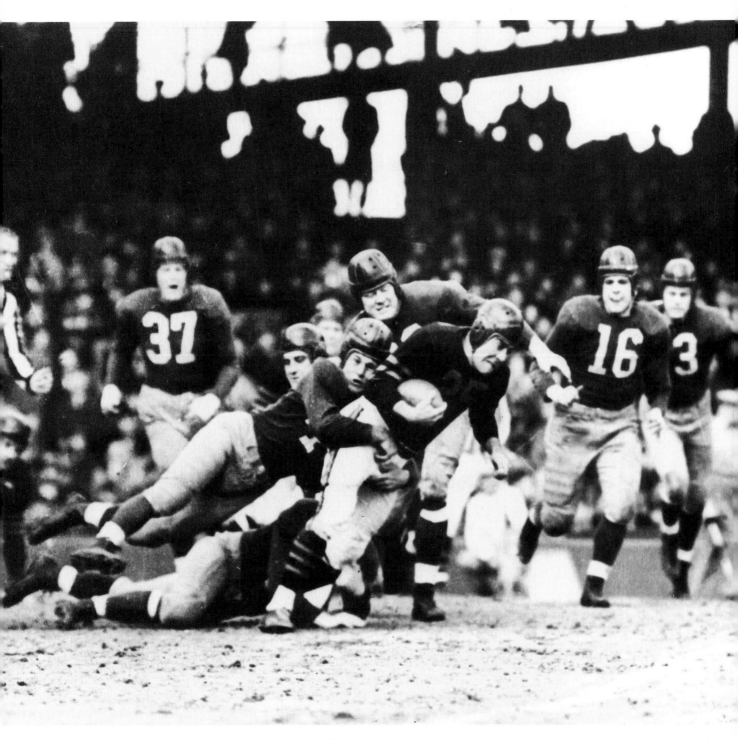

Washington defensive back Andy Farkas wrestles Chicago Bear back Ray Nolting to the ground in the 1942 NFL title game at Griffith Stadium. About to aid in the effort is tackle Wee Willie Wilkin. (HOF/NFL Photos)

SECTION TWO
SPORTS   MARKETS
WANT ADS

Chicago Daily Tribune
THE WORLD'S GREATEST NEWSPAPER

Tribune Phone Numbers
SUPerior 0200 Public Information Service
SUPerior 0260 Sports Bulletin Service
SUPerior 0100 Want Ads—General Business

MONDAY, DECEMBER 14, 1942.   21

BEARS LOSE TITLE GAME TO REDSKINS, 14 TO 6

SCHWOEGLER NEARS ALL-STAR BOWLING CHAMPIONSHIP

LONG PASS AND 43 YARD MARCH WHIP CHICAGO

Artoe Takes Fumble for Touchdown.

LEADS COMINS BY 25 POINTS; VARIPAPA THIRD

Winner Will Receive $1,500 and Trophy.

All-Star Standings

	W.	L.	Pins.	Pin.
Schwoegler	.44	16	12962	305.92
Comins	.33¼	36½	12248	279.33
Varipapa	.31	27	12177	276.72
Crimins	..32½	21½	12204	274.19
Day	..31	29	12167	274.17
Benkovic	..29½	30½	12148	272.30
Nelson	..32	28	12014	272.14
Krumske	..29	31	12007	270.12
Young	..30	30	11907	267.47
Sulik	..27	33	11800	264.10
Bomar	..25	35	11768	259.43
Rusch	..15	45	10745	239.45

BY C. H. BEUKEMA.

A 1,303 count in his 10th match late yesterday gave Connie Schwoegler of Madison, Wis., 305.02 points in the national match game bowling tournament. Dawes Comins of Kansas City, Mo., shot a 1,287 series and won five games from Billy Rusch Jr. of Gary to increase his second place point total to 279.33. He trailed Schwoegler by 25 points, while Andy Varipapa moved into third place by winning four games from Ned Day. He had 276.72 points.

Schwoegler knocked down 1,304 pins to win five out of six games from Buddy Bomar and score 31.04 points in the first afternoon block. That gave him such a margin that he was certain of stepping up later in the evening to receive the acclaim due a champion, along with a check for $1,500 and a trophy.

While Connie, therefore, was assured of becoming the national individual match game bowling champion, the first new one since Ned Day was crowned in November, 1938, Dawes Comins of Kansas City, who was 25.29 points behind him, had much more of a struggle ahead before winning second money, $750. Dawes topped a list of eight bowlers who still had a chance of getting the check that goes to the runner-up.

Prize Money Totals $7,500.

At the close of yesterday's play all 24 men in the championship and consolation fields were to receive prize money, a grand total of $7,350. That amount included $1,500 to Ned Day for winning his 50 game match with John Crimmins of Detroit, and $750 to Crimmins. The prize money scaled down to $25 each for the last four men in the consolation flight. Distribution of prize money was the final number on the nine day program which opened Dec. 5 with Day bowling Crimmins as 100 All-Stars from 42 cities in 16 states shot for 10 places in the championship field and 12 more dropped into a consolation flight.

The tournament, sponsored by the Chicago Tribune Charities, Inc., and the Bowling Proprietors Association of America, was conducted on 12 new alleys in the huge theater and was the most spectacular in the history of bowling. It attracted bowling fans from all over the midwest, including Mayor Kelly, Mayor Edward J. Jeffries of Detroit, President Martin Unmacht of the American Bowling Congress who resides in Dubuque, and other ABC officials.

Schwoegler in Form.

There's little to be said about Schwoegler's performance in defeating Bomar yesterday, except that he simply continued to display the form he has shown thruout the show—form which Day himself declared was outstanding in the game's history, the caliber of the field considered. In piling up 1,304 pins, Connie included 255 and 244 games among his efforts.

Comins, who went into the day's play with a small margin over Day, increased it slightly in his match with the champion. Each won three games, but Dawes dropped 1,232 pins to Day's 1,218, scoring 27.32 points to 27.9 posted for Ned. At the end of the block he had 248.36 points and Day had 248.01, which, since figures on the right side of the decimal point are computed in pins, with one point given for every 50 pins, means Dawes led Ned by 35 pins.

Frank Benkovic of Milwaukee and Andy Varipapa also put on a spirited match. Frank got 1,240 pins to Andy's 1,238 and, as they split six games, Frank got 27.4 points and Andy 27.38. Crimmins submitted the best total of the first round, 1,308, and won four games from Chicago's Paul Krumske, even tho Paul's total of 1,247 for the six games was highly respectable. Crimmins' high game was 246, and his low game 202.

Wilman Wins Consolation.

With only the three games position found remaining, Joe Wilman had taken the consolation title. He had won 33 games and lost 10 and had knocked down 6,746 pins to score 158.46 points. In his last round robin match he won two out of three from Chris Schirof of St. Louis to run his record for the day to seven won and two lost.

In the final position round he met

MAROONS FACE MARQUETTE AT HOME TONIGHT

Chicago Makes 3d Bid for First Victory.

College Basketball

GAMES TONIGHT.
Marquette at Chicago.
Missouri at Illinois.
Fort Knox at Indiana.
Carleton at Iowa.
Butler at Purdue.
Wisconsin at Notre Dame.
Camp Grant at Illinois Wesleyan.
Illinois Tech at Wheaton.
Culver Stockton at Macomb.
Drake at Grinnell.
Hamline at St. Olaf.
Illinois Professional Schools at 87th Street Navy school.
Wabash at Earlham.

The University of Chicago will open its home basketball schedule against Marquette tonight at 8 o'clock in the Midway fieldhouse. Marquette expects to experience little difficulty against Chicago, whose two defeats this season have run the string of consecutive losses to 23.

Marquette, still smarting from the 42 to 32 beating received at Ann Arbor Saturday night, will be seeking its first victory over Big Ten opposition. Previously the Hilltoppers had been beaten, 45 to 36, by Wisconsin. Substitution of Howard Kallenberger forward to replace Ernie Kivisto was expected as a result of the 15 point total compiled by Kallenberger against Michigan.

The Maroons, twice beaten in games with navy opponents this season, will attempt to re-create the flash of team unity which accounted for a surprise victory over a favored Marquette team two years ago, and which has been conspicuously missing ever since. Ed Nelson, senior forward elected captain Saturday as the Maroons wound up practice for tonight's contest. He was outstanding as a long shot artist in his sophomore year, but experienced only a mediocre season in 1942.

CHICAGO.		MARQUETTE.
Nelson	F	Kallenberger
Zimmermann	F	Skul
Ellman	C	Konkel
Oakley	G	Schodrowski
Crosby	G	Brei
Officials—Jack Truswell [Armour], and James Enright [Chicago].		

Bears Express Desire to Play in Charity Game

[Chicago Tribune Press Service.]

Washington, D. C., Dec. 13.—The Chicago Bears joined today in vigorously denying reports current in the last few days that they refused to play against the National Football league All-Stars in a charity game Dec. 27 in Philadelphia, proceeds to go to the United States marine corps.

"The reason the winner, of to-day's Bears-Redskins title play-off game is to meet the league All-Stars thus eliminating the Bears, as a team, as the charity game participants. Players, however, before losing to the Redskins, were unanimous in expressing their desire to take

MOON MULLINS—DOUBLE EXPOSURE

YOU MEAN TO SAY THAT THEM SLITHER SISTERS IS TWINS, MOON?

YEH—BOTH OF 'EM.

OH-OH!

OH, WELL, I GUESS I'LL GIVE EMMA CANDY THIS CHRISTMAS

GOOD GRIEF, GIRL! ARE YOU IN EVERY SHOP IN TOWN?

Reg. U. S. Pat. Off.
Copyright, 1942, by News Syndicate Co. Inc.

BAUGH FIRES AWAY FOR A REDSKIN BULLSEYE!

Dick Todd, No. 41 (left), Redskin half back, comes in fast to get under Sammy Baugh's pass for a 12 yard gain in second quarter of yesterday's play-off battle for the National Football league championship in Washington, D. C. Baugh is at right (No. 33). | back to camera. Receiver Todd, no down. | Broken line shows flight of Baugh's throw and black arrow indicates Clyde Turner of the Bears (center) comes in too late to knock down. The Redskins won, 14 to 6.

In the Wake of the News

BY ARCH WARD.

TRAVELING SECRETARY JOE BARRY of the White Sox and Joe Farrell, press agent of the Blackhawks, friends since boyhood, are a feudin'. . . . It seems that some of the Blackhawks asked Barry Farrell's exact age, and with his customary sincerity Joe B. said Joe F. was 67. . . . Joe F., who says he is a tender 63, told his missus. Leona, what Joe B. had said. . . . "I'll snatch all the luxuriant white hair right out of his model scalp the next time I see that wicked Barry," said Mrs. Farrell. . . . Donie Bush says his resumption as manager of the Indianapolis Indians of the American association is for another reason besides retrenchment. . . . Says Donie: "I simply can't sit in the grandstand and watch a game in which I have an interest." . . . Marvin [Bud] Ward has been commissioned a second lieutenant in the army air corps and is now stationed at Santa Ana, Cal. . . . In case it's troubling you, Mason Dixon, sophomore guard on Northwestern's basketball team, is not from the south. . . . He's from Flora, Ind., where he starred on his high school quintet. . . . Omar Crocker, former University of Wisconsin and national intercollegiate boxing champion, is now a captain in the artillery and is taking some solid punches at the Japs in the Solomons.

Jack Doyle, Cub scout who discovered Gabby Hartnett and other Cub stars, was brought to Chicago from his home in Holyoke, Mass., to serve as receptionist in the club's headquarters during the recent major-minor league conventions. . . . A man of gentle culture, Doyle made every one feel at home, provided they didn't pay any attention to his quaint greetings and social chitchat. . . . Branch McCracken, Indiana basketball coach and the first Monroe county USO chairman to reach his $10,000 quota, has won more Big Ten basketball games during his four years in the league than any rival. . . . Professional boxing shows in Cleveland have grossed more than half a million dollars in the last two years. . . . Gunboat Smith, old time heavyweight fighter, is a sergeant of civilian guards in a Brooklyn shipyard. . . . The Baseball Writers' Association of America is its national meeting in Chicago, Dec. 2, froze all honorary memberships thru 1944. . . . The reason was not made public. . . . Charley Finney, a member of Alabama Polytechnic's 1942 football team, is a brother of Lou Finney of the Red Sox. . . . Henry [Dutch] Dehnert, who devised the pivot play while he was with the original Celtics, is coaching basketball in a Brooklyn high school.

Daffynitions.

Coordinator: A person who brings organized chaos out of regimented confusion.
—Bill Gloer.
* * *
The Wake Depends Help!
Upon Its Friends. Help!
* * *
Gypsy Rose Lee Influence?
From ChiTrib: "Miss Catherine Ryan, principal of Freeman High school, said girls may wear slacks to school, but must remove them in locker room before going to classes." Who's going to furnish the fans?

A Champion!
It seems that Barney Ross not only knocked out the Jap opponents for the 10 count. He's knocking at Japs by the counts of 10.
—Joe Liberti.
* * *
Notre Dame's Opponents Know.
We had the CCC, WPA, NRA,—but the latest is CC. If my guess is correct, CC will cause lots of trouble in the fall of 1943. Got it? Corwin Clatt, of course.
—Jimmy Mahoney.

BETTING, CROWD RECORDS BROKEN AT FAIR GROUNDS

New Orleans, La., Dec. 13 (AP).—The historic old Fair Grounds here, where many of the turf's immortals performed during the last 70 years, is off on a war buoyed boom that promises to eclipse all modern records and attendance.

Thanks to the appearance of Whirlaway, the Fair Grounds finished its first 13 days of winter racing with its average daily handle 100 per cent above last year.

Day's Betting Is Record.

Black Gold and Pan Zareta probably twisted a little in their graves in the lake dotted infield when an estimated 20,000 fans jammed the track to see Whirlaway. They pushed $301,537 thru the mutuel windows, betting $56,064 on the Whirlaway race alone. All the figures were new records in the memory of racing followers here. The state racing commission's tabulation for the first 13 days of the 75 day season shows a handle of $1,459,783, more than half the $3,625,424 total of the entire 44 day meeting a year ago.

The daily average of $112,291 is almost twice as large as the $59,668 last season and estimated attendance figures show about the same percentage of increase.

No Transportation Problems.

The Fair Grounds Breeders and Racing association, which brought back the sport last year when the track was about to be sold for residential lots, does not have the transportation problem some plants face. Located squarely in the center of crescent shaped New Orleans, the track is within walking distance of Canal street. And officials believe the high caliber of racing this year has had a lot to do with the boom. Many of the country's leading stables are

AAU Completes Plans for Competitive Sports Program

BY WILFRID SMITH.

The delegates to the 54th annual convention of the Amateur Athletic union completed their reports and legislation yesterday with a program of competitive athletics for 1943 that will compare favorably with last year's calendar. The convention, while indorsing the victory program for physical fitness as set up by the federal authorities, also proposed to set up its own project for all activities over which the AAU has direct jurisdiction.

Altho the track and field committee did not select a site for the outdoor meet, the indoor games again were assigned to New York and will be held Feb. 28. Sites were chosen for nearly all national competitions, altho the exact dates in many of these instances will be announced later by the associations to whom the events were assigned.

The convention also delivered an ultimatum yesterday to the Amateur Softball association, an affiliate of the AAU, that it will be suspended unless it brings its rules into line with those of the AAU. The ASA was given a year of grace, but a mail vote of the members of the softball group on amateur restrictions must be held by Jan. 1. Relationships between the AAU and the ASA also involve joint recognition of suspension of athletes by each organization.

Di Benedetto Is Reelected.

Lawrence di Benedetto of New Orleans, representing the southern association, was reelected president. Other officers for 1943 are Daniel J. Ferris of New York, secretary-treasurer; and Lyman Bingham of Chicago, assistant to the president, do not expire until 1944. The site of the 1943 convention will be selected by the board of governors. St. Louis, Columbus, O., and Pittsburgh have made bids, but two other cities also are seeking the convention. The projected sites for national competition follow:

Indoor track and field, New York, Feb. 28.
Junior cross-country, Bowling Green, O. (November).
Senior cross-country, Baltimore, Md. (November).
Women's track and field, Cleveland, O. (July).
Gymnastics, New York (May).
Boxing, Boston, Mass. (April).
Outdoor men's and women's swimming, Indianapolis, Ind., or Columbus, O. [August].
Women's basketball, Denver, Colo., March 14-20.
Men's basketball, probably St. Joseph, Mo. [March].
Handball, either four wall, San Francisco, Cal. [May]; senior one wall, New York [September].
Junior weight lifting, Boston [April or May].
Senior weight lifting, St. Louis; 15 kilometers, New York, and 22.
Junior horseshoe, Columbus, O. [September].

Sites Still Unselected.

In addition to the outdoor track and field meet, AAU committees failed to select sites for national competitions in wrestling, ice hockey, senior weight lifting, volleyball, and code ball. The latter sport may be abandoned because of lack of equipment.

All-Around Championships.

The schedule of junior indoor and outdoor national championships, which allots individual events to various associations which then build local meets around each attraction, also was completed.

Indoor track and field, New York, Feb. 6.
Boxing, Boston, March.
Swimming, New Haven, Conn., Connecticut.
Outdoor track and field, New York; 20 kilometers, Detroit; 50 kilometers, Cincinnati.

Section Two
Redskins Settle a Score.

Two years ago in this same park, 36,000 and fans booed the Washington Redskins while they were being humiliated by the Chicago Bears, 73 to 0. Today they came back, as did the Redskins, to settle the score in a game which started with the two-time champions the 5 to 1 favorites.

Twenty-four consecutive victories had netted the Bears 39 points—yet, today, these Redskins were so inspired that the only points the ability clapping champions could make came on a 50 yard run by Tackle Lee Artoe, who picked up a Redskin fumble early in the second quarter. After that they twice ponded at the gates, but there was no entrance, and an inspired Washington eleven passed to one touchdown. Then, showing their contempt for the mammoth Chicago line, which, with ridiculous ease, had turned back opponents in 11 league games, yielding less than 600 yards, the Redskins drove 43 yards for their second touchdown.

Redskins' Line Proves Superior.

With a 14 to 6 lead, the Redskins, now in command, threw back two desperate scoring efforts of the fading champions. Once the Bears had a first down on the 2 yard line and here the Washington line proved its superiority, at least, on this wintry but sunny afternoon.

There are many loose ends to be picked up. Newspaper men were ready to write another chapter in the Bears' storybook appendix. It was to be the 26th straight victory. It was to be the third straight league title for the Bears. It was to enrich each of the Chicago players by $966.87. They took the losers' portion, $639.12 to a man.

It was said before the game that it would be a battle of two of the league's all-time great lines. So it proved just that. The 'Chicago forwards took a sound beating, and that's where the game was lost. They couldn't hold back those charging Redskins, who made a beeline for Sid Luckman, the Bear passer, and either sneered him or made him throw so hurriedly that there was no connection at the other end.

Sid was harried on every pass. He was strictly on his own as he faded back, watching those mammoth red shirts closing in on him and desperately trying to rid himself of the ball. In other games he almost had time to light a cigaret and read the evening paper before deciding on his target. Today he had to throw it in sheer self-defense.

Another Avenue to Victory.

There still was one other avenue to victory open. This was the famed quick openers of the 'T' formation which send backs thru the line. The fans saw this quick opener at its best only once. Early in the first quarter, Ray Nolting sped right down the middle for 17 yards. After that the Redskins completely hemmed in the backfield on this maneuver. Instead of Bear streaking out of the line for scrimmage there was a tremendous

Stunned!

BEARS [6].		REDSKINS [14].
Nowaskey	L.E.	Masterson
Kolman	L.T.	Wilkin
Fortmann	L.G.	Farman
Turner	C.	Aldrich
Bray	R.G.	Slivinski
Artoe	R.T.	Young
Nolting	R.E.	Cifers
Luckman	Q.B.	M. Hare
Mullins	L.H.	Baugh
Galimberti	R.H.	Justice
Famiglietti	F.B.	Farkas
Chicago		0 6 0 0—6
Washington		0 7 7 0—14

Points after touchdowns—Masterson [2].
Substitutions: Chicago—Left ends, Siegal; left tackle, Stydahar; left guard, Drulis; center, Matuza; right guard, Akin, Musso; right tackle, Hoptowit; right end, Pool; quarter back, O'Rourke; left half, Clark, Maznicki; right half, McLean; full backs, Osmanski, Petty.
Washington—Left tackle, Belcari; left guard, Shugart; right tackle, Davis; quarter back, C. Hare; right half, Moore; full backs, Todd, Seymour.
Referee—Ronald Gibbs. Umpire—Carl Brubaker. Field judge—Chuck Sweeney. Head linesman—Charles Berry.

BY EDWARD PRELL.
[Chicago Tribune Press Service.]

Washington, D. C., Dec. 13.—A football dynasty fell with a thud today on the frozen turf of Griffith stadium where two years ago it rose in power. A pistol shot rang out and a beaten troupe of Chicago Bears sought the exits while a jubilant swarm of Washington Redskins clapped each other on the back in midfield and took a look at the scoreboard just to see that it really read: Washington, 14; Chicago, 6.

Hundreds of the 36,006 who watched in unbridled joy the fall of the old title holders cut off at no distance, shook the goal posts from their moorings and broke them up so much kindling wood. Long after the two-time National Football league championship had walked disconsolately to their dressing room the rebel-like cheers of the half-delirious Redskin fans came echoing across the field.

Packers, Steve Owen of the Giants, and Jimmy Conzelman of the Chicago Cardinals; Sen. A.B. "Happy" Chandler, who would later become commissioner of major league baseball; and a host of other politicians and brass-laden military officers. Even Lt. Cmdr. George Halas had swung a temporary leave from his station at Norman, Oklahoma, to watch his Bears at play.

The game was broadcast on radio by Harry Wismer and Russ Hodges to 178 stations throughout the country, the most widespread coverage of a pro football game up to that time.

The Bears struck first, led by their defense instead of their heralded offense. Dick Todd fumbled the ball on the 50-yard line and Bears tackle Lee Artoe scooped it up and ambled all the way downfield for a touchdown. But Artoe, perhaps out of breath from his unusual sprint, missed the extra point.

Unlike in 1940, however, the Redskins came right back, returning the ensuing kickoff to the Bears' 42-yard line. Three plays later, Sammy Baugh hit halfback Wilbur Moore with a 38-yard touchdown pass. Bob Masterson's extra point made the score 7–6 and the half came to an end.

It appeared the Bears would regain the lead in the third quarter when they marched down the field and Hugh Gallarneau plunged in for a touchdown, but it was nullified because the Bears were penalized, one of their backs having been in motion. The Redskins defense then staged a magnificent goal line stand and took over the ball.

A Washington drive was more successful. It moved the ball down to the Bears' one-yard line, where Andy Farkas carried it in for the score. The Redskins' 14–6 lead going into the final period proved all that was necessary. There was no scoring in the fourth quarter and, with the final whistle, the Bears' win streak came to an end in the cold environs of Griffith Stadium, and the Washington Redskins had their second NFL title.

OPINION

Sports columnist Bob Considine loved the championship game of '42 but hated the halftime. As he wrote the day after it:

George P. Marshall was so subdued . . . that he didn't make a single call to the bench on the telephone he has in his box. He seems to have some curious idea that Ray Flaherty can coach, which the result did nothing to diminish.

Marshall hit his all-time high and vaudeville suffered another 10-year setback during the halftime show. First the loudspeaker boomed that the National Football League was extending the wish of a Merry Christmas to our soldiers and sailors, which will come as a great comfort to the boys in foxholes and probably bring Hitler to his knees. Then to cap it all, George's 100-plus-piece Indian band came out on the field with long white beards playing "Jingle Bells." At a late hour last night a war council of the Sioux, Iroquois, Blackfeet, and Choctaw nations was considering secession.

NAVY'S GAIN, REDSKINS' LOSS

After the Redskins had, with sweet revenge, won the 1942 NFL championship by defeating the Chicago Bears, they also suffered a loss. Coach Ray Flaherty put down his whistle and clipboard and left for the U.S. Navy and World War II.

Flaherty, who had been at the helm of the Redskins since 1936, led them to their first title in 1937 and their second in 1942, and logged an enviable record of 56–23–3 (.709). Only subsequent pilots Joe Gibbs and George Allen have won more games for Washington than Flaherty.

This tribute in the 1942 championship game program summed up the feelings for Flaherty of fans and team alike. "They call him the Knute Rockne of pro football. The guys in the know ... they say that Ray Flaherty, head coach of the Washington Redskins, is the smartest coach in football today.

"The thousands of Washington fans who have seen Ray in every game play as hard from the bench as most of the boys do on the field, will miss him next year when he's playing that real tough ballgame for Uncle Sam. . . .

"The big redhead from Spokane, Wash., will be missed by the fans, but he'll be missed even more by the Redskins players. There is not a man on the squad who wouldn't fight his heart out for Flaherty. . . .

"Flaherty is big and tough and hard; but he's fair and he's kind. He's going into a tough scrap. He will take with him the admiration and respect and good wishes of every Redskin fan and player."

Redskins Players Express Their Gratitude for Unwavering Support of District Fans

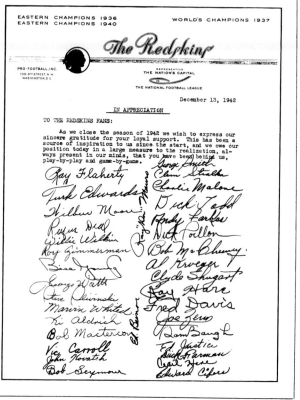

7

The War Years

It took the Redskins until 1942 before they were able to shed the shroud of that 1940 title game in which they embarrassedly sat at the zero end of a 73–0 score. And, of course, they did it with a certain panache, wreaking revenge on the perpetrators of that disaster, the Chicago Bears themselves, in the championship game of 1942, beating the Bears by the score of 14–6 and securing for Washington its second NFL crown.

What The Big Chief wanted now was a repeat: back-to-back championships. Up to that time, only the Chicago Bears had won two consecutive titles (1940 and 1941). Marshall confronted the sports press: "We have proven we are the team to beat. We will now show just how true that statement is by launching a string of championships unprecedented in the National Football League."

World War II had depleted the rosters of most teams in the NFL by the start of the 1943 season, to the degree that the Philadelphia Eagles and the Pittsburgh Steelers were forced to combine their two teams in the NFL East and became known around the league as the Phil-Pitt Steagles.

The Redskins were not as badly drained of talent as many teams, however. They still had Sammy Baugh, Andy Farkas, Wilbur Moore, Joe Aguirre, Bob Masterson, and Wee Willie Wilkin, among others. They had, however, lost to military service such regulars as Dick Todd, Frank Filchock, Wayne Millner, Charley Malone, Ed Justice, Ed Cifers, and Fred Davis. In fact, 44 Redskins in all would serve in World War II at one time or another during the years 1942 through 1945. Only one did not return, halfback Keith Birlem, who was killed in battle May 7, 1943.

The most noticeable absence, however,

Andy Farkas bulled in for the game's first score. Baugh engineered a similar drive a little later that also ended up on the two, and Farkas again toted the ball in for a touchdown, enabling the Redskins to retire to their locker room with a 14–0 halftime lead.

In the third quarter, the Giants' offense came alive and moved the ball to the Washington 32, but there the Washington defense doused the drive, and the period remained scoreless. In the fourth quarter, New York's Tuffy Leemans dropped back and rifled a pass that Baugh intercepted and carried 28 yards to the New York one-yard line. Farkas plunged in for the touchdown on the next play. And finally, to add the proverbial icing to the cake, Baugh tossed a touchdown pass to Ted Lapka. The final score: Redskins 28, Giants 0, and Baugh had his revenge. He completed 16 of 21 passes that day for 199 yards.

With the win, the Redskins earned the right to play in their fourth NFL championship game in seven years. And for the fourth time, they were to face the Chicago Bears.

While Sammy Baugh was having one of his finest years, so was Bears quarterback Sid Luckman. Both, in fact, were named All-Pro, Luckman at quarterback and Baugh at halfback. Luckman had set several NFL records that year when he became the first quarterback ever to pass for more than 400 yards in a game (433) and to throw seven touchdown passes in one game, both of which he accomplished in a 56–7 decimation of the New York Giants. He had also set single-season standards by passing for 2,194 yards and 28 touchdowns.

Because the Bears had lost a good number of their regulars to the war effort, they induced Bronko Nagurski, now 34 years old, to end his five-year retirement and once again don a Bears uniform. He was still an awesome force.

PEP TALK

Several decades after the 1943 playoff game between the Redskins and Giants to determine the NFL East title, Dutch Bergman explained to *Washington Evening Star* columnist Lewis F. Atchison how he tried to spur the Skins after they had lost two consecutive games to the Giants on the two preceding Sundays. Atchison duly reported it in his column in 1964.

It was a cheerless, dispirited group when Bergman entered the room for his pre-game. A definite "let's get it over with" atmosphere was in the air and he sensed it.

"I just want to say," he began in slow, precise words, "that we have some good ballplayers on this squad and we have some yellow-bellied, gutless ones too. I know that some of you already have bought train tickets and are leaving for home right after the game. You're going out there, take your beating, and slink home like whipped dogs. You don't want to play the Bears. You're yellow, gutless. . . ."

"Wait a minute there, you can't call me yellow," Sammy Baugh angrily broke in. "Nobody's gonna call me a quitter."

The rangy quarterback took a couple of menacing steps forward, but Dutch held his ground.

"All right, Sam, if you want to fight go out and fight the Giants," he calmly replied. "I'll be here in this room after the game. I'll be waiting for you."

It worked. The Redskins went out and scalped the Giants 28–0, and Baugh, with his passing, is credited with having led them to the victory.

crucial, pressure-filled games in a row. The gamblers wondered which would dull the edge, or perhaps if both might exact a toll.

When the day had ended, it was safe to say that three intense games in succession had been more damaging than four weeks of rest and relaxation. That, and the fact that Sammy Baugh had staggered to the sideline after the opening kickoff when someone had kicked him in the head. He remained there with a mild concussion for the rest of the first half, replaced by George

An injured and dejected Sammy Baugh sits on the bench during the NFL championship game of 1943 against the Chicago Bears. Despite a concussion, Baugh made it back onto the field in the second half. (HOF/NFL Photos)

The Bears had ended their season with a record of 8–1–1, their only loss dealt to them by the Redskins, 27–14, a game in which coach Bergman surprised the Chicagoans with the old Statue of Liberty play in which end Wilbur Moore snatched the ball from a poised-to-pass Sammy Baugh and ran 20 yards for a touchdown.

The NFL championship game was set for Sunday, December 16, at Wrigley Field in Chicago. Both teams figured they had something going against them before they even took the field. Because the Bears had begun their season two weeks before the Redskins and because the title game had to be pushed back a week to accommodate the NFL East playoff game, Chicago had not played a football game in a month. On the other hand, the Redskins were coming off three

Marshall had also decided he was through with the single wing, and that the Redskins—as most of the other teams in the league had already done—were going to convert to the T formation, which the Chicago Bears had reintroduced to pro football in 1940. To accomplish the transformation, Marshall hired Clark Shaugnessy, who had orchestrated the T successfully at Stanford University before helping George Halas develop the formation with the Bears.

So Sammy Baugh, who had been a tailback for four years in college and seven in the pros, and Frank Filchock, who was just returning after two years of service in the Coast Guard, faced a major adjustment in leading their team on the field.

It did not work all that well for Marshall's tribe that first year, 1944, the Redskins turning in a 6–3–1 record and a third-place finish behind the New York Giants and the Philadelphia Eagles. Baugh and Filchock had been platooned at quarterback, as they had as tailbacks in 1939. Filchock adjusted more readily to the new system than Baugh, who admitted he was very much steeped in his old ways. The adaptation on Filchock's part was so good that he ended up leading the entire NFL in passing that year, completing 84 of 147 passes for 1,138 yards and 13 touchdowns. He was, for some reason, denied All-Pro honors, although his favorite receiver, end Joe Aguirre, was so honored.

Marshall was thoroughly disenchanted

The Redskins gang up on All-Pro halfback Steve Van Buren of the Philadelphia Eagles in this 1945 game at Griffith Stadium. The Washington defenders at Van Buren's legs are defensive back Bob Seymour (20) and end Doug Turley. (Washington Redskins)

Vaulting over a Boston Yanks defender in a 1945 game is halfback Steve Bagarus, who wore the unorthodox number 00 during his years as a Redskin, 1945 through 1948. Bagarus, an exciting and obviously high-stepping runner, was also a fine receiver. (Washington Redskins)

with the 1944 season, as he made clear in a variety of statements to the press, but not enough to replace DeGroot as his coach. He made it abundantly clear, however, that he expected a better showing in 1945.

Coach DeGroot accommodated him—almost, anyway. Sammy Baugh helped considerably, having now fully mastered the profession of T-formation quarterback. He felt so comfortable in the role by 1945 that he quipped, "I could play it in top hat and tails."

The Redskins opened up in Beantown against the Boston Yanks, a team that had

joined the NFL just the year before. Washington was a heavy favorite to beat the NFL neophytes from Boston, who had turned in a meager record of 2–8–0 in their maiden season. But the Boston Yanks apparently had not been informed and had not heard Marshall's statements to the press that the Redskins were the clear favorites to win the NFL East that year, and stunned them, 28–21.

After that, however, there was nothing to stop the marauding Redskins. They knocked off their next six opponents, including a fine Philadelphia Eagles team that showcased All-Pro halfback Steve Van Buren; the always difficult New York Giants, a game in which Baugh completed 20 of 24 passes for 265 yards and two touchdowns; and the perennially powerful Chicago Bears.

Their success was founded around the skills of Baugh, who was no longer being platooned with Frank Filchock and was having one of his best years ever as a Redskin. Baugh's unsurpassed passing was supplemented by the powerful running of fullback Frank Akins, the fleetness of rookie halfback Steve Bagarus, and the placekicking of Joe Aguirre. In those six victories, the Redskins averaged 25 points a game.

Their offense failed them, however, when they went to Philadelphia to face the Eagles in a crucial game; if they had won it they would have practically wrapped up the NFL East title. Washington was 6–1–0 and Philadelphia was 5–2–0, while the normally pesty Giants were out of the running with a record of 2–4–1. But the Eagles mounted a fortification that day that even Baugh could not breach, and the Redskins fell, 16–0.

It proved of little importance, because Washington rebounded and shut out their last two opponents of the year, the Steelers 24–0 and the Giants 17–0, while the Eagles lost to the Giants. With an 8–2–0 record, Washington had earned its fifth NFL East title.

A little face slapping went on in this 1945 game as Redskins halfback Bill deCorrevont (29) charges by Chicago Cardinal defensive back John Knolla (33). The Skins won the game 24–21. (Washington Redskins)

Baugh, enjoying his first selection as an All-Pro quarterback (his previous such honors were as a halfback), had set an NFL record by completing 70.3% of his passes, a mark that has only been surpassed once in NFL history (Kenny Anderson of the Cincinnati Bengals completed 70.55% of his passes in 1982). Slingin' Sam's 128 completions were the most in the NFL that year, and only Sid Luckman of the Bears gained more yards passing than Baugh's 1,669 yards (1,725).

Frank Akins was second in rushing to Philadelphia's Steve Van Buren, gaining 797 yards, the most a Redskin had earned since Cliff Battles ran for 897 in 1937. Akins also posted an impressive average of 5.4 yards per carry. Halfback Steve Bagarus led the team in pass receptions with 39 and in yards gained receiving with 637, both Washington records at the time. And Joe Aguirre led the league with seven field goals and was successful on 23 of 24 conversion attempts, both setting new team marks.

The Redskins would not be facing the Chicago Bears as they had in their four

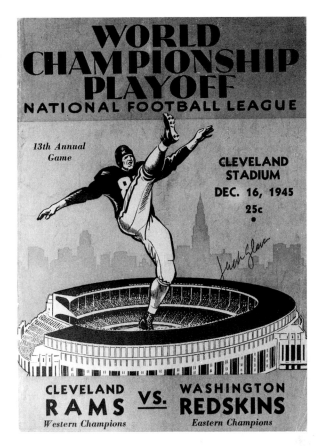

PRIORITIES

The late Jack Mara, former president of the New York Giants football team, often told the story of George Preston Marshall and his football priorities.

The Giants were in Washington one year in the mid-1940s to play the Redskins when a freak snowstorm left the field under about a foot of snow. An hour before the teams were to take the field for pregame warm-ups, Mara was surveying the situation from the sideline, wondering if indeed it would be possible to play a game in all that snow.

His thoughts were interrupted, however, when he saw Marshall trudging across the field in the knee-high snow. As he approached, Marshall shook his head. "Don't worry, Jack, they're coming," he said. "They'll be here in plenty of time."

"Snowplows?" Mara asked.

"Snowplows, hell," Marshall said with a look of great disbelief. "I'm talking about overshoes for the band."

It wasn't hay for the Redskins on the bench that cold and fateful day. Just a lot of straw.

Jim Gillette, Rams, gains four. Ki Aldrich (55), is stopper.   Bagarus Redskins for 2nd quarter score.

Scenes from the bitterly cold NFL championship game of 1945 between the Redskins and the Cleveland Rams.
(HOF/NFL Photos)

116

Joe Aguirre attempts a game-winning, 25-yard field goal in the last minute, but the ball falls just short of the crossbar. (HOF/NFL Photos)

previous title-game appearances. Instead they were to meet the Cleveland Rams, who, with a record of 9–1–0, had glided through the NFL West. The Rams were quarterbacked by rookie Bob Waterfield, destined for the Pro Football Hall of Fame, who was third that year in yards gained passing behind Luckman and Baugh. Waterfield also led the league in touchdown passes (14) and in yards gained per pass attempt (9.4), and was a distinct threat with his bootleg runs around end.

The game was set for Municipal Stadium in Cleveland, an amphitheater that could seat 80,000. The setting was less than comfortable, however. Five inches of snow were on the ground the day before the game. And, on the day of the game, as Shirley Povich described it in his *Washington Post* column: "Pretty soon they'll line up for the kickoff but the heroes of this Redskins–Rams game for the pro league championship are already established. They're the 32,178 fans who paid as much as $6 to watch this thing in zero weather. They're peddling hot coffee in the stands, and the lucky fans

are getting it spilled all over 'em. When one clumsy vendor attempted to apologize he was told, 'Never mind, the pleasure is all mine.' "

On that gelid afternoon in Cleveland, the Rams were the first to march. Halfback Fred Gehrke picked up 16 yards on a crossbuck, then Waterfield connected with All-Pro end Jim Benton on a 30-yard pass to the Washington 14-yard line. Cleveland bulled it down to the five, but disdained a field goal attempt and was held on fourth down.

Instead of the three points the Rams might have gotten, they managed to get two. Sammy Baugh dropped back into the end zone to pass, but when he threw the ball it hit the goalpost crossbar and bounced back at him, which, according to the rules of the day, constituted a safety, so the Rams took a 2–0 lead into the second quarter.

Worse than that, Baugh did not appear on the field for the second period, benched with some badly bruised ribs and replaced at quarterback by Frank Filchock. But it was not all bad news in that period of play. Redskins linebacker Ki Aldrich intercepted

In what could pass for a statue commissioned for the Pro Football Hall of Fame, Steve Bagarus goes up to grab a Sammy Baugh pass in the 1946 game against the Chicago Bears. (HOF/NFL Photos)

take over head-coaching chores for the AAFC's Los Angeles Dons. With DeGroot, Marshall had been at his most meddlesome, and the telephone from Marshall's booth to the sideline was ordinarily as busy as that of most bookmakers. As DeGroot explained later, "I couldn't stay on as coach of the Redskins and keep my self-respect. Marshall took too many privileges. He gave the assistant coaches too much direct authority. I found myself head coach in name, but I had the authority only to substitute the quarterback, the center, and the ends." Assistant

coach Turk Edwards was moved up to replace DeGroot.

Wayne Millner, after seven years as a Redskin, retired. He would later be inducted into the Pro Football Hall of Fame for his outstanding career as an offensive and defensive end. Also gone was sometime-platooning and always-threatening backup quarterback Frank Filchock, traded by Marshall to the New York Giants. Filchock would evince his deep sense of ingratitude to Marshall by turning in an All-Pro season, leading the Giants to the NFL East title, and humiliating the Redskins 31–0 in the last game of the regular season.

With Sammy Baugh ailing much of that 1946 season, the Redskins, for the first time since coming to Washington in 1937, did not have a winning season, their 5–5–1 record only good enough for third place in the five-team NFL East.

The following season the Redskins proved they could score a lot of points and lost most of their games at the same time. The 295 points they scored in their 12 games in 1947 was by far the most in team history at the time, but the 25 points they averaged per game was below the average of 31 they allowed their opponents.

Sammy Baugh had a magnificent year, setting two NFL passing records. He became the first player to complete more than 200 passes in a season, his 210 considerably more than the previous record of 146 by Cecil Isbell of the Packers. The 2,938 yards he gained on those passes far surpassed the record of 2,194 set by Sid Luckman of the

Bears in 1943. In one game alone, played on "Sammy Baugh Day" at Griffith Stadium against the Chicago Cardinals, Slingin' Sam completed 25 of 33 passes for 355 yards, six for touchdowns. The Skins trounced the Cardinals—a team, incidentally, that was destined to win the NFL title that year—45–21, but it was one of only four victories they could claim in 1947.

Three Redskins gained more than 500 yards catching Baugh's passes that year: halfbacks Eddie Saenz (598) and Bob Nussbaumer (597) and end Hugh "Bones" Taylor (511), a rookie from Oklahoma City University. Nussbaumer, rookie from the U. of Michigan, caught 47 passes, a club record that would remain until Fred Dugan snared 53 in 1961.

The Redskins' record of 4–8–0 in 1947 was the worst since the 2–8–1 season of 1935 back in Boston, and left them in fourth place in the NFL East. After the season, Marshall, when asked if the year had any highlights, remarked: "One comes to mind

Dick Todd (41) picks up a few yards for the Skins in a 1947 game against the New York Giants at Griffith Stadium. Todd was one of Washington's best offensive and defensive backs during his eight years with the Redskins (1939–42, 1945–48). The Redskins prevailed in this game, 28–20. (HOF/NFL Photos)

The Redskins Review ★ ★ ★ THE OFFICIAL PUBLICATION

OF THE WASHINGTON REDSKINS, REPRESENTING THE NATION'S CAPITAL IN THE NATIONAL FOOTBALL LEAGUE

The 12th Year   PUBLISHED BY PRO FOOTBALL, INCORPORATED
739 NINTH STREET N.W., WASHINGTON, D. C.   **Dec. 5, 1948**

Season Tickets Make Lasting Christmas Gifts
(SEE PAGE 28 FOR INFORMATION)

How to Get Season Books for 1949

We have had numerous queries on when . . . where . . . and how to obtain season books for the six home games on our 1949 National Football League schedule.

Except for a limited block of seats for each visiting team and its fans, all seats in Griffith Stadium will be offered on a season-book basis.

This will be done on a first-come, first-served basis with (1) 1948 season-book holders being entitled to renew their present seats; (2) present book-holders being entitled to improve their locations wherever possible; and (3) new applicants being taken care of in the order in which they apply.

The following prices will prevail:

Grandstand	Established Price.. $16.50	Upper Boxes	Established Price.. $21.00
South Field Stand	Federal Tax 3.30	Field Boxes	Federal Tax 4.20
East Field Stand		Side Line Boxes	
Lower Boxes	Total $19.80		Total $25.20

War II. Whelchel was known to be a firm disciplinarian, but had the most limited of coaching credentials. He was so inexperienced that Marshall sent him to South Bend, Indiana, where Notre Dame coach Frank Leahy was commissioned to teach him the rudiments of the T formation (Whelchel, in his short career at Navy, had employed only the single wing).

Whelchel, who was as authoritarian and opinionated as Marshall, clashed with the owner from the start, which earned for him the distinction of having the shortest career ever as a Washington head coach. After the seventh game of the season, with a record of 3–3–1, it was announced that the admiral had resigned. He was replaced by assistant coach and scout Herman Ball. After the season, in which the Redskins' record dropped to 4–7–1, a sportswriter asked Marshall if perhaps he might have been a bit premature in unseating Whelchel as head coach. Marshall shouted his answer: "Hell, I hired him for a disciplinarian, not for a goddamn coach."

At any rate, the Redskins were back in fourth place, and with few postseason statistics to boast about. Only the passing of Sammy Baugh (145 of 255 for 1,903 yards and 18 touchdowns) and the receptions of Bones Taylor (45 for 781 yards and nine touchdowns) were noteworthy. Taylor's reception yardage and touchdowns were team records, and the latter was also the NFL high in 1949.

The 1950s

If the second half of the 1940s had been dismal, the decade of the '50s was to offer little relief. There would be the appearance of a variety of colorful players and some very exciting games, and at least one season reminiscent of the early '40s Redskin teams, but for the most part it would be a dreary segment of team history.

The AAFC had departed with the '40s, although three franchises—the Cleveland Browns, San Francisco 49ers, and Baltimore Colts—were absorbed into the NFL. The resulting reorganization turned the NFL East and West divisions into the NFL American and National conferences. Because the New York Bulldogs (successor to the Boston Yanks) went out of business like the AAFC, the NFL now had a total of 12 teams. The Redskins were slotted into the American Conference with the Giants, Eagles, Steelers, Cardinals, and Browns.

Herman Ball was kept on as head coach, much to the surprise of many observers. Marshall brought All-Pro halfback "Bullet" Bill Dudley to Washington in a trade that sent defensive back and kick returner Dan Sandifer to the Detroit Lions. Dudley, who would eventually make his way into the Pro Football Hall of Fame, had been coveted by Marshall since the days when The Big Chief used to watch him play at the University of Virginia before the war. The Bullet was a

The most exciting draft choice in many a year, halfback Charlie "Choo Choo" Justice (22) arrived in 1950. Runner-up for the Heisman Trophy the year before, North Carolinian Justice was a consensus All-America and found an immediate spot in the Redskins backfield. (HOF/NFL Photos)

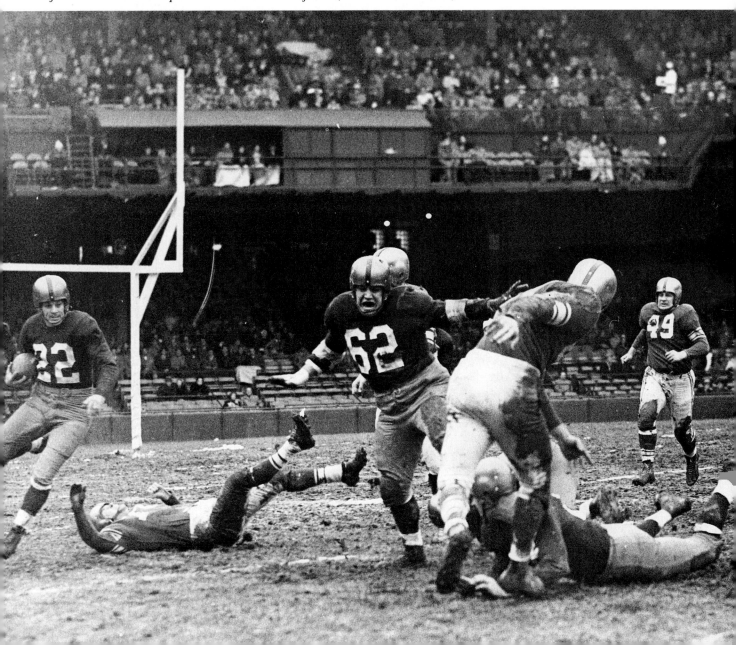

fine runner, kicker, and kick returner, but he was also approaching the age of 30 and had been in the league since 1942, with two years off during the war to serve as a fighter pilot.

Prospects for the '50s were decidedly improved by the drafting of some very talented college players as well. The biggest name to come to Washington was consensus All-America halfback Charlie "Choo Choo" Justice from North Carolina. The additions of Virginian Dudley and Tarheel Justice fueled the popularity of the Redskins throughout the middle and deep South, where Skins games were regularly broadcast on radio; in fact, Washington had come to be considered *the* pro football team of the South. Mar-

shall's systematic exclusion of blacks from his team was also a factor in Redskin popularity in that area of the country at that particular time in our history.

Rob Goode, in his second year with Washington, was switched from a halfback to fullback and would lead the team in rushing. Another important draft pick was linebacker Chuck Drazenovich of Penn State, who would have a fine 10-year career in Washington. Also helping the defense was veteran tackle Paul Lipscomb, acquired from Green Bay.

The big name that Charlie Justice brought to the Redskins, however, didn't land on a contract. He decided to eschew football for business.

Eddie Saenz takes off around left end in a 1950 game against the Baltimore Colts. Saenz was a key running back from 1946 through 1951. The Redskins beat the Colts that muddy afternoon, 38–28. (HOF/NFL Photos)

The Redskins opened the season with a lot of new faces in the starting lineup, but the team was still built around the arm of Sammy Baugh, which was well weathered as it entered its 14th season. The Redskins appeared well, too, when they went to Baltimore to face the Colts on opening Sunday. They drubbed the former AAFC team, 38–14.

In the wake of victory came collapse, however. Eight straight losses followed, games in which the Redskins gave up an average of 29 points while averaging only 14 themselves. They sunk to the cellar of the NFL American Conference, where they remained even though they won two of their last three games. Their three victories were the second-fewest wins in the club's then 19-year history.

Choo Choo Justice had decided business was not as much fun as football and had come back after the fifth game of the season to join Baugh, Dudley, and Goode in the backfield. As a result of the running potential the Redskins now had (although it failed to materialize) and the attempt to involve Harry Gilmer in the offensive attack, Baugh did not throw the ball as frequently in 1950 as he had in previous years. He did complete 90 of 166 passes for 1,130 yards and 10 touchdowns. His favorite receiver, as well as Gilmer's, remained Bones Taylor, who set two club records by gaining 781 yards receiving and catching nine touchdown passes. Both Charlie Justice and Harry Gilmer, so heralded in college, had not lived up to expectations. Justice was dissatisfied enough to drop out of football after the season, but would come back again in 1952.

Whether the Redskins improved in 1951 or the American Conference simply got worse is a debatable question. They did improve somewhat by adding end Gene Brito from Loyola University of Los Angeles, who would later specialize as a defensive end and prove to be one of the finest in Redskins history.

Herman Ball, after leading the Redskins to three defeats in their first three games (in which they lost by a collective score of 115 to 31), incurred Marshall's intense displeasure and was replaced by assistant coach Dick Todd, who had been a mainstay in the Washington backfield during most of the 1940s.

Todd managed to compile a 5–4–0 record during the remainder of the year, which was good enough to land the Redskins in third place in their conference. But they finished far behind the 11–1–0 Cleveland Browns, who showcased such future Hall of Famers as Otto Graham, Marion Motley, Dante Lavelli, Lou Groza, Len Ford, Bill Willis, and Frank Gatski.

It proved to be Sammy Baugh's last year as starting quarterback, even though Gilmer again failed to show the greatness he had as a college player. Rob Goode again led the team in rushing yardage, the 951 yards he gained eclipsing the record of 874 that Cliff Battles had set the first year the Redskins played in Washington.

Dick Todd returned as head coach in 1952, at least for part of the preseason. He found, however, that working for Marshall in that capacity was unbearable, and he quit.

Marshall quickly hired Curly Lambeau, the founder of the Green Bay Packers and their head coach from 1919 through 1949, who for the two previous years had piloted the hapless Chicago Cardinals (8–17–0 under Lambeau).

Another casualty of the preseason was Sammy Baugh, who broke his hand. For the regular season, the quarterbacking duties fell to rookie Eddie LeBaron, with Harry Gilmer again serving as backup. LeBaron, out of the College of Pacific and one of the littlest quarterbacks to ever play the game (5'9", 170 pounds), had been drafted two

Dick Alban (42) intercepts a pass in a 1954 game against the New York Giants. The intended receiver, Frank Gifford, looks back at his passer Charley Conerly, but it is too late. (Washington Redskins)

years earlier but had had a Marine Corps obligation to fulfill before coming to Washington.

Bill Dudley had retired. Military service snagged Rob Goode, as well as rookie and former Heisman Trophy winner Vic Janowicz of Ohio State. The depleted Redskins offense was no match for its American Conference opponents that year, and they were 2–8–0 when Baugh came back to quarterback for the last two games of the season. Behind the old slinger, they defeated the Giants 27–17 and the Eagles 27–21. With that, Baugh, now 38 years old, retired after entertaining and exciting Washington football fans for 16 years, and returned to his ranch in Texas.

The 4–8–0 season tied the Redskins for last place in the American Conference with the Chicago Cardinals. Bones Taylor had become Eddie LeBaron's favorite target, too, and he set two team receiving records when he gained 961 yards on his receptions and caught 12 touchdown passes. The latter is still the Redskins standard, although Taylor shares it now with Charley Taylor, who caught his 12 in 1966.

It was a better year in 1953. With the quarterbacking shared between LeBaron and rookie Jack Scarbath, an All-America from Maryland, the Skins posted their first winning season since 1948. One of the reasons was a fine defense anchored by linebackers Chuck Drazenovich and Al Demao;

front linemen Gene Brito, Paul Lipscomb, and rookie Dick Modzelewski, also from Maryland; and defensive backs Dick Alban and Don Doll, a rookie out of Southern Cal. In addition, Choo Choo Justice, back again, chugged with the ball in the manner that everyone had been hoping he would since he'd joined the Redskins in 1950, leading the team in rushing with 616 yards, with average carries of 5.4 yards. Bill Dudley had come back for a final year, too, principally as a kicker. He contributed 11 field goals and 25 of 25 extra points. The Redskins' 6–5–1 record, however, was only good enough for third place in the American Conference.

Coach Lambeau was far from beloved by his players, something he had experienced in his later years at Green Bay and in Chicago as well. As it turned out, he did not get along with George Marshall either. Their animosity toward each other flared before the 1954 regular season got under way and Curly was out. After having coached in the NFL every year since its inception in 1920, Lambeau hung up his whistle for good. The 230 victories he coached the Packers, Cardinals, and Redskins to were second at that time only to George Halas of the Bears.

His replacement was Joe Kuharich, who had replaced Lambeau at the Chicago Cardinals in 1952. Kuharich was about to begin the longest tenure of a Redskins head coach since the days of Ray Flaherty in the late 1930s and early '40s. He would last five full years, no mean feat in those days of transient coaches in Washington.

He began his Redskins career without two key players, however. Quarterback Eddie LeBaron and All-Pro defensive end Gene Brito had defected to the Canadian Football League. The quarterbacking responsibilities fell to Al Dorow, a rookie from Michigan State, and Jack Scarbath.

Scatback Billy Wells, another rookie from Michigan State, and fullback Rob Goode, back in the fold, proved to be the most productive rushers (516 and 462 yards, respectively), and Bones Taylor was the top receiver (37 for 659 yards). But the Redskins as a whole were sadly lacking and won only three of their 12 games that year. One loss, a 62–3 debacle to the Cleveland Browns, was the worst defeat since that dreadful 73–0 massacre perpetrated in the 1940 championship game by the Bears. The only thing that kept Marshall from a total funk that year was the fact that he had enticed Washington's prestigious National Symphony Orchestra, under the direction of Dr. Howard Mitchell, to perform at halftime in a game against the Giants at Griffith Stadium. After the concert was over, however, the Redskins continued fumbling their way to a 51–21 defeat.

In what now appeared to be a coming-and-going tradition, LeBaron and Brito returned to the Redskins for the 1955 season. Also moving into the starting lineup was halfback and placekicker Vic Janowicz. But gone to retirement was the then-leading receiver in Redskins annals, Bones Taylor.

The Redskins got revenge for their humiliation at the hands of the Browns the preceding season by knocking off the defending NFL champions in the opener by a score of 27–17. The following week, with Washington down 16–0 to the Eagles in the third quarter, the Redskins scored an astonishing 21 points in just over two minutes of play to precipitate one of the great comebacks of team lore. First Gene Brito recovered a fumble on the Philadelphia 32, then Eddie LeBaron, on the first play from scrimmage, lofted a touchdown pass to Vic Janowicz. On the ensuing kickoff, the Eagles fumbled the ball in the end zone and it was recovered by Redskins end Ralph Thomas. After the next kickoff, Philadelphia again fumbled, and this time the ball was re-

REDSKINS vs. CLEVELAND BROWNS
October 16, 1955   Price 50c Incl. Tax

Lions scored 96). And Joe Kuharich was named NFL Coach of the Year, preempting Marshall's habit of keeping his coaches' careers very brief.

The promise offered by the exceptional play of Vic Janowicz would disappear, however, on a dark and ill-fated night in 1956 near training camp at Occidental College in California. The talented halfback was thrown from a car that evening and suffered brain damage, serious enough to end his football career. Injuries to Eddie LeBaron and backup quarterback Al Dorow also contributed to the faltering of the Redskins in '56. Still, they managed a 6–6–0 season and a third-place berth in the NFL Eastern Conference, as it was now called.

In 1956, the Redskins had found a new kicker in Sam Baker, who filled in for Janowicz in that capacity. He set a team record that year by kicking 17 field goals, considerably more than the previous record of 11 by Bill Dudley in 1953. Baker and his foot would lead the team in scoring for four years before he was traded to Cleveland.

Two notable additions to the team in '56 were guard Dick Stanfel (who would earn All-Pro honors each of his three years with the Redskins), acquired in a trade with the Lions, and halfback Dickie James, drafted out of Oregon.

The Skins, however, resumed their losing ways in 1957, an unhappy state of affairs that would carry on well into the 1960s. As it had the year before, the preseason began on a tragic note. Defensive back Roy Barni was shot to death while trying to break up a brawl in a bar he owned on Telegraph Hill in San Francisco.

LeBaron had an entirely new backfield with him in 1957, made up of three rookies: fullback Don Bosseler from Miami (Florida), who would lead the team in rushing with 673 yards and a four-yard average gain; and halfbacks Jim Podoley, who had played at

covered by Washington linebacker LaVern Torgeson. Moments later Janowicz carried the ball in for the Redskins' third touchdown. Washington went on to win the game, 31–30. It was the first time the Skins had won their first two games of the season since 1948.

The Redskins of 1955 went on to post a record of 8–4–0, second to the Browns, who took the conference title with a record of 9–2–1. It was the most victories a Washington team had rung up since the divisional champion Redskins won eight in 1945. The biggest hero of the year was Janowicz, who set a club record by scoring 88 points on seven touchdowns, six field goals, and 28 extra points. It was the second-most points in the NFL that year (Doak Walker of the

A retired but always inspirational Sammy Baugh, replete with cowboy hat, joins the team on the Redskins bench in 1955, three years after he retired. (HOF/NFL Photos)

little-known Central Michigan, and Ed Sutton of North Carolina.

The Redskins managed to win only two of their first nine games that year, then swept the last three, but their record of 5–6–1 entrenched them in fourth place in the NFL Eastern Conference.

They ended up in the same slot in 1958 as well, this time with an even less-inspiring record of 4–7–1. The only bright spot was the blossoming of end Joe Walton, who had been acquired in the draft the year before,

and who led the team in pass receptions (32) and yardage gained on them (532).

Joe Kuharich deemed it time to leave and took the head-coaching job at Notre Dame. His assistant, Mike Nixon, was named successor.

During the season, the Redskins Alumni Association was organized with a formal constitution, bylaws, and an open invitation to all former players to join.

Kuharich had chosen the right time to depart. The faltering Redskins could win

SANTA CLAUS IS COMING TO TOWN

Under George Preston Marshall, the last home game of each season took on special traditional significance. It was at halftime of that game that Santa Claus would arrive to take part in the intermission festivities.

He would arrive a different way each year, and it became a great local guessing game to figure out what imaginative way Marshall would have him make his entrance. The first time Santa tried to parachute onto the field at Griffith Stadium during the half, a gusty wind carried him out over the right field wall and he had to settle for landing on the rooftop of a nearby apartment building.

Only in Washington—George Preston Marshall's Washington, that is.

vided a home to many other noteworthy receivers. In the Baugh era, there was Dick Todd, Bob Masterson, Wilbur Moore, and Steve Bagarus; in the 1950s, Johnny Carson and Joe Walton; and more recently, Jerry Smith, Larry Brown, Joe Washington, Clint Didier, and Ricky Sanders.

Charley Taylor was Washington's most productive pass catcher eight times, four times in the 1960s and four times in the '70s. His namesake (though no relation), Bones Taylor, was tops six consecutive years, 1949–54, while Bobby Mitchell took the honors in four straight, 1962–65. Charley Taylor claims all career pass-reception marks, with 609 catches for 9,140 yards and 79 touchdowns. Art Monk set an NFL record for receptions in a season when he snared 106 in 1984. And Bobby Mitchell accounted for the most yards gained on receptions in a single season, collecting 1,436 in 1963.

Wayne Millner

An All-America end from Notre Dame, Wayne Millner, at 6'1", 190 pounds, joined the Boston Redskins in 1936. His coach, Ray Flaherty, also in his first year with the team, was so elated at signing him that he sent boss George Preston Marshall a one-sentence wire: "With that Yankee playing end, please accept my resignation if the Redskins do not win the championship this year."

Millner could not only catch the ball well, he was also an outstanding defensive player, difficult to block and a ferocious tackler. He was also an excellent blocker. His teammate and fellow Hall of Famer Cliff Battles said of Millner, "I always knew if I could get out in the open, Wayne would be there to throw a block for me. It was Wayne's blocks that determined whether or not I would get away for a long run."

Wayne Millner (40) joined the Redskins in Boston in 1936 and stayed with them in Washington through 1941. After a stint in the U.S. Navy in World War II, he came back and played the 1945 season. Millner was inducted into the Pro Football Hall of Fame in 1968. (Washington Redskins)

During his seven-year career with the Redskins, Millner played in four NFL title games (1936, 1937, 1940, and 1945). He missed the 1942 championship match because he was serving in the U.S. Navy, as well as the next two years. When asked what he felt was his most memorable game, Millner said, "Has to be the 1937 championship against the Bears." Millner made it memorable for all Washington football fans. With the Skins trailing Chicago in the third quarter, 14–7, he grabbed a 20-yard pass over the middle from Sammy Baugh and raced another 35 yards for a touchdown. Later that same period, Washington down this time 21–14, Millner again teamed with Baugh. Slingin' Sam dropped back from his own 22-yard line and rifled it to Millner at midfield, who carried it 50 yards into the end zone. Having been burned twice in the same quarter, the Bears were all over Millner, so Baugh used him as a decoy and tossed another touchdown pass to Ed Justice. At day's end, Millner had caught nine passes for 179 yards, and the Redskins were victorious, 28–21. To this day only Art Monk has caught more passes in a playoff game (10, in the divisional playoff game against the Bears in 1984).

The most passes Millner caught in a single season were the 22 he gathered in during the 1940 season; the most yardage he chalked up was 294 in 1939. His career stats with the Skins: 124 receptions, 1,578 yards, 12 touchdowns.

As a result of his exceptional play on offense and defense, Wayne Millner was elected to the Pro Football Hall of Fame in 1968.

Charley Malone

George Preston Marshall went all the way down to Texas A & M to get a rather large end in 1934. He was Charley Malone, and

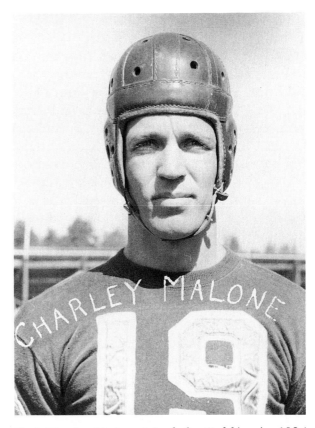

End Charley Malone joined the Redskins in 1934 after a noteworthy college football career at Texas A & M. At 6'4" and 200 pounds, he was a chief flanker for Washington through the 1940 season and led the team in pass receptions in 1934, 1935, 1937, and 1938. (HOF/NFL Photos)

he stood 6'4" tall and weighed in the vicinity of 200 pounds.

Malone moved right into the starting lineup that rookie year and immediately became the principal receiver—which in those days meant he caught an incidental 11 passes for 121 yards and two touchdowns. In 1935, however, with the addition of tailback Bill Shepherd, who was not a bad passer, and an invigorated emphasis on passing from new coach Eddie Casey, Malone doubled his catches with 22. The 433 yards he gained on them were the most in the NFL that year.

With the arrival of Wayne Millner in 1936, the Redskins could boast the most solid and dangerous flanks in football, although they were still a year away from obtaining a passer worthy of the two receivers. That, of course, was Sammy Baugh, and in Slingin' Sam's rookie year, 1937, Malone became his favorite target. Charley caught 28 passes for 419 yards, and only Don Hutson of the Packers, Bill Hewitt of the Eagles, and Gaynell Tinsley of the Chicago Cardinals scored more than Malone's four touchdowns on pass receptions.

Malone again led the Redskins in the receiving department in 1938, this time with 24 catches for 257 yards. Charley stayed with the Redskins through the 1942 season, although he missed 1941. When he retired, Charley Malone had caught a total of 137 passes for the Redskins for 1,922 yards and 13 touchdowns. His mark of 433 yards on receptions in 1935 stood until Steve Bagarus broke it in 1945 with 637.

Hugh "Bones" Taylor

Arriving in Washington as a free agent in 1947, Hugh Taylor was a gangly 6'4", 198-pound end from Oklahoma City University who brought with him the appropriate nickname of "Bones." Rawboned and wiry, with craggy features, he seemed almost an extension of Sammy Baugh. And the long-legged, long-striding Taylor was soon to become Baugh's favorite target. As Baugh later said of him, "Bones had the body of a basketball player, but a pair of hands that just naturally belonged around a football."

The walk-on Taylor not only made the team, but won a starting position in '47. He was the third most productive pass receiver (the most productive end) after halfbacks Eddie Saenz and Bob Nussbaumer—Baugh had taken a liking to throwing to them coming out of the backfield. Taylor led the

team in TD catches, though, with six, then the second most in club history.

By 1949, it was clear that Bones Taylor was the premier receiver on the Redskins. In that year, he set two Washington records when he gained 781 yards on receptions, demolishing the mark of 637 set by Steve Bagarus in 1945, and scored nine touchdowns to take the honor from Joe Aguirre, who had caught seven touchdown passes in 1943. That was the first of six consecutive years in which Taylor would lead the team in pass receptions.

Taylor broke his own reception-yardage record the following year with 833 and tied

Hugh "Bones" Taylor was Washington's top receiver for five consecutive years, 1949–54. (HOF/NFL Photos)

the TD mark with another nine. His finest year, however, was 1952, a season during which he was catching passes from a quarterback who could walk under his outstretched arm without ducking, Eddie LeBaron. That year Bones set two auspicious records. He caught 12 touchdown passes, a standard that remains today the all-time high (Charley Taylor tied it in 1966, as did Jerry Smith in 1967), and gained 961 yards on his catches, a mark that would stand until Bobby Mitchell ran off 1,384 in 1962. His average of 23.4 yards per reception that year was the highest in the NFL.

When Bones Taylor retired after the 1954 season, he had rewritten the Redskins record book for career pass receiving. Bones had pulled in 272 passes, which stands today as the fifth most in club history. He gained a total of 5,233 yards, again ranked fifth. His 58 touchdown receptions have only been exceeded by Charley Taylor (79) and Jerry Smith (60). In his eight years with the Skins, Bones Taylor was credited with 348 points scored, the sixth most in club annals.

Bobby Mitchell

Bobby Mitchell was already an established star when he came to the Redskins in 1962. He had played four years in the Cleveland Browns backfield with the legendary Jim Brown and was considered one of the most explosive runners in the game.

The Redskins wanted him badly. In fact, they traded their first-round draft choice, the first pick in that year's draft, Heisman Trophy winner Ernie Davis of Syracuse, to the Browns for Mitchell and running back Leroy Jackson, the first two black players ever to wear Washington Redskins uniforms. Shirley Povich in his column in *The Washington Post* nailed it down: "The Redskins' fascination for Mitchell, to the point of giving up the most publicized number one draft choice of the decade, is understandable. In the period since Mitchell abandoned his Olympic sprint ambitions and came into the league from U. of Illinois, he has wrecked the Washington team. The Redskins have scouted him mostly from the rear." Proof of that particular pudding came early, in one of Mitchell's first encounters with the Redskins, during his rookie year of 1958: He rushed for 232 yards that day and added another 20 on pass catches.

At 6' and 195 pounds, Mitchell was graced with three exceptional talents: speed (he ran the 100-yard dash in 9.7 seconds in college), an uncanny faking ability, and perfect balance. Combining them, he became a pure hellion on the football field.

Washington coach Bill McPeak announced that Mitchell would be slotted as a flanker instead of a running back, a move that would prove to be both wise and heartily welcomed by Mitchell (he had wanted to play flanker at Cleveland). In his first game against the Browns, with their coach Paul Brown very aware of what Mitchell could do on a football field, he was double-teamed, which proved effective . . . until the last two minutes of the game, when a stymied, frustrated Mitchell bounced off one defender into another, somehow got his hands on a Norm Snead pass at the 50-yard line, broke a tackle, put moves on several other would-be tacklers, and streaked into the end zone for the game-winning touchdown. He gave further testimony of the sagacity of the conversion to flanker that first year in Washington when, on the receiving end of Snead's passes, he led the NFL in receptions and found a place in the Redskins record book with 72 catches for 1,384 yards, becoming the first Skin to break the 1,000-yard receiving mark. Also devastating on kickoff returns, Bobby was a unanimous choice for All-Pro.

Bobby Mitchell (right) came to Washington from the Browns in 1962 and became one of the most dangerous receivers in the NFL. Here he has a step on New York Giants defensive back Erich Barnes and is about to haul in one of his 65 career touchdown pass receptions. (Fred Roe)

The following year was equally dazzling. Although he caught three fewer passes, he gained 1,436 yards with them, the NFL high and a Washington record that has yet to be matched. Ninety-nine of those yards came on an NFL record-tying touchdown pass from George Izo in another contest with his former employer, the Browns. In a game against the Steelers, Mitchell gained 218 yards on pass catches, the third most in Washington history.

A simple fact that Mitchell proved beyond a doubt in his first two years at flanker was that an opponent's troubles were just begin-ning *after* he caught a pass—he was recognized as the most difficult receiver in the league to corral and ground once he got his hands on the ball. He had his own philosophy: "You've got to go out there with confidence. If you come hesitating, that defenseman he has you in his back pocket. You got to aim at him with authority and make him worry about *you,* and not you worry about *him.*"

As it turned out, Mitchell, in his seven years with the Skins, gave defenders a great deal to worry about. He was forever a threat to break the big play, a 60-yard touchdown

140

here, a 45-yarder there, leaving a defender flat-footed with a move, breaking away from the pack with an explosive burst of speed, inevitably gobbling up great chunks of yardage.

Mitchell retired from the game after the 1968 season, but his Redskins career did not end there. He moved into the front office, where he has served in a variety of capacities, from director of pro scouting to assistant general manager.

As a player with the Redskins, Bobby ranks fourth in pass receptions (393), third in yards gained receiving (6,491), and third in touchdown receptions (tied with Bones Taylor at 58). He maintains the highest average kickoff return in club annals (28.5).

His combined net yards gained of 8,162 ranks fourth in the Redskins record book, and no one has yet exceeded the 1,852 combined net yards he posted in 1963.

In 11 seasons in the NFL, Bobby Mitchell rushed for 2,735 yards and gained 7,954 yards on pass receptions, 2,690 on kickoff returns, and 699 on punt returns. He scored a total of 91 touchdowns (65 on receptions, 18 rushing, five on kickoff returns, and three on punt returns). In 1983, he was inducted into the Pro Football Hall of Fame.

Charley Taylor

The Redskins and coach Bill McPeak had no reservations about who their first-round draft pick would be in 1964. It was the 6'3",

Wide receiver Charley Taylor making a spectacular catch in a 1973 game against the San Francisco 49ers. Taylor caught more passes (649) for more yards (9,140) than any player in Washington history. He was enshrined at the Pro Football Hall of Fame in 1984. (Washington Redskins)

210-pound speedster from Arizona State named Charley Taylor. The question kicked around backstage in Washington, however, was where to play him—at running back, where he had excelled in college, or, as some lobbied, at defensive cornerback. No one, at the time, was thinking wide receiver.

The running-back advocates prevailed. He was thrust into the backfield his rookie year and became *the* running game to augment the passing game of Sonny Jurgensen, another first-year Redskin in 1964. Taylor responded and exhilarated the Washington fans by turning in the most exciting and productive season by a Redskins ball-carrier in a decade and a half. He not only churned out 755 yards rushing, the most since Rob Goode set the team standard of 951 in 1950, but also caught 53 passes for 814 yards, only a whisper behind flanker Bobby Mitchell in both those categories. He contributed 10 touchdowns, five running and five catching the ball. And for it, he was named the NFL Rookie of the Year.

Taylor also led the Skins in rushing the following year, but in 1966 a coaching change put Otto Graham, one of the game's greatest quarterbacks in his day, at the helm, and increased the emphasis on passing in the Redskins' offensive scheme. He looked at Charley Taylor and came to certain conclusions: "Charley was poetry in motion," Graham observed, "but he couldn't gear his speed to his interference. More often than not he'd be out in front of the guard who should have been leading the running play, or climbing up the back of a slow tackle. He was devastating once he had room to run, so we kept asking ourselves what was the best way to get Taylor out into the open field. The answer was obvious: Put him outside as a receiver."

That shrewd decision changed Charley Taylor's life and eventually inked a new name and new figures in the NFL record book. In the second half of the 1966 regular season, Taylor ceased to be the Skins' leading ground gainer and began a stint as top receiver that would span the next 11 years in Washington. In his first effort split out at end, a game against the Baltimore Colts, he hauled in eight passes for 111 yards; the following week against Dallas, he tied Bobby Mitchell's team record of 11 receptions in a game. After one of those catches he shook off three would-be tacklers and raced to a 78-yard touchdown. Taylor ended the 1966 season with 72 receptions, the most in the NFL that year, which also tied the team record set by Bobby Mitchell four years earlier. Of the 72, 54 came in the six games he lined up as a wide receiver. His 12 touchdowns on pass catches also tied the club record, set by Bones Taylor in 1952.

George Allen came on the scene in 1971 and brought along a raft of veterans, dismantling the lineup almost completely in the process. One post he had no desire to tamper with, however, was wide receiver. He had a definite fondness for Charley Taylor, and later, when he wrote a book about the greatest pro football players, he ranked Charley the fourth-best receiver of all time, behind Don Hutson, Lenny Moore, and Crazylegs Hirsch. "Charley was very disciplined," Allen said. "He had good moves, and ran perfect routes. He could catch the ball long or short. He could make the tough catch over the middle. He had sure hands and could catch the ball one-handed. He was also a tremendous blocker."

Taylor missed much of the 1971 season and all of 1976 because of injuries. Other than those years he was always at or near the top of the NFL receiving charts. He endeared himself to Redskins fans by consistently being at his best in games against the abhorred Cowboys. In the 1972 NFC title game against Dallas, for example, he grabbed seven passes and scored the game's only two touchdowns, on passes of 15 and 45 yards, to insure a 26–3 Washington victory. Charley Waters, the Cowboys' All-Pro safety who spent much of his career chasing Taylor, said of him, "I hate to say it, but I sure wasn't crying when Charley couldn't play. . . . He's a helluva competitor, and his competence is overwhelming. We'll jaw back and forth at each other; he's always trying to psyche me out. He's one guy who talks a good game and can also back it up."

When Charley Taylor ended his pro football career after the 1977 season, he was the NFL all-time-leading pass catcher, having gathered in 649 passes. To this day, only Charlie Joiner, who broke the record in the 1980s, has caught more passes. Taylor set another NFL record by catching more than 50 or more passes in seven seasons.

Taylor owns all Washington career pass-catching records. The 649 he snared accounted for 9,140 yards and 79 touchdowns. He teamed with Sonny Jurgensen to produce three of the nine longest pass plays in team history, an 88-yarder against the Dallas Cowboys in 1969 and two for 86 yards, against the Atlanta Falcons in 1966 and the Los Angeles Rams in 1967. His total of 90 touchdowns is the most ever by a Redskin, and the 540 points Taylor scored is second only to the 1,204 amassed by kicker Mark Moseley.

Charley Taylor earned his way to the Pro Bowl eight times and into the Pro Football Hall of Fame in 1984.

Roy Jefferson

George Allen, in his first year as head coach in 1971, went after veteran wide receiver Roy Jefferson before he realized how desperately he would need him. The 6'2", 195-pound Jefferson had played with the Pittsburgh Steelers for five years and the Super Bowl champion Baltimore Colts of 1970 before becoming a member of the Over-the-Hill Gang in Washington.

Jefferson, who played his college ball at Utah, was 27 when he donned the burgundy and gold and was anything but over-the-hill. Teaming him at the other end of the line from All-Pro Charley Taylor, Allen envisioned the most threatening double barrel in the NFC. And to complement it, he had the ever-reliable Jerry Smith at tight end. Allen told the press he had "a trio of targets beyond compare" for his quarterbacks Sonny Jurgensen and Billy Kilmer.

The way they lined up that first season of "The Future Is Now" was with Jefferson and Smith on the strong side and Taylor on the weak side. Unfortunately, it did not stay that way for long, because injuries benched both Taylor and Smith for a good part of the season and Jefferson became *the* object of attention coming off the line of scrimmage. He carried the burden well and hauled in 47 passes for 701 yards, both team highs that year.

From the time he came to Washington, it became clear that Jefferson was especially dangerous on a quick-post pattern. As he explained it, "I've made a living off the quick post. Go straight down the field about 10 yards, then cut toward the goalpost on about a 45-degree angle. Of course, I put a few jukes along the way to get the defender off balance."

The next year, with Billy Kilmer handling most of the quarterbacking chores due to injuries to Sonny Jurgensen, the passing game was beautifully balanced, with a healthy Taylor and Smith back to join Jefferson, and Larry Brown coming out of the backfield as well. Between the four of them, they caught 137 passes for 2,849 yards to energize the Redskins as they hurtled toward their first divisional title since 1945. In the regular season, Jefferson, with 35 catches for 550 yards, was the second most

143

Displaying perfect form, Roy Jefferson hauls in a pass for the Redskins against the Dallas Cowboys in 1972. In the background is Washington tight end Jerry Smith (87). Jefferson was acquired by the Redskins in 1971 and remained through 1976. (Washington Redskins)

productive receiver, behind Charley Taylor. In the first playoff game that year, against the Green Bay Packers, Jefferson struck with his favorite quick-post pattern—after a juke, darting across the middle to take a pass from Kilmer for a 32-yard touchdown. Roy caught five of Kilmer's seven passes that day for 83 yards as the Skins scalped the Pack, 16–3. Jefferson was also the top receiver for Washington a few weeks later at Super Bowl VII, making five receptions for 50 yards, although the Redskins fell short that day against the Miami Dolphins, 14–7.

After missing all but six games of the 1975 season because of a knee injury, Jefferson came back in '76, had a credible year, and then retired from the game. He caught 208 passes for the Redskins in his six years in Washington, ranking number seven in that category, and gained 3,119 yards, sixth best.

During 12 years in the NFL, Roy Jefferson caught a total of 451 passes for 7,539 yards and 52 touchdowns, placing him among the all-time top 40 receivers in all three categories.

Art Monk

The day to remember for Art Monk, Washington's first-round draft choice of 1980 out of Syracuse, was December 16, 1984, at RFK Stadium, the last game of the season against the St. Louis Cardinals. With the divisional title on the line and the game well into the

Art Monk tries to grab a pass in the end zone in a 1981 game against the New York Giants. Monk had arrived in 1980, and in 1984, he would set the all-time NFL record for receptions (106) in a season. (Washington Redskins)

third quarter, Monk lined up out on the left at the St. Louis 36-yard line while Joe Theismann barked the signals. Suddenly he was racing a fly route down the sideline, then curling to the inside a step ahead of the defender to grab the ball in his sure hands and cross the goal line.

A touchdown was signaled, the game was stopped, and the announcement was made: "Art Monk has just caught his 102nd pass this year and broken the NFL record for receptions in a single season." The record, which had been held for the previous 20 years by Charley Hennigan of the Houston Oilers, was further shattered when Monk snared another four passes before the game

Art Monk
1980–present (Washington Redskins)

was over. Besides setting a major pro football record that day, Monk's 11 receptions for 136 yards and two touchdowns were instrumental in the Skins' 29–27 triumph to earn the NFC East title for 1984.

Monk, at 6'3" and 209 pounds, made his presence felt right from the very beginning in Washington. Winning a starting role in 1980, Art proceeded to wipe out the rookie receiving record of 53 grabs set by Charley Taylor in 1964 with the 58 he caught for 797 yards, both team highs that year. He was honored as the NFL's Offensive Rookie of the Year.

Nicknamed "Money" for his ability to catch clutch passes and pull off the crucial play, Monk led the team in yardage gained on receptions the following year, toting up 894, the most since Charley Taylor earned 990 yards 14 years earlier.

In the strike-torn season of 1982, Monk again led the team in catches, but in the last game he broke his foot and missed the playoffs and Super Bowl XVII. Other injuries plagued him during the first part of the 1983 season, but Monk came back to help the Skins win the eastern divisional title. In the playoff game against the Rams, Monk caught two touchdown passes for 40 and 21 yards as the Skins triumphed, 51–7.

After Monk's record-setting season of 1984, Joe Gibbs said, "I don't think you can ask a football player to do more. He played every down and caught nearly every pass thrown to him, from training camp on." The totals were surely impressive—106 receptions for 1,372 yards and seven touchdowns. He was a unanimous All-Pro and was voted by his coaches and teammates as the Redskins' Most Valuable Player. Later, the unassuming Monk said of his grand performance, "Last year I did catch more passes . . . and there were a few reasons. The receptions came partly because Charlie Brown [the Redskins' other starting wide receiver] was injured, and partly because when I was open, the ball was coming my way. Lots of times you get open, but the quarterback has already thrown the ball to someone else, or is getting sacked, or just doesn't see you. This past year the ball was always there."

By the end of the 1989 season, Art Monk had caught 662 passes surpassing Charley Taylor's record of 649 career receptions. He had gained 9,165 yards, again topping the mark set by Charley Taylor who had earned 9,140 in his 13-year Redskins career. Art Monk's most prodigious single game came in December 1985 at RFK Stadium against the Cincinnati Bengals, when he caught 13 passes, a club record he now shares with Kelvin Bryant, and gained 230 yards, the third most in club annals.

Gary Clark

A featherweight in terms of pro football's weights and measures, Gary Clark in 1985 was a mere 5'9" and 173 pounds. A refugee from the USFL, he had been overlooked in the one NFL draft for which he had been eligible. But he was signed by Washington as a free agent that year, mostly on the recommendation of Larry Csonka, former Miami Dolphin fullback and general manager of the Jacksonville Bulls in the USFL, who had had to release Clark because both the franchise and the league were in the process of going bankrupt. Csonka told Coach Joe Gibbs he thought the elusive, if miniature, Clark might be the perfect complement to Art Monk in the Redskins receiving corps.

"Quick-footed and filled with an unpredictable array of moves" was one description offered early that first year in a Redskins press release, while a Washington newspaper suggested South American soccer might be a better field for a person of his physical endowments.

Clark, however, did not take long to prove that professional football, in the United States, was indeed the perfect milieu for him. After breaking into the starting lineup in the fifth game of the regular season, he set about illustrating in dramatic fashion that Larry Csonka had indeed had an eye for talent.

Clark, once he got the chance, turned in three 100-yard-plus games that rookie season, including an effort against the New York Giants that netted him 11 receptions and 193 yards. When the regular season came to a close, Clark had pulled in 72 passes, the fifth most in the NFC and the fourth highest in Redskins history. He gained 926 yards for Washington on those

Gary Clark (Washington Redskins)

147

A diving Gary Clark clutches the football with his little fingers; amazingly he hung on to it. This catch was one of the 340 pass receptions he has made for the Redskins since joining the team in 1985. (Washington Redskins)

receptions and led the team with five touchdowns.

In 1986, Clark hop-skipped, sidestepped, and leaped to the top of the Washington pass-receiving ledger. Two games in particular tell the crux of the story. Against the New York Giants, he shook off all defenders to snatch 11 passes for 241 yards, the latter setting a new club record (Art Monk had gained 230 yards against the Bengals the year before). Wounded and sidelined the following week, he came back from the bench in overtime to make a game-winning touchdown catch against the Vikings.

When the season was over, Clark led the Redskins in receptions with 74, fifth best in the NFC, and yardage gained (1,265), second in the conference and fourth best in Redskins history.

By the start of the 1987 season, Gary Clark had so established himself that former Oakland Raiders coach and television commentator John Madden said, "If I was starting a team and had to pick one wide receiver, I'd pick Gary Clark. . . . He really impresses me. He seems to be one of those guys who keeps his motor running the whole time. Nobody thinks of him when they think of the best receivers, but he's always there to make a play when you need it. He's the guy who keeps the first downs coming, then he'll lull you to sleep and slip behind you for a deep one. He just knows how to play the game."

He lived up to the accolade that year, ending up with a team-high 56 receptions for 1,066 yards and seven touchdowns. In the NFC championship game of 1987, Clark caught the game-winning touchdown toss from Doug Williams, and grabbed three for 55 yards and a touchdown in the Skins' victory in Super Bowl XXII.

By the end of the 1989 season, Gary Clark was well established in the Washington record books for receiving. In five years with the Skins he has caught 340 passes for 5,378 yards and 35 touchdowns.

10

The 1960s

A week before the 1960s were to officially begin, the Redskins' front office announced a positive step. After Congress had approved a bill to construct a new stadium to be called D.C. Stadium, the Redskins signed a 30-year lease to play there. It would be ready for the 1961 season.

The fans, however, would hardly be ready for the '61 season, coming off a decade-opening year that was the worst ever in Washington Redskins history.

Another new league also appeared in 1960, the American Football League, destined to take up the competitive cudgels for top-flight players who disappeared when the AAFC folded a decade earlier. There was no AFL franchise slotted for Washington to vie for football fans' attention, but there were new teams staking territory in New York, Boston, Buffalo, Dallas, Hous-

ton, Denver, Los Angeles, and Oakland, and the salary wars were about to begin in earnest.

There was also a new team in the NFL that year, the Dallas Cowboys, who would provide the only glimmer of light in what otherwise stands out as the bleakest of years for the Redskins. Dallas was the only team that Washington was able to defeat in 1960, and that was hardly an exceptional feat in light of the fact that the newborn Cowboys lost 11 games and tied one that year.

The Redskins wallowed in the cellar of their conference with a season's record of 1–9–2. Head coach Mike Nixon exited and Bill McPeak, his assistant, was sentenced to succeed him.

The brand-new D.C. Stadium was ready in 1961. Unfortunately, the Redskins were not. After losing their first two games on the

The Redskins new home in 1961, then the 55,004-seat D.C. Stadium which evolved into the 55,750-seat RFK Stadium. (Washington Redskins)

road, to the 49ers and Eagles, they debuted on their new home field and promptly blew a 21-point lead and lost to the Giants, 24–21.

Leading McPeak's pallid offense was rookie quarterback Norm Snead, from Wake Forest. If the offense was pale, however, the defense was deathly ashen. Going into the last game of the 1961 season, the Redskins were 0–12–1. They had given up a total of 362 points, an average of 29 per game, and had scored a mere 140. They managed to avoid a shutout year by defeat-

ing the Cowboys in the last game of the season, 34–24, a game in which Dickie James set a club record by scoring four touchdowns.

A cellar-dweller for the second consecutive year, Washington had so far in the 1960s won two games, lost 21, and tied three. As it turned out, those two forgettable years are the only two in Redskins history in which the team failed to win more than one game.

Despite the awful year of '61, Snead

Center Len Hauss, who played his college ball at Georgia, was a ninth-round draft choice of Washington in 1964. He won the starting position in his rookie season and gave it up only when he retired after the 1977 season. In his 14-year career with the Redskins he played in 196 consecutive games, the most in club history. As one of the finest offensive linemen ever to wear a Redskin uniform, he earned a trip to the Pro Bowl six times. (HOF/NFL Photos)

showed a lot of promise, connecting on 172 of 375 passes for 2,337 yards, the best passing statistics turned in since Sammy Baugh was tossing the ball for the Redskins in the late 1940s.

Surprisingly, in view of Marshall's low threshold of patience with coaches who turned in losing seasons, Bill McPeak was on the sideline for the start of the 1962 season. And on the field for the first time in Redskins history, wearing the familiar burgundy and gold of Washington, were black players.

There had been pressure from the U.S. Department of Interior regarding the Redskins' exclusion of black ballplayers—all other NFL teams had been integrated during the 1950s—and there were strong hints that the government might evict the team from D.C. Stadium because of discrimination. It was also obvious that the all-white Redskins were a certified disaster on the field. Marshall could not have failed to notice the extraordinary talents of many blacks on teams his Redskins faced during the 1950s and early '60s, players such as Marion Motley, Bill Willis, Len Ford, and Jim Brown of Cleveland; Joe Perry of the 49ers; Dan Towler and Tank Younger of the Rams; Ollie Matson and Dick "Night Train" Lane of the Chicago Cardinals; Rosey Brown,

third quarter: Washington 48, New York 28.

And on it went. In the final period, Rickie Harris took a Giants punt at his own 48-yard line, zigzagged his way to the sideline, and ran it in for another Washington touchdown. New York, now its own worst enemy, came back and threw a pass into the hands of Washington's Brig Owens, who raced 60 yards for his second touchdown of the day, and the score was 62–28, Redskins.

The Giants, out of the game at this point but not giving up, came back with two touchdowns. Then Dick Shiner, replacing Sonny Jurgensen at quarterback for Washington, hit Bobby Mitchell for a 45-yard touchdown.

As the game moved inexorably toward its end, with Washington leading 69–41, the Redskins got the ball and moved it again into New York territory. Then, with seven seconds remaining, they called for a time-out. Graham, perhaps remembering Sam Huff's halftime plea, motioned Char-lie Gogolak onto the field. The little soccer-style kicker trotted out and kicked a 29-yard field goal to end the scoring for the day.

With the final score of 72–41, two NFL records were set that afternoon. The 72 points scored by the Redskins was the most ever in a regular-season game, breaking the mark set by the Los Angeles Rams in 1950 when they tallied 70 in defeating the Baltimore Colts. And the 113 total points scored easily outstripped the record of 98, set when the Chicago Cardinals beat the Giants 63–35 in 1948.

The 72 points remains by far the most ever scored by a Washington Redskins team (the 59 scored against the Boston Yanks is the closest to it).

After the game, when reporters asked Otto Graham the inevitable question as to why he had added a last mortification in the waning seconds of the game, he shrugged and with a straight face said, "Gogolak needed the practice."

SCORING

	1st Qtr	2nd Qtr	3rd Qtr	4th Qtr	Final Score
Giants	0	14	14	13	41
Redskins	13	21	14	24	72

There was little question now that the Redskins indeed had a formidable passing attack. Their kicking game had picked up considerably with the drafting of the Skins' first soccer-style kicker, Charlie Gogolak, the year before. He set two team records in 1966 by kicking 22 field goals (the previous record of 17 was set by Sam Baker in 1956) and 39 extra points, bettering the mark of 35 kicked by Jim Martin in 1964. Still, there was the ineffectual running game and the porous defense to counterbalance things.

In spite of their extraordinary aerial attack, the Redskins were not able to win more than five of their 14 games in 1967, and their record of 5–6–3 left them ahead of only the first-year Saints in the NFL Capitol Division.

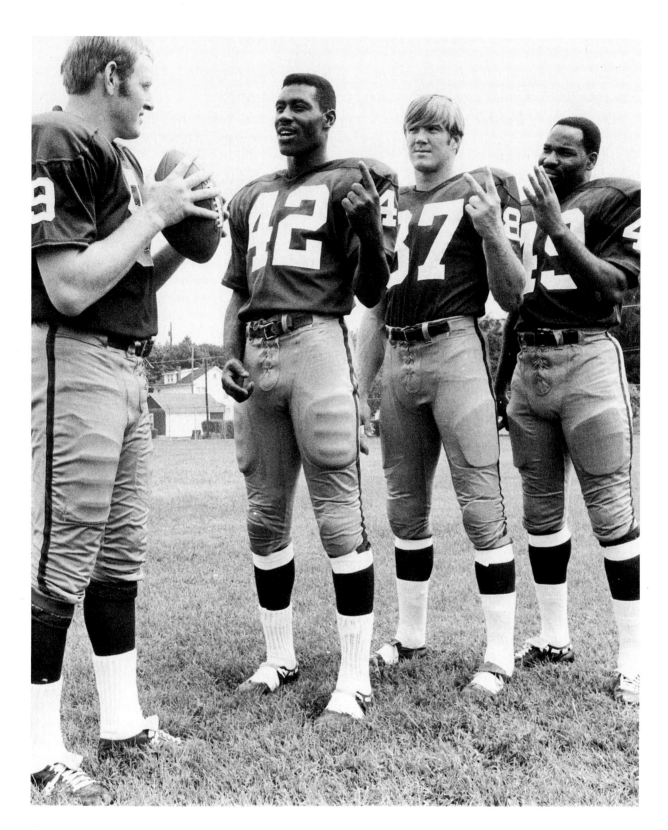

The year of the pass in Washington, 1967. Sonny Jurgensen, along with his receivers, set two NFL records when he completed 288 passes for 3,747 yards and a club mark of 31 touchdowns. His receivers, indicating their rank in the NFC in '67 were No. 1 Charley Taylor, 70 for 990 yards; No. 2 Jerry Smith, 67 for 849 yards; and No. 4 Bobby Mitchell, 60 for 866 yards. (Washington Redskins)

Sonny Jurgensen on the sideline. He entertained Washington football fans on and off the field for 11 years, 1964–74. (Washington Redskins)

It was surely not the fault of Sonny Jurgensen, who turned in a record-setting year. The "rotund rifle," as one scribe referred to him, set NFL records by completing 288 passes (in 508 attempts) for 3,747 yards and established a club record of 31 touchdown passes.

Jurgensen's three favorite receivers remained Charley Taylor (70 catches, the league high, for 990 yards), Jerry Smith (67 receptions for 849 yards), and Bobby Mitchell (60 snares for 866 yards).

In 1968, middle linebacker Sam Huff retired and All-Pro safety Paul Krause was traded to the Vikings for linebacker Marlin McKeever. Washington acquired Heisman Trophy-winning quarterback Gary Beban, who had shone at UCLA, but, as it would turn out, could not maintain that luminescence as a pro.

Jurgensen was plagued with rib injuries for much of the season, and the running game was practically nonexistent. The result was a disappointing 5–9–0 season.

It was time for a change, decreed Edward Bennett Williams, and it was one that reverberated through the nation's capital. It was not the departure of Otto Graham, which had in fact been expected. It was the hiring, as head coach and general manager, of the legendary Vince Lombardi, who had engineered the Green Bay Packers' turnaround from a disaster of the 1950s to the dynasty of the 1960s.

Fans referred to it as the "coming of St. Vince" and looked forward to a plethora of miracles.

But with the arrival of Lombardi, there was also the departure of George Preston Marshall. The Big Chief, after a long illness, died in August 1969.

The first miracle Lombardi pulled off was the drafting and development of running back Larry Brown from Kansas State. Brown would add life to a running attack that had lain stagnant for more than a decade.

Next, he took an uninspired, undisciplined group of players, integrated them with some new blood, and turned the entire mixture into a well-trained, motivated football team.

After 24 years of lackluster football, a savior was expected in 1969. (Washington Redskins)

The result was a heightened level of excitement and a renewed anticipation of winning among Redskins fandom, feelings that had rarely been there during the previous 20 years.

The Redskins got off on the proverbial proper foot in '69 by defeating the New Orleans Saints. But by the time they made their debut that year at D.C. Stadium, they were 1–1–1. It did not deter a sellout crowd from watching Lombardi's Skins devour the St. Louis Cardinals, 33–17, and make believers of fans and skeptics alike.

The team was truly the most exciting in many years and the fans were more exuberant than they had been in an age. It lasted through the entire season, and when it was over a grinning, gap-toothed Vince Lombardi celebrated a 7–5–2 record and a second-place finish in the Capitol Division.

Lombardi had successfully developed a balanced offensive attack and had inspired a defense to be intimidating, although it was clearly not as strong as he would have liked. At season's end, Lombardi vowed it would be better in 1970. No one doubted their sainted leader.

Jurgensen had been allowed to do what

160

Vince Lombardi, the legendary coach of the Green Bay Packers dynasty of the 1960s, took on the challenge of the Redskins in 1969, and made it clear from the outset who was in charge. In his first and only year in Washington, Lombardi gave Redskins fans their first winning season since 1955, a 7–5–2 record and a second place finish in their division. (Washington Redskins)

Fullback Charley Harraway "takes the fall" for a touchdown in a 1970 game against the St. Louis Cardinals. Blocking for him here is halfback Dave Kopay (40) and on the ground beneath Harraway is tackle Jim Snowden. (Washington Redskins)

he did best and had ended up the league's top passer in 1969, completing 274 passes for 3,102 yards and 22 touchdowns. Charley Taylor caught the second-most passes in the NFL that year, 71 for 883 yards. Rookie Larry Brown rushed for 888 yards and Charlie Harraway ran for 428. All told, six Redskins went to the Pro Bowl, the most in some time: Sonny Jurgensen, Larry Brown, Jerry Smith, Chris Hanburger, Pat Fischer, and Len Hauss.

The emphasis on defense for 1970 was apparent in the draft, when Lombardi took defensive end Bill Brundidge of Colorado as his first pick, followed by defensive tackle Manny Sistrunk from Arkansas A&M.

Just when everything seemed to be going right for the Redskins, tragedy struck. The seemingly immortal Vince Lombardi proved only too mortal when he was struck down by cancer. He would not be with the team for training camp, he explained, and the head-coaching duties would be handled by his chief assistant, Bill Austin. Two weeks before the 1970 regular season, Vince Lombardi died and a football nation mourned the passing of one of the game's greatest coaches and most inspiring figures.

Austin, who had been second in command to Lombardi for many years at Green Bay, had a difficult job trying to carry on in the wake of Lombardi. After they lost the first two games of the 1970 regular season and then five in a row later in the year, it appeared that the Skins had reverted to their pre-Lombardi doldrums. Their record of 6–8–0 left them in fourth place in the NFC East, clearly outclassed by the Cowboys, Giants, and Cardinals.

The one bright note of the year was the rushing of Larry Brown, who became the first Redskin runner to breach the 1,000-yard mark. Brown led the NFL with 1,125 yards, an average carry of 4.7 yards.

The clouds that had shrouded Griffith Stadium and D.C. Stadium since 1946, however, were about to be swept away. The first blast of wind would come with the hiring of volatile and victory-oriented George Allen as head coach, and the second on the wings of his unorthodox philosophy:

"The Future Is Now."

QUOTE TO REMEMBER

John Wilbur, an offensive lineman for the Cowboys (1966–69) and the Redskins (1971–73), was quoted in *Sports Illustrated* regarding the Washington–Dallas rivalry.

"It got to you. I mean he [George Allen] never referred to the Dallas Cowboys without calling them the goddamn Dallas Cowboys. I can't think of them as anything else now. My nine-year-old son, Nathan, even calls them that."

THE RIVALRY

There has never been any mutual affection found between the Washington Redskins and the Dallas Cowboys, neither among the teams, coaches, and the front offices nor among the fans. When the two teams go at each other, as they do twice each year, it summons memories of the old Redskins–Giants fueds and the Redskins–Bears postseason hostilities of the 1930s and '40s. Those rivalries seem tame, however, compared to the Redskins–Cowboys battles, which make one think of a cobra and a mongoose, or a pair of pit bulls in a ring. Columnist Art Buchwald summed it up succinctly: "It boils down to one thing: Hate. Hate for reasons that nobody understands."

How it all began or why the fire has stayed fueled for so long is anybody's guess. Certainly it reached epic proportions in the 1970s, when George Allen and Tom Landry and others at Cowboys headquarters hissed at each other with specially nurtured venom in the press and before the television media.

Landry and especially his boss in Dallas, Tex Schramm, fueled the conflagration when they suggested Allen approached football as if he were stocking a nursing home, and implied that Allen and his new colleagues in Washington were a bit behind the times.

Allen responded. As Mark Nelson and Miller Bonner explained in their book *The*

Cowboy quarterback Craig Morton (14) is in the grasp in a 1967 game at the Cotton Bowl in Dallas. Doing the grasping is Washington defensive end Ron Snidow (78), while Bill Briggs (86) struggles to get in on the act. Washington defeated the Cowboys 27–20. (Washington Redskins)

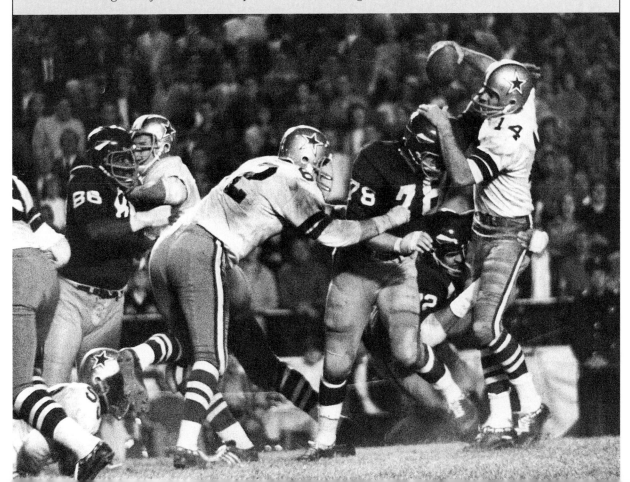

The Cowboys were always envious of the Redskins uniforms, witness Dallas's Jethro Pugh trying to steal Billy Kilmer's jersey. (Washington Redskins)

Semi-Official Dallas Cowboys Haters' Handbook (Macmillan, 1984), "Allen turned hating the Dallas Cowboys into a religious experience. He made it personal. The Cowboys, with their computerized organization, didn't know how to react. They accused him of spying, lying, and cheating. Allen's Redskins beat Dallas the first time they played and they whipped the Cowboys on six other occasions, including the 26–3 humiliation of the Cowboys in the 1972 NFC championship. To add insult to injury, Allen compiled a personal list of pro football's 25 Greatest Games and listed six games involving Dallas among his greatest. Naturally all six were Dallas losses."

It would not be unsafe to say that the rivalry began the very first year the Cowboys joined the NFL. That was 1960, and they lost every game they played except one, which they tied. The Redskins met them only once that year and soundly thrashed them, 26–14. But what burned Dallas the most was that it was the Skins' only victory that year, giving them a better record at 1–9–2 than Dallas's 0–11–1.

Since then there have been a series of highlights in the rivalry, which has grown into an arch-rivalry. Here are some of them—from a Redskin fan's point of view, or course.

Highlights:

1961 The Redskins do not win a game until the last of the season, when they drub the Cowboys, 34–24, to give Washington a record of 1–12–1 (the tie was also with Dallas, 28–28).

1971 After six straight losses to Dallas, George Allen turns the tide and defeats the Cowboys, 20–16, in his first encounter with the infernal enemy.

1972 The Redskins destroy the Cowboys in the NFC championship game, 26–3.

1973 On Monday night football, before a national television audience, safety Ken Houston makes a spectacular tackle at the one-yard line to prevent Walt Garrison from scoring a touchdown and the Skins win, 14–7.

1975 Washington defensive tackle Diron Talbert calls Roger Staubach a "fag" and becomes the only player in NFL history to cause the Dallas quarterback to cuss on the football field.

1975 In their first overtime game, the Redskins prevail, 30–24.

1978 Again on Monday night, the Skins scalp the Cowboys before the nation's football fans, this time 9–5, which sounds more like a baseball score.

1979 The Redskins clobber the Cowboys, 37–20, and incur their unyielding wrath when with 14 seconds left and the score 34–20 they kick a field goal.

1982 The Redskins dispatch the Cowboys in the NFC title game, 31–17, and go on to Super Bowl XVII.

1984 Washington defeats Dallas twice in the regular season for the first time since they began playing each other in 1960, by scores of 34–14 and 30–28.

1986 The Redskins annihilate the Cowboys, 41–14, their biggest margin of victory ever in the rivalry.

1987 For the second time, the Skins beat the Cowboys twice in the regular season, 13–7 and 24–20.

Behind some picturesque blocking, Larry Brown (43) sets out to rack up a little yardage for the Redskins in a 1970 game against the Cowboys. Blocking for him are guard Paul Laaveg (73) and tackle Jim Snowden (74). (Washington Redskins)

11

The Great Defenders

One of the game's greatest advocates of defensive football, George Allen, once said —maybe pontificated—"Great defenses stop great offenses, and win football games." It is a maxim subscribed to by many successful pro football coaches, and its veracity has been corroborated over the years by the list of NFL championship teams who have unmistakably been anchored by fearsome defenses: the Chicago Bears of the 1930s and early '40s, the New York Giants of the 1950s, the Packers of the '60s, the Steelers of the '70s, Tom Landry's flex-defense Cowboys, Minnesota's Purple People Eaters, and every title-bearer of the '80s.

In the good years, the Redskins have fielded exceptional defensive teams with a memorable assortment of All-Pros, from Turk Edwards, who was there in Boston on the very first opening day, to Dexter Man-ley, who continues to set sack records in the late 1980s.

In the early days of the franchise, defensive players were never designated as such because they also played offense—the legendary 60-minute men. Sammy Baugh was not merely a great tailback and quarterback, he was also an outstanding defensive back. Wayne Millner could not only catch passes, he also lined up at defensive end and was known to be a devastating tackler.

Turk Edwards was the first acknowledged great defender to wear the Redskins' burgundy and gold, toiling in the trenches of both Boston and Washington. He was followed by Wee Willie Wilkin, who played into the 1940s. Then there was Al DeMao and Gene Brito. They were all two-way players, battling from both sides of the line of scrimmage each Sunday.

With the age of defensive specialists came such luminaries as Chris Hanburger, Ken Houston, Dave Butz, and Dexter Manley—all accurately defined as great.

There were many others, too, who should not be overlooked, their contributions well grounded in Washington football lore. In the earlier days, there were, of course, Baugh and Millner, but also others such as interior linemen Jim Barber, Dick Farman, and Fred Davis, ends Bob Masterson and Joe Aguirre, linebacker Ki Aldrich, and defensive backs Wilbur Moore, Dick Todd, Dan Sandifer, Dick James, and Jim Steffen.

After 1950, there were linebackers the likes of Chuck Drazenovich, LaVern Torgeson, and Sam Huff; linemen with the caliber of Paul Lipscomb, Bob Toneff, Joe Rutgens, and Karl Kammerer, and such defensive backs as Don Doll and Dick Alban.

More recently there have been the leaders of the Over-the-Hill Gang: Jack Pardee, Myron Pottios, Verlon Biggs, Diron Talbert, Coy Bacon, Deacon Jones, Rich Petitbon, Ron McDole, and Dave Robinson. Other memorable defenders include Paul Krause, Harold McLinton, Pat Fischer, Bill Brundige, Mike Bass, Brig Owens, Eddie Brown, and Lemar Parrish.

The 1980s featured such standouts as Mark Murphy, Vernon Dean, Barry Wilburn, Charles Mann, Rich Milot, Neal Olkewicz, Darryl Grant, Monte Coleman, Wilber Marshall, and Alvin Walton.

Defensive statistics were never kept in the early years of pro football. Sacks and interceptions, though, would have been relatively inconsequential because of the dearth of passes thrown by tailbacks or quarterbacks in those days.

Since such stats have been collected, Dexter Manley has ravaged the most quarterbacks, collecting 97⅓ sacks. Brig Owens holds the record for the most career interceptions, 36. The most sacks in a season belongs to Manley, who downed quarterbacks 18 times in 1986, and the most picked-off passes in one year were snatched by Dan Sandifer, 13 in 1948. Sammy Baugh still holds the record for the most interceptions in a game, four in a 1943 contest with the Lions, which Sandifer tied in 1948 against the Boston Yanks. And Diron Talbert can claim most sacks in one contest, when he scored five against the Giants in 1975.

Glen "Turk" Edwards

In an age when behemoths were the exception rather than the rule in pro football, tackle Turk Edwards was known as a monstrosity to all who tried to block him. At 6'2" and 260 pounds in the late 1930s, he was truly the immovable object, and when he chose to move he was indeed an irresistible force.

Edwards, who was an All-America lineman for the University of Washington, re-

Turk Edwards played for the Redskins when they began as the Braves in Boston and stayed through the 1940 season in Washington. A four time All-Pro tackler, Edwards was enshrined in the Pro Football Hall of Fame in 1969. (HOF/NFL Photos)

ceived offers from the New York Giants, the Portsmouth Spartans, and that newcomer to the league in 1932, the Boston Braves. He chose the latter. "They offered me the most money, $150 a game for 10 games," Edwards explained. "That was a lot of money for a young man in those days."

Turk then began a career that started in Boston and ended in Washington, and one that was illustrious, to say the least. He was named All-Pro four times, in 1932, 1933, 1936, and 1937. As Don Smith wrote for the Pro Football Hall of Fame, "Edwards typified overwhelming strength and power, rather than speed. Yet he was agile enough to get the job done as well or better than all but a mere handful who have played the tackle position in pro football."

Edwards was the typical iron man of the day—in one 15-game season in Boston he was on the field all but 10 minutes of play during the entire year.

In 1940, after the ceremonial coin toss before a game with the New York Giants, he pivoted to trot off the field and his knee went out on him. It ended Turk's playing career, but he remained with the Skins as an assistant coach and took on the head-coaching duties from 1946 through 1948. Turk Edwards was inducted into the Pro Football Hall of Fame in 1969.

Wee Willie Wilkin

His name was Wilbur Byrne Wilkin, but he was known as "Wee Willie," as inappropriate a nickname as could be levied, because he was 6'6" and weighed as much as 280 pounds at the girth of his career.

Wilkin had played college ball at St. Mary's in California and was signed by the Redskins in 1938. From the very beginning he was as awesome on the field as he was uncontained off it. In the *Washington Star-*

Wee Willie Wilkin (6'6", 265 pounds) snares Chicago Bears fullback Bill Osmanski in the 1940 NFL title game. It was one of the few times Washington stopped the Bears in that 73–0 debacle. (HOF/NFL Photos)

Center/linebacker Al DeMao (53) appears to be intercepting a pass from Johnny Lujack of the Bears in a 1949 game at Griffith Stadium. DeMao was an integral part of the Redskins defense and offense from 1945 through 1953. (HOF/NFL Photos)

News it was reported that in "Wilkin's rookie pro year he was fined $25 nine times for training infractions during the 11-week season, and there was no assurance that he was on his good behavior those other two weeks."

In battle, he was equally unrestrained. Harry Sheer, writing for The Associated Press, noted, "His first mark of distinction came early, in his second pro game. It was against the Detroit Lions in 1938 and the Redskins were trailing 3–0. The Lions, however, were deep in their own territory and a punt was called. Willie plowed through, picked up the blocker, Ace Gutowsky, and threw him head-on into the kicker. The punt was blocked, a Redskin fell on it for a touchdown, and the Washingtons had won."

Wilkin was named All-Pro in both 1940 and 1941. Coach Ray Flaherty said that having him on the line in a football game was like having a tank in combat. His ulti-

mate boss, George Preston Marshall, complained that he spent more time bailing Wee Willie out of trouble off the field than he did enjoying his play on the field. Wilkin's NFL career came to an end in Washington after the 1943 season, although he came back and played one last year for the Chicago Rockets in the AAFC in 1946.

Al DeMao

Al DeMao has the distinction of being the first Redskin lineman ever to have a "Day" held in his honor. It was November 2, 1952, and before that day only two Washington ballplayers had ever been so honored, Sammy Baugh and Bullet Bill Dudley.

By 1952, DeMao had centered both the offensive and defensive lines for the Redskins for eight years. He had come to the Redskins in 1945 directly from the U.S. Navy, which he had entered after playing a little college ball at Duquesne University. On his "Day," he was described this way: "On offense, he is a cunning, bruising blocker; on defense, he has been a shrewd, deadly tackler. And at all times, he has been a true team player."

DeMao, at 6'2" and 215 pounds, was the perfect example of the all-around lineman who lived in relative obscurity for most of his career. It was not until the proverbial twilight of his career that he began to receive the recognition he so richly deserved as a splendid contributor to the Washington Redskins. "Al is fast, strong, and has an absolutely perfect instinct for the game" is the way Curly Lambeau, one of DeMao's six head coaches with the Redskins, put it.

The team and fans honored him that day in 1952. After the following season, Al De-Mao retired, leaving behind an honored career on both sides of the Redskins line.

Gene Brito

When Gene Brito joined the Redskins in 1952, there were 12 ends in camp seeking a job. At the start, Brito, who came out of Loyola of Los Angeles and was drafted in the 18th round, ranked 12th. After the cuts were made, however, the 6'1", 215-pound Brito was still there.

For the first two years in Washington, Brito was used mostly on offense, but in 1953 coach Curly Lambeau decided to play him mostly as a defensive end. The switch worked so well that Brito earned his first of five invitations to the Pro Bowl. In 1954, along with Redskins quarterback Eddie Le-Baron, Brito defected to the Canadian Football League and played for Calgary.

The following year, 1955, they were both back in Washington, and Brito, earning All-Pro honors, fully established himself as one of the premier defensive ends in pro

Defensive end Gene Brito is feted with a day in his honor at Griffith Stadium in 1958. Handing him the keys to a new car is Vice President Richard M. Nixon. Brito had two stints with the Skins, 1952–53 and 1955–58. (HOF/NFL Photos)

Linebacker Chris Hanburger (55) neckties Cleveland Brown quarterback Frank Ryan in a 1967 game at Municipal Stadium in Cleveland. A nine-time Pro Bowler, Hanburger played 14 years with the Redskins, 1965–78. (Washington Redskins)

football. An opposing player once described him this way: "You're wasting your time with a delaying block. He's got so many moves he'll leave you flat on your back. The only way to contain him is to go after Gene aggressively—and hope you've got the strength to keep from landing flat on your rear anyhow."

The story has also been told that Ted Marchibroda, when he was quarterbacking for the Pittsburgh Steelers in the mid-1950s, once pulled his tackle from the huddle and said, "I can't take much more of that Brito. I don't care if the ref is looking—if you can't keep him out, hold him."

"You kidding?" the tackle shrugged in reply. "I've *been* holding him."

Gene Brito brightened the Redskins defense through the 1958 season. Besides 1955, he also earned All-Pro recognition in 1956, 1957, and 1958.

Chris Hanburger

The defense-minded George Allen, Chris Hanburger's coach at Washington from 1971 through 1977, ranked him among the top 13 linebackers ever to have played in the NFL, comparing him to the likes of Chuck Bednarik, Dick Butkus, Sam Huff, Ray Nietschke, and Jack Lambert. "He played the right side as skillfully as almost anyone I ever saw," Allen said of Hanburger. "Chris was a little light for a linebacker (6'2", 218 pounds). But he was seldom knocked off his feet. He had real good balance and excellent agility. But quickness was his biggest asset. He could really push the passer and he covered a lot of ground on pass defense."

Hanburger, like All-Pro Gene Brito before him, was almost overlooked by the Redskins, and was not drafted until the 18th round in 1965. He broke into the starting

Known for his bone-jarring tackles, strong safety Ken Houston shadows Dallas's Drew Pearson. A perennial Pro Bowler, 12 times in all, Houston was elected to the Pro Football Hall of Fame in 1986. (HOF/NFL Photos)

lineup at right linebacker in the 10th game that rookie year and remained there through 13 more seasons. The following year he earned a trip to the Pro Bowl, the first of nine such junkets he would make during his late career with the Redskins.

Hanburger was responsible for changing the outcomes of many games for Washington. A player profile from a *GameDay* program in 1973 described him this way: "Starting from his post as a right linebacker . . . he is liable to turn up anywhere on the field, usually hitting harder than anybody in the near vicinity. Unlike the normal run of linebackers, Hanburger has a gift for the spectacular play. He stole the ball out of Ron

Johnson's arms, for instance, to set up a Washington win over New York. And in the playoffs (1972), he blitzed the Dallas Cowboys, leaped completely over a blocker, and landed on Roger Staubach, for a crucial sack."

Hanburger himself shrugged off the assessment. "I don't think of myself as a big-play type. To me every play is important. . . . I just try to keep involved, to be in the middle of the action every time."

And that he was. For 14 years, Hanburger was stopping running backs, sacking quarterbacks, and breaking up pass plays for the Redskins. Only Sammy Baugh and Dave Butz played more seasons in Washington

(16 and 15, respectively), and only Butz and Len Hauss played in more games than Hanburger's 187. No Redskin, however, has gone to as many Pro Bowls as the nine attended by Hanburger. He intercepted 19 passes, recovered 12 fumbles, and scored five touchdowns. Three of those five touchdowns were on fumble recoveries, which ranks him second on the all-time NFL list in that category.

Ken Houston

The Redskins wanted safety Ken Houston so badly they traded five players to the Houston Oilers for him in 1973. Already an established All-Pro defensive back who shared the NFL record for interceptions returned for touchdowns in a season (four in 1971) and in a game (two against the San Diego Chargers in '71), Houston had six pro football seasons behind him when he came to Washington. George Allen, who acquired him, said, "Everyone said I had given too much to get him. Well, he gave me five years the others wouldn't have given me combined." And he gave the Redskins three more than he gave Allen.

At 6'3" and 198 pounds, with speed, strength, and a natural propensity for punishing tackles, Houston had all the natural endowments to become a superb strong safety—which, of course, he did. From Prairie View A. & M. in Texas, Ken was a late-round draft choice by the Oilers in 1967, but it took him only three games to secure a starting role in their secondary.

Houston had eight super seasons with the Redskins. His value to the team was evinced in many ways, but perhaps one play dramatizes it better than any other. It was October 8, 1973, and the Redskins were locked in a bitter struggle with the arch-rival Dallas Cowboys at RFK Stadium. Washington led 14–7 with 16 seconds left to play, but the Cowboys had the ball on fourth and goal to go. Craig Morton tossed a short pass to powerful Walt Garrison just outside the goal line. Garrison whirled toward the end zone, but Houston hit him high and wrestled him to the ground less than a yard from a touchdown. "It was the most important tackle I ever made," Ken said after the game. I knew I had to get him down or it was the ballgame." It was *so important* it won a special place in *The Semi-Official Dallas Cowboys Haters' Handbook*. To the delight of Redskins fans everywhere, Houston consistently came up with big plays against the Cowboys—returning a punt 58 yards for a touchdown to insure a 28–21 win in 1974, intercepting a Roger Staubach pass in overtime to set up a 30–24 win in 1975, making several key defensive plays to save a 9–5 victory in 1978, among many others that have tormented Dallas fans during Houston's tenure in Washington.

With Washington, Houston was either All-Pro or All-NFC every year he played. He was invited to eight consecutive Pro Bowls while a Redskin and 12 straight counting the years with the Oilers (only Merlin Olsen has been to more).

Houston retired after the 1978 season and still holds the NFL record for the most career touchdowns on interception returns—all nine of them, surprisingly, coming in his six years with the Oilers. During his 12-year NFL career, he intercepted 49 passes, returning them for a net of 898 yards. But in Washington he will probably be best remembered for his bone-jarring tackles and all those things he did to the Cowboys. Kenny Houston was elected to the Pro Football Hall of Fame in 1986.

Dave Butz

Over on Pennsylvania Avenue, Gerald Ford was in the White House when Dave Butz came to Washington in 1975. When the

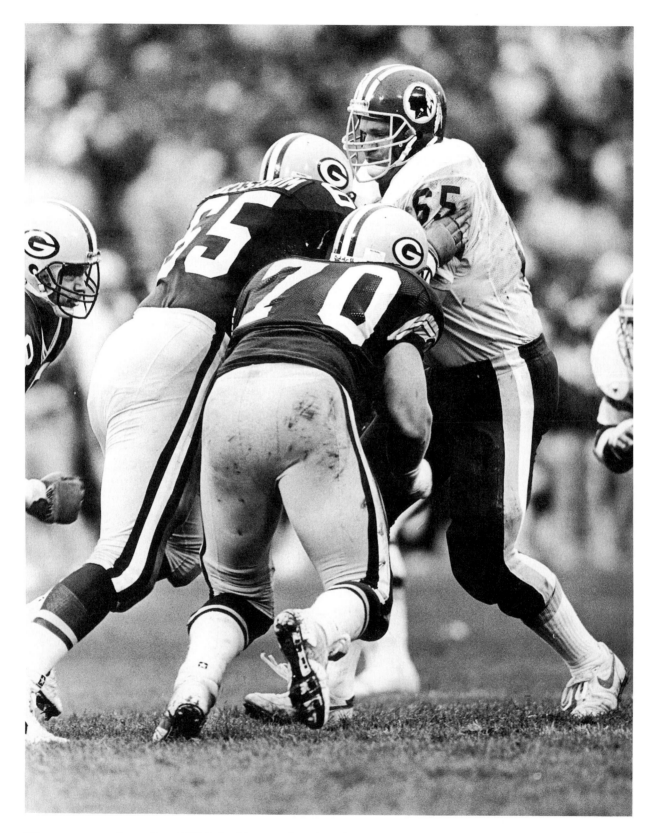

The gargantuan Dave Butz (65) is double-teamed against the Green Bay Packers. As durable as he was powerful, Butz played in more games for Washington than any other Redskin in history, 216 between 1975 and 1988. (Washington Redskins)

enormous tackle announced his retirement, George Bush was living there.

At 6'7" and 295 pounds, with a 19½" neck, Butz has always captured attention wherever he went. An All-America defensive tackle from Purdue, he caught the eye of the St. Louis Cardinals, who drafted him in 1973, and he made himself visible enough to NFL official observers to land on that year's NFL All-Rookie team.

After a year on injured reserve in 1974 and an ensuing contract dispute, with his option played out, Butz signed with the Redskins in 1975 for double the salary he had been paid in St. Louis. The league later decided that Washington had to give the Cardinals two first-round and one second-round draft choices for Butz, in what was one of the largest compensation deals in NFL history.

Fourteen years later, having watched Butz, "The Master of Intimidation," disassemble offenses, pulverize running backs, terrorize quarterbacks, and display a seemingly endless endurance in Washington's front line, most Redskins fans agree he was easily worth the compensation.

George Allen loved him for his unsparing devotion to the game of defensive football. Joe Gibbs respected him for his total concentration, dedication, and durability.

In the off-season, Butz liked to sit quietly and carve duck decoys; during the regular season . . . well, as kicker Mark Moseley tells it: "All season, Dave, Joe Theismann and I drive to the [home] games together. Dave drives, and he always likes to find some dead animal in the road to run over. It gets him psyched before the games."

In the Super Bowl season of 1982, Butz led the team with 55 tackles in the regular season and 19 in the playoffs. The following year he led the team with 11½ sacks, forced a team-leading five fumbles, and made 69 tackles. An All-Pro, he was voted Defensive

Lineman of the Year by the NFL Alumni Association.

Defensive statistics with the Redskins were not logged before 1979, but since then Butz has always been at or near the top of all categories. His best year for tackles was 1986, when he gathered 91, and his 11½ sacks of '83 was a career high.

When Dave Butz retired after the 1988 season, he had recorded (since 1979) 742 tackles and 59½ sacks, recovered seven fumbles, and forced 15½.

Dexter Manley

Since Dexter Manley staked a claim as one of the Redskins' defensive ends in 1981, he has earned two Super Bowl rings, set the all-time team standard for quarterback sacks, graduated from an alcohol-abuse program, admitted being a functional illiterate despite having spent four years on a football scholarship at Oklahoma State, and been referred to as the team's "designated talker."

"I like football, I like fun, I like talking," he said before Super Bowl XXII. His teammates understand him. Charles Mann, the Skins' other defensive end, shrugged, "Dexter's kind of flamboyant and boisterous." Offensive lineman Raleigh McKenzie mentioned, "Sometimes Dexter likes to let his man know he's there."

Manley has, of course, been there, physically and vocally. The 6'3", 257-pounder was a fifth-round draft choice in 1981 and contributed 63 tackles and six sacks his rookie year. In 1982, he was an integral part of the Super Bowl champion Redskins, especially during the NFC title game against the Cowboys. First he descended on Dallas quarterback Danny White, leaving him with a concussion. Then, in the fourth quarter, with the Skins trailing 17–14, he tipped a pass from Gary Hogeboom, White's replace-

Fearsome pass rusher Dexter Manley (72) sacked more enemy quarterbacks than any other Redskin in history. (Washington Redskins)

ment, into the hands of teammate Darryl Grant, who carried it in for the game-winning touchdown.

In 1985, Manley tied the team mark of 15 sacks in a season, set by Coy Bacon back in 1979, and the following year set a new standard with 18, which still stands today.

Along the way, he has consistently provided the press with stories and quotes. Before the 1987 playoff game with the Chicago Bears he called their coach Mike Ditka a bum, which prompted Ditka to respond, "Dexter has the IQ of a grapefruit," which prompted Dexter to respond, "Mike Ditka, with that ugly face of his, I got something for him—a case of grapefruit." Grapefruit notwithstanding, Manley and the Redskins eliminated Ditka and the Bears from the playoffs the following Sunday.

More recently, fans will remember when he told reporters during the summit meeting between President Ronald Reagan and the USSR's Mikhail Gorbachev that the Soviet leader should "get the hell out of town and stop drawing attention away from a bigger event," the upcoming Redskins–Cowboys game.

Besides his vocality, Dexter Manley has used many other talents to make himself well known around Washington. All-Pro, Pro Bowl, NFL Players Association Defensive Lineman of the Year: The honors keep coming.

By the end of the 1989 season he had accounted for 471 total tackles. Manley's 97⅓ tackles are by far the most in team history. Unfortunately for Manley, the All-Pro defensive end was banned from professional football by the NFL after testing positive for drugs a third time in 1989.

12

Allen and Super Bowl VII

After another losing season in 1970, the Redskins' chief of staff, Edward Bennett Williams, and other powers of note in the organization decided on still another coaching change. And available was just the kind of leader they wanted, a coach with a history of single-handedly turning a poor team into a consistent winner.

George Allen had that reputation; controversy, however, was also part of his portfolio. In Chicago, where he had served as defensive coordinator for the Bears under George Halas, he had been given the game ball when the team's niggardly defense had systematically thwarted the Giants' offense in the 1963 NFL title game. The Bears won it, 14–10. But he was known around town as a "Contract Breacher" because he broke his contract with Halas and the Bears in order to take the head-coaching job for the Los

Angeles Rams. Halas sued Allen and won the suit in court. Then, with his point made, he released Allen from the contract.

The Rams team Allen inherited had won only four of 14 games in 1965 and finished in the cellar of the Western Conference. He invoked his deeply rooted but unorthodox philosophy immediately: Trade for proven performers, regardless of their age. It worked. In his five years in Los Angeles, Allen won two division titles and never had a losing season. He was just the kind of reformer that Williams wanted to turn his ball club around.

Allen was hired not only as coach but as general manager as well, and he set about instituting on the East Coast the philosophy that had served him so well on the West Coast. Bringing in a lot of weathered faces who were at the peak of their earning power

Coach George Allen confers with his new starting quarterback Billy Kilmer, who took over after an injury sidelined Sonny Jurgensen in 1971. (Washington Redskins)

Redskins Park, the training facility near Dulles Airport commissioned by George Allen and still in use today. (Washington Redskins)

rather than a slew of rookies who would earn apprenticeship-level salaries, however, was costly. In addition, Allen demanded and got a commitment to build a self-contained practice facility, replete with offices, training and locker rooms, and two practice fields. It all prompted Edward Bennett Williams to remark later, "I gave George an unlimited expense account and he exceeded it in the first month with us."

But, with a new face and philosophy on the sideline and a bevy of new-but-old faces on the field of play, Washington was about to enter a new era in its NFL life.

The turnaround came swiftly. The Skins, now known as the Over-the-Hill Gang, knocked off their first five opponents in the 1971 season: the Cardinals twice, the Giants, the Oilers, and even the arch-rival Cowboys, who had gone to the Super Bowl the year

before and were destined to win it later that season. It was the first time the Redskins had won their first five regular-season games since 1940.

Sonny Jurgensen had been injured in the preseason, so the quarterbacking duties fell to 31-year-old Billy Kilmer, who Allen had acquired from the New Orleans Saints. In the sixth game of the season, Kilmer lost his favorite target when wide receiver Charley Taylor ended his season with a broken ankle. It was also the game in which the Washington win streak came to an end, at the hands of the Kansas City Chiefs, 27–20.

Injuries also hampered the running of Larry Brown and the pass catching of tight end Jerry Smith. But the defense was vastly improved, and when the season was over it ranked second in the entire NFL.

The 1971 football year did not end for

A little jocularity in the locker room among the Redskins quarterbacks of the early 1970s, Sonny Jurgensen (left) and Billy Kilmer, who has the ball and got the starting job. (Washington Redskins)

Larry Brown cuts behind the block of tight end Jerry Smith in a 1971 game against the St. Louis Cardinals. Both Brown and Smith were instrumental in getting the Redskins to their first playoff appearance in 26 years. (Washington Redskins)

Washington with the last game of the regular season, as it had each of the previous 26 years. The Redskins were playoff-bound. Their record of 9–4–1 was not good enough to capture the NFC East, which was taken by Tom Landry's Dallas Cowboys, who won 11 of their 14 games. But it qualified them for a wild-card berth and their first playoff appearance since 1945.

The nine victories that George Allen gave to Washington fans in 1971 were the most since Ray Flaherty's 1942 world champions posted a 10–1–0 record. Kilmer had quite ably filled in for Jurgensen, especially in light of injuries to key receivers, and threw 166 completions for 2,221 yards, including 13 touchdowns. Larry Brown rushed for 948 yards, somewhat short of his club record of 1,125 the year before, but still the fourth best in the NFL. Wide receiver Roy Jefferson, an Allen acquiree from the Colts, was the top receiver, with 47 catches for 701 yards. And one of the most delightful surprises of the year was place kicker Curt Knight, who had his best year since coming to Washington in 1969. Knight led the league with 29 field goals, then a club record. His 114 points scored was a team record that would stand for more than a decade. In two games that year, Knight kicked five field goals, against the Oilers (15, 36, 13, 17, and 39 yards) and a month later against the

Linebacker Chris Hanburger (55) is not about to let the elusive scrambler Fran Tarkenton get away in this game with the Giants in New York. Moving in to help are Over-the-Hill-Gang members Diron Talbert (72) and Manny Sistrunk (64). (Fred Roe)

Defensive back Richie Petitbon (16) breaks up a pass intended for Giants' wide receiver Bob Grim, and thrown by former Redskins quarterback Norm Snead. Petitbon, a charter member of the Over-the-Hill Gang played for Washington in 1971 and '72. Presently the Assistant Head Coach—Defense, Petitbon has been on the Redskins coaching staff since 1978. (Washington Redskins)

Bears (30, 12, 37, 9, and 27). No Redskin has ever kicked more in a single game, although Mark Moseley tied the mark in 1980 and Knight kicked another five in a 1973 contest.

For the playoffs, the Redskins had to travel to San Francisco to face the 49ers at Candlestick Park the day after Christmas. San Francisco, quarterbacked by John Brodie, had won the NFC West with a record of 9–5–0.

The Redskins jumped to the lead in the first quarter. After blocking a 49ers punt, Washington moved the ball to the San Francisco five-yard line; Kilmer then hit tight end Jerry Smith for a touchdown. Bruce Gossett booted a field goal to put the 49ers on the scoreboard in the second quarter, but Washington countered with one of its own, a 40-yarder from the toe of Curt Knight.

The momentum turned in the third quarter, however, when Brodie connected with All-Pro wide receiver Gene Washington for a 78-yard touchdown. In the same quarter, Brodie added another, this one a two-yarder to tight end Bob Windsor, after 49ers defensive back Roosevelt Taylor had intercepted a Kilmer pass. Knight added a 36-yard field goal, but the Redskins trailed 17–13 going into the final period.

The Redskins' tepee collapsed, however, in the fourth quarter when punter Mike Bragg could not handle a bad snap from center and the 49ers' Bob Hoskins recovered it in the end zone for a Frisco touchdown. Kilmer engineered a drive at the end of the game that resulted in a touchdown on a 16-yard pass to Larry Brown, but the final score stood San Francisco 24, Washington 20.

DEDICATION

The headline in the Christmas Day 1971 edition of *Pro Football Weekly* read:
Kilmer Leaves Jail to Rally
Following it was columnist Dave Brady's incisive look into a story of true dedication.

Kilmer had been called upon to replace the heralded Sonny Jurgensen and lead the Redskins through the 1971 regular season after Jurgy suffered a fractured shoulder in the final preseason game that year.

Kilmer had risen to the occasion admirably by piloting the Redskins to five consecutive wins at the outset of the season and keeping them in first place until the 10th game that year. With the glint of a playoff berth twinkling about RFK Stadium, nothing was going to keep him from his appointed rounds—even jail.

Here is how Dave Brady described the incident, which occurred late in the season:

The first report of his altercation in an Arlington, Va., coffee shop knocked the India-Pakistan war off page one in the city's afternoon tabloid newspaper.

All he did was have a few drinks, stop for some eggs and coffee, and have the misfortune to have only a hundred-dollar bill to pay the check in a spot where he was not at all famous.

A guy with deep conviction, as he is in the huddle, Kilmer argued his case with a no-nonsense waitress, even offering to leave the C note with her, along with his name and address. The fuss attracted a policeman who was unacquainted with Kilmer. Kilmer thought he was so right that he told the copper, "If you think I am in the wrong, put me in jail."

The policeman took the hint, Kilmer briefly was caged, but was released after officials at the pokey were able to make change for another C note so he could post $15 in collateral.

The next day he forfeited the collateral, showed up at the Redskins headquarters to sweat out the night before in a sauna, watch game films at 8:30 A.M., and all at once every guy in town who ever celebrated too enthusiastically identified with Kilmer.

The quarterback was the most popular Redskin in town by the time he disclosed that he had suffered a jammed neck the day before and was trying to ease the pain. He arranged for the waitress to keep the disputed $100, and said in jest, "Pete Rozelle probably will put that whole chain of coffee houses off limits."

Billy Kilmer barely gets this pass off in a 1971 game against the St. Louis Cardinals. The Skins throttled the Cards in both their encounters that year. (Washington Redskins)

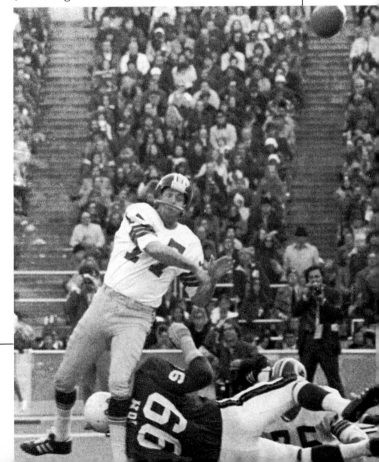

Redskins fans had quickly adjusted to winning and, as the 1972 football season approached, there was more excitement wafting about Washington and the surrounding environs than at perhaps any time since Sammy Baugh had gone back to Texas.

Preseason predictors, however, were touting the Cowboys, who had defeated the Miami Dolphins, 24–3, in Super Bowl VI the preceding January to again capture the NFC East crown. The Cowboys were an awesome force led by Roger Staubach at quarterback (although a shoulder injury would keep him on the bench most of the year), ably backed up by Craig Morton. They also had running back Calvin Hill, wide receiver Bob Hayes, tight end Mike Ditka, defensive tackle Bob Lilly, defensive

backs Herb Adderley and Cliff Harris, and linebackers Lee Roy Jordan and Chuck Howley, to name just a few who often appeared on the All-Pro listings.

George Allen was undismayed, however, and announced before the season, "This is the year Dallas falls from grace, and the Redskins are going to be the ones doing the pushing."

As it turned out, he was correct.

Sonny Jurgensen was healthy again at the start of the season, but he was now 38 years old. Despite his reverential regard for aged ballplayers, Allen decided that the 32-year-old Billy Kilmer would lead the tribe. Charley Taylor and Larry Brown were back in first-rate shape, and the defense—old, wily, gritty, and menacingly experienced—seemed ready for any offensive onslaught.

Linebacker Jack Pardee (32) goes up to bat away a pass intended for Calvin Hill (35) of the Cowboys in the first meeting of these two rivals in 1972. Washington won it 24–20. (Washington Redskins)

And so the Redskins charged into the season with the same vivacity they had the year before. Granted they did not win their first five straight, but they won four of them, defeating the Cardinals twice, the Eagles, and the Minnesota Vikings, who had stormed through the NFC Central the year before. Their only loss was a frustrating, depressing surprise at the hands of the New England Patriots. Curt Knight had kicked a field goal in the waning minutes of the game to tie the score at 24–24. But an overzealous Patriot defender had bumped into Knight. The penalty gave the Redskins a first down if they chose to take it. Coach Allen said to go for the win, so the Redskins canceled the field goal and set out to score a touchdown for the victory. Only they did not get the ball into the end zone. Knight came back onto the field after three fruitless downs, but this time he missed the field goal and the Redskins succumbed of their own volition, 24–21.

The sixth game of the season brought the Cowboys to Washington. Dallas, like the Redskins, came into the game with a 4–1–0 record. Sonny Jurgensen was Washington's starting quarterback now, with Kilmer benched after the loss to New England. And Craig Morton was the Cowboys' full-time quarterback while the injured Staubach watched from the sidelines. Morton, though, appeared to be on the way to one of his best seasons ever. Despite Washington's home-field advantage, the oddsmakers favored Dallas by a touchdown.

It looked as if they were correct, at least through the first half. A field goal and a Morton touchdown pass gave Dallas a 10–0 lead at the end of the first quarter, which was extended to 13–0 in the second period. Jurgensen led a Washington drive that climaxed with a pass to Larry Brown for a touchdown, but at the half the Redskins trailed by the oddsmakers' six points.

Another seven points were added to the lead in the third quarter when true-life cowboy and Dallas Cowboy Walt Garrison burst in for a touchdown. But then, true to George Allen's preseason prediction, the Cowboys began their fall from grace and the Redskins were doing the pushing.

Larry Brown broke one for 34 yards and a touchdown to bring the score to 20–14. Curt Knight kicked a 42-yard field goal to make it 20–17. Charley Harraway barreled 13 yards to make the score 24–20, Redskins. And during all this offensive derring-do, the Over-the-Hill Gang defense totally shut down the Cowboys. At the final gun, Washington had defeated the despised Texans and was in sole possession of first place in the NFC East.

The Skins continued their winning ways, taking the next six games in a row. With two games remaining, Washington was 11–1–0, and more importantly had clinched the NFC East title. Ensuing losses to the Cowboys and the Buffalo Bills were meaningless. It was the first time since 1965 that the Dallas Cowboys had not triumphed in the NFC East. And the Redskins' 11 victories would remain their most ever until another Super Bowl-bound Washington team won 14 in 1983.

The entire team contributed to the 1972 regular-season glory. The defense gave up the fewest points in the NFC, 218, for a per-game average of 15.6. Larry Brown led the NFL by gaining 1,216 yards rushing, which was also a new club record. Billy Kilmer, who had regained the starting job at quarterback after Sonny Jurgensen suffered a season-ending injury in the seventh game that year, was the fourth-ranked passer in the league. Charley Taylor gained 673 yards on 49 receptions, and Roy Jefferson picked up 550 on 35 catches. And six Redskins earned invitations to the Pro Bowl: Larry Brown, Billy Kilmer, Charley Taylor, Len Hauss, Chris Hanburger, and Speedy Duncan.

The playoff alignment for 1972 pitted Washington against the Green Bay Packers, who had won the NFC Central Division with relative ease and a 10–4–0 record. The Pack was far from the powerhouse it had been during the '60s in the Lombardi years, when Hornung, Starr, Taylor, and all the others had terrorized the league. The Packers did have a brute of a fullback in John Brockington and a good runner/receiver in halfback MacArthur Lane, but they had not looked all that impressive in falling to the Redskins at RFK Stadium, 21–16, earlier in the year. Their second meeting was also scheduled for RFK Stadium, on Christmas Eve.

George Allen's game plan focused first on stopping the Green Bay running game. He had great faith in his defense, but he added nose guard Manny Sistrunk to help stifle the Packer rushing attack. Offensively he wanted a ball-control game; keep it on the ground, use the pass only when needed or as a surprise.

The plan worked perfectly, although Green Bay was the first to get on the scoreboard. But Chester Marcol's field goal in the second quarter provided the only points the Packers would score all afternoon.

The Redskins came right back, and Kilmer did indeed surprise the Pack, with a 32-yard toss to Roy Jefferson for a touchdown. A Washington field goal just before the half lifted the lead to 10–3. Curt Knight added two more field goals for the Skins in the fourth quarter, and the final score was Washington 16, Green Bay 3.

The defense had done just what George Allen had asked of it. The Packers rushed for only two first downs and a meager 78 yards all day.

The victory, of course, sent the Redskins to the NFC championship game. They would not have to travel very far, however. It, too, was to be played in RFK Stadium.

The opponent was none other than the Dallas Cowboys, a wild-card entry, who was the most veteran of veterans in terms of the NFL playoffs during the late 1960s and

The 1972 NFC champs. (Washington Redskins)

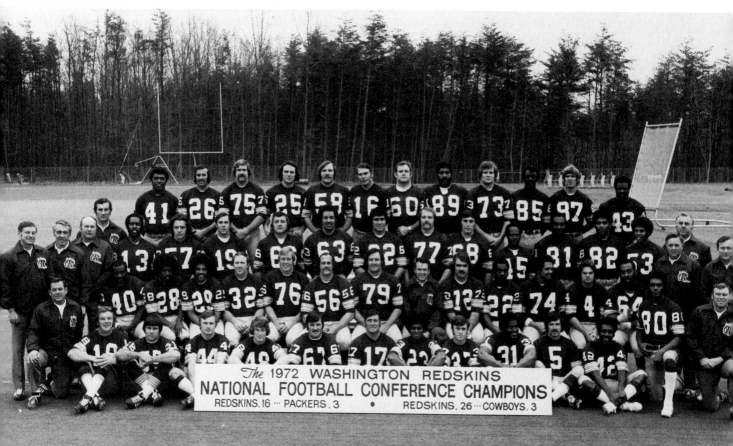

The 1972 WASHINGTON REDSKINS
NATIONAL FOOTBALL CONFERENCE CHAMPIONS
REDSKINS, 16 ··· PACKERS, 3   •   REDSKINS, 26 ···COWBOYS, 3

QUIZ, 1972

Columnist Steve Guback of the *Sunday Star* and the Washington *Daily News* concocted this quiz for fanatical fans of the Redskins in 1972. "How well do you REALLY know the Redskins?" he asked.

Not very well, he implied, if you could not match the following players with the nicknames they are known by in the confines of Redskin Park and the locker room at RFK Stadium.

Jerry Smith	A. Sweet-Pea
Jack Pardee	B. Grumpy
Roy Jefferson	C. Whisky
Ron McDole	D. Gabby
Brig Owens	E. Rubber-Man
Chris Hanburger	F. Twiggy
Larry Brown	G. Babycakes
Charley Harraway	H. Pigpen
Billy Kilmer	I. Rap
Terry Hermeling	J. Rev.

Answers to the Nickname Quiz

Smith	G. Babycakes
Pardee	D. Gabby
Jefferson	A. Sweet-Pea
McDole	E. Rubber-Man
Owens	F. Twiggy
Hanburger	B. Grumpy
Brown	I. Rap
Harraway	J. Rev.
Kilmer	C. Whisky
Hermeling	H. Pigpen

early '70s. The Cowboys, who had been runner-up to the Redskins in the regular season, had put on their postseason game face and defeated the NFC West Champs, the 49ers, 30–28, when a recovered Roger Staubach came off the bench to throw two touchdown passes in the waning minutes of the game.

The title tilt took place on New Year's Eve afternoon, a chilly, damp, overcast day in D.C. Staubach was in the saddle, so to speak, for the Cowboys, and Dallas fans were thrilled to have him back, especially after he'd plucked victory from the claws of defeat the week before.

But it was not Staubach's star that would shine in the darkened sky above RFK Stadium. It was the quarterback on the Redskin side of the line of scrimmage, Billy Kilmer. After a Curt Knight field goal got the scoring started for Washington, Kilmer connected with the ever-reliable Charley Taylor on a 15-yard touchdown pass, and took a 10–3 lead into the locker room at halftime.

In the fourth quarter, Kilmer again went to Taylor, this time for a 45-yard touchdown. Knight added three more field goals that period, and the Over-the-Hill Gang defense was as stingy as it had been in the playoff game the week before, allowing only a second-quarter field goal. The final score was Washington 26, Dallas 3.

Next stop: that most glittering of sports events, the Super Bowl.

Super Bowl VII

When the Miami Dolphins arrived in Los Angeles, they brought with them a note of distinction. They had won all 14 of their regular-season games. Only one other team in the history of the National Football League, which had been in operation for over half a century, had posted a perfect regular season. The Chicago Bears had done it twice, in 1934 (13–0–0) and 1942 (11–0–0). The Bears, however, had lost the title game both years, to the Giants in '34 and to the Redskins in '42.

Miami, who by Super Bowl time had won 16 straight games, including its two playoff triumphs, stood on the threshold of making NFL history by becoming the first championship team with a totally unblemished record.

Surprisingly, however, the Dolphins were not the favorites. The oddsmakers favored Allen's Over-the-Hill Gang by two points. Coach Allen raised his eyebrows more than once when that fact was brought up in the two hype-filled weeks before the Super Bowl game. Allen knew he had to contend with Miami's explosive passing game, which featured Bob Griese throwing to the likes of Paul Warfield, Howard Twilley, and old vet Marv Fleming. Then there was the powerful running attack, centered on Larry Csonka,

Jim Kiick, and Mercury Morris. And the Miami defense was ranked the best in the entire NFL, yielding the least number of points per game (12.2), the least number of first downs (186), and the second-least number of yards rushing (1,548, or a mere 111 per game).

Allen, as was his nature, remained steadfastly positive and confident. Experience would prevail in this most pressure-packed of games, he told the assembled press and media corps, whom he found most distracting and annoying.

It was a sunny but typically hazy day in smoggy Los Angeles, and uncomfortably hot for a football game (84 degrees at kickoff), that mid-January afternoon when the Redskins and Dolphins took the field at the Coliseum to decide the 1972 NFL title.

The ball exchanged hands five times before any real action took place. There was just under three minutes to play in the first quarter when the Dolphins began to march. They ate up yardage on the ground, then Griese connected on a 14-yarder to Warfield. At the Washington 28-yard line, Griese threw a perfect strike to Twilley near the goal line, who carried it in for the game's first score. Garo Yepremian's extra point gave the Dolphins a 7–0 lead.

The Redskins had as much trouble in the second period moving the ball as they had had in the first quarter. At the same time, the defense was holding its own, shutting down the Miami attack, with the exception of a 47-yard touchdown bomb from Griese to Warfield that, fortunately for the Skins, was called back because of a penalty.

The Redskins were not so fortunate in the last two minutes of the period. Kilmer dropped back to pass, but threw it into the hands of Miami's All-Pro linebacker Nick Buoniconti, who returned it 32 yards to the Washington 27. After a pair of running

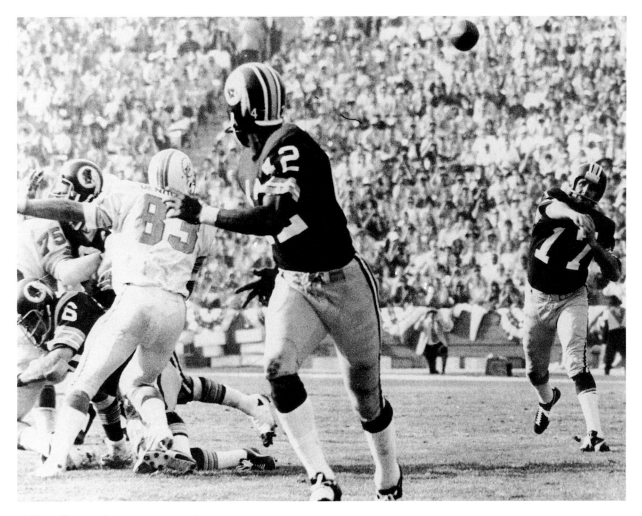

Billy Kilmer (17) tosses to a wide open Charley Taylor (42) in Super Bowl VII. Kilmer completed 14 out of 28 passes, but the offense could not put a score on the board against the Dolphins that Super Sunday, and the Skins lost 14–7. (HOF/NFL Photos)

plays, Griese picked up a first down by hitting receiver Jim Mandich on the Redskins' two-yard line with a little less than 30 seconds to go in the half. Moments later, Jim Kiick bulled it in for the touchdown, and Miami took a 14–0 halftime lead.

The Redskins had a chance to score early in the third period when they got within field goal range, but Curt Knight's attempt was wide. The Dolphins also had a chance to put some points on the board in the same quarter after Csonka broke free and carried

the ball 49 yards to the Washington 16-yard line. But a Griese pass into the end zone was picked off by Redskins safety Brig Owens.

In the fourth quarter, the Skins marched 79 yards to the Miami 10-yard line. But when Kilmer threw into the end zone, it was snared by Dolphins safety Jake Scott, who ran it all the way back to the Redskins' 48-yard line. Miami moved the ball into field goal range and Yepremian lined up for a 42-yarder. Then, in one of the classic football follies of all time, Yepremian booted the

SUPER BOWL VII

Site: Memorial Coliseum, Los Angeles, CA

Date: January 14, 1973

Weather: 84 degrees, clear and sunny

Attendance: 90,182

Gross receipts: $4,180,086.53

Player shares: $15,000 winner, $7,500 loser

LINEUPS

Washington Redskins	Offense	Miami Dolphins
Charley Taylor	WR	Paul Warfield
Terry Hermeling	LT	Wayne Moore
Paul Laaveg	LG	Bob Kuechenberg
Len Hauss	C	Jim Langer
John Wilbur	RG	Larry Little
Walt Rock	RT	Norm Evans
Jerry Smith	TE	Marv Fleming
Roy Jefferson	WR	Howard Twilley
Billy Kilmer	QB	Bob Griese
Larry Brown	RB	Jim Kiick
Charley Harraway	FB	Larry Csonka
Curt Knight	K	Garo Yepremian

	Defense	
Ron McDole	LE	Vern Den Herder
Bill Brundige	LT	Manny Fernandez
Diron Talbert	RT	Bob Heinz
Verlon Biggs	RE	Bill Stanfill
Jack Pardee	LB	Doug Swift
Myron Pottios	MLB	Nick Buoniconti
Chris Hanburger	LB	Mike Kolen
Pat Fischer	CB	Lloyd Mumphord
Mike Bass	CB	Curtis Johnson
Brig Owens	S	Dick Anderson
Roosevelt Taylor	S	Jake Scott
Mike Bragg	P	Larry Seiple

	Coaches	
George Allen		Don Shula

SCORING

	1st Qtr	2nd Qtr	3rd Qtr	4th Qtr	Final Score
Redskins	0	0	0	7	7
Dolphins	7	7	0	0	14

The Super Bowl coaches of 1972. George Allen congratulates Miami Dolphin coach Don Shula at a Touchdown Club luncheon in Washington. (Washington Redskins)

ball straight into the hand of onrushing Redskin Bill Brundige. The blocked kick rolled around before Yepremian picked it up, juggled it in panic, and then—in a mixture of lob and bobble—threw it right into the hands of Washington cornerback Mike Bass, who raced 49 yards with it for a Redskins touchdown.

Washington got the ball back with a little more than a minute to play at its own 30-yard line. Kilmer, however, could not overcome the Miami defense, which had been outstanding all day. When the game

ended the Skins were back on their own 15 and the scoreboard read Miami 14, Washington 7.

Miami had made football history at the Redskins' expense. It was a game best summed up by Washington linebacker Jack Pardee after it was over. "We were never really in the game . . . and we were never really out of it." So, with disappointment but the notion that they were a certifiable contender, Allen and his Over-the-Hill Gang headed home to begin preparations for the 1973 season.

COACH TALK

After Super Bowl VII, both coaches summed up their sentiments.

George Allen: "It doesn't do any good to play in the Super Bowl if you don't win. Miami is not a team that impresses you on film because they execute so well. Our kicking game was not up to par. We just lost to a team that played a better game. . . . I can't get out of here [Los Angeles] fast enough. We will stay overnight and leave tomorrow morning. There will be a lot of hours of agony tonight."

Don Shula: "When you do not go all the way, there is an empty feeling, even if you are Coach of the Year. But there is no empty feeling this year. This is the ultimate. . . . This is the greatest team I have been associated with."

SPIES

Was George Allen the perpetrator of clandestine deeds, the employer of surreptitious agents? Only Allen himself knows—or if he was, only Allen and his undercover army know—but many an NFL coaching rival would swear that Allen and/or members of his coaching staff were prone to spy on the closed practice sessions of his upcoming opponents.

There was the time in Philadelphia, for example, when Eagles trainer Otho Davis swore that he saw a member of Allen's staff, dressed in dungarees and wearing a welder's hat, lurking about the otherwise empty stands of Veterans Stadium while the Eagles were preparing for a game against Washington.

Another incident of similar repute occurred when Allen was guiding the Rams in 1967. It seems Tex Schramm, then Dallas Cowboys general manager, announced to the press that a suspicious-looking yellow Chevrolet had been parked across from the team's practice field. He had taken down the license number and after a little investigation had determined that it was a Hertz rental car that had been rented to, of all people, Johnny Sanders—then chief of the Rams' scouting system.

Allen immediately retorted with a countercharge. He said that his coaching staff had observed a man sitting up in a eucalyptus tree with binoculars, spying on the Rams' practice session. They had chased the man but had not caught him. According to Allen, however, the man looked an awful lot like Frank "Bucko" Kilroy, the former Philadelphia Eagle All-Pro guard who was now employed by the Cowboys as a scout.

If the two teams were spying on each other, Allen's secret service must have been more adroit, because the Rams annihilated the Cowboys the following Sunday, 35–13.

Sonny Jurgensen joined the Redskins in 1964 and led the team at quarterback until 1972. (FRED ROE)

George Allen and his philosophy of "The Future Is Now" took Washington by storm in 1971. (FRED ROE)

Larry Brown (43) goes in for a touchdown behind the blocking of all-pro tight end Jerry Smith (87). (FRED ROE)

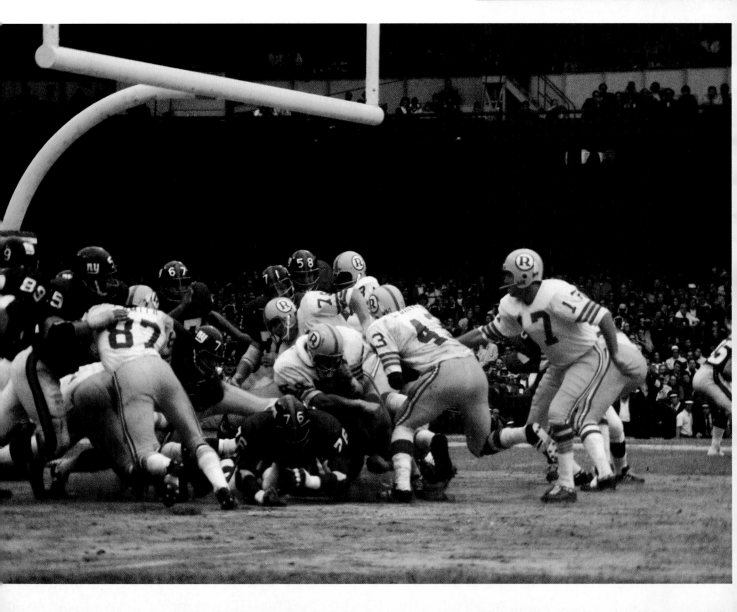

Billy Kilmer, a fearsome competitor, fades back to pass in Super Bowl VII. (FRED ROE)

Roy Jefferson (80) brings down a reception between Miami defenders. (FRED ROE)

Joe Theismann rolls to his left in a 1979 game. (WASHINGTON REDSKINS)

*John Riggins, the Redskins' all-time leading rusher, cuts upfield
and into the clear.* (WASHINGTON REDSKINS)

MVP Doug Williams looks downfield for a receiver in Super Bowl XXII. (FRED ROE)

Timmy Smith cuts off-tackle in Super Bowl XXII on his way to 204 yard performance. (FRED ROE)

All-pro linemen Dexter Manley and Charles Mann. (FRED ROE)

On the sideline, "Hogs" Jacoby, May, Bostic, Thielmann and McKenzie. (FRED ROE)

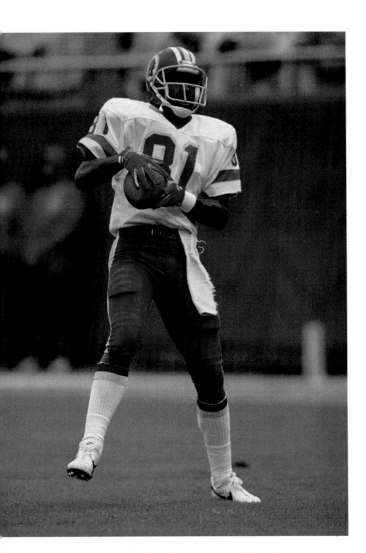

Joe Gibbs, the Redskins' winningest coach, pacing the sidelines. (FRED ROE)

All-pro wide receiver Art Monk brings down a touchdown reception. (WASHINGTON REDSKINS)

Mark Rypien throws downfield in the face of a heavy rush by Lawrence Taylor. (FRED ROE)

GEORGE ALLEN

"All the past is future."

ROBINSON JEFFERS, 1924

"The future is now."

GEORGE ALLEN, 1971

When George Allen took over as head coach and general manager of the Washington Redskins in 1971, he decided immediately that the future indeed had to be *now*. The previous two and a half decades had produced a dizzying series of failures (only four winning seasons since 1945). The present was hardly any better, with Allen inheriting a young team that had lost five of its last seven games the season before.

After five winning years as head coach of the Los Angeles Rams, George Allen signed a contract with Washington that made him the highest-paid coach in NFL history. His annual salary of $125,000 was also supplemented by a variety of perks and incentive bonuses.

One of Allen's first moves was to initiate the construction of Redskins Park, a $750,000, multi-use training facility and office complex that featured two practice fields, one natural grass and the other artificial surface.

Then came the trades. Allen's philosophy was to build a team around proven veterans. And he went after them with gusto. As author David Slattery observed, "He sent future draft choices around like pellets from a shot gun. When he finished, he had taken the team from a young, rebuilding group to a covey of veterans soon known as the 'Over-the-Hill Gang.'" In 1971, Allen's bartering activity totaled 19 trades, involving 24 draft choices and 33 players (eight of whom had played for Allen in Los Angeles). The most notable oldster/newcomers were quarterback Billy Kilmer from the Saints,

linebackers Jack Pardee and Myron Pottios and defensive tackle Diron Talbert from the Rams, wide receiver Roy Jefferson from the Colts, defensive ends Verlon Biggs from the Jets and Ron McDole from the Bills, and defensive backs Richie Petitbon from the Rams and Speedy Duncan from the Chargers. Allen even managed to talk former star Green Bay Packer receiver Boyd Dowler out of retirement.

Allen also arrived in the nation's capital with a caseful of inspirational slogans. "Every year is the most important year." "What we do in the off-season will determine what we do in the regular season." Etc. They were carefully logged by everyone from the beat sports reporter to columnist Art Buchwald.

"When I came to Washington, I had to *sell* winning," Allen later said. "Even whether or not I had to, I felt it was proper and the time to do it was right away. If not, it would not become a way of life, and I believe that it must. I found cooperation in this respect, though some people weren't used to working hard to achieve it. . . . To have a job and not be one of the best . . . well, in my mind, there is something wrong with anyone who thinks that way."

The roots of Allen's enthusiasm for football and devotion to winning can be traced to his undergraduate college days at Alma College in Michigan and Marquette University, where he played end. (Allen also received a master's degree from Stanford.) He began college-level coaching at Morningside in Iowa (1948–51), then moved to Whittier College in

George Allen leading his troops into battle. (Washington Redskins)

California in 1952 and remained there for five years.

In 1957, Allen began his NFL coaching career as an assistant to Sid Gillman with the Los Angeles Rams. The following season he went to the Chicago Bears to assist "Papa Bear" George Halas as defensive coordinator. In 1963, Allen's league-leading defensive platoon battered and stifled every opponent, and proved to be the key ingredient in bringing the Bears that year's NFL crown (so instrumental that Halas awarded Allen the championship game ball).

In 1965, Allen accepted the head-coaching job with the Rams and was promptly sued by George Halas for breach of contract, but the Bears' legendary owner and coach finally relented and released Allen from his contract.

With the Rams, Allen developed the reputation of being a "player's coach,"

one which served him well when team owner Dan Reeves tried to fire him after the 1968 season. A player revolt forced Reeves to reinstate Allen, who then led the Rams to the playoffs in 1969.

"I think I can handle all my players," said Allen. "I treat them like I hope I would be treated. I take time and I spend time with them. Part of the misunderstanding that grows up in this business is not doing that, not helping them better themselves."

While Allen will be forever remembered as a champion of veterans, he also pioneered the free-agent camps that gave unknowns and the overlooked a chance at playing in the NFL.

Allen turned down offers from the Green Bay Packers and the Houston Oilers to accept the Redskins job in 1971. He added a new coaching staff, three of whom would later become NFL head

Defensive strategist Allen leads an impromptu defense council on the sideline with cornerback Brig Owens (23), tackle Myron Pottios (helmetless), and linebackers Jack Pardee (32) and Chris Hanburger (55). In his seven years as head coach of the Redskins, Allen produced a record of 67–30–1 (.689) and took Washington to the playoffs five times. (Washington Redskins)

coaches themselves: Marv Levy, Ted Marchibroda, and Mike McCormack.

The Over-the-Hill Gang provided the seasoned squad that Allen felt would lead Washington back into contention. Allen's emphasis on discipline and defense, coupled with his many-faceted motivational tactics, spurred the Redskins to a 9–4–1 mark his first year on the job and earned Washington its first playoff berth since 1945. Allen was a unanimous selection as NFC Coach of the Year, an award he would also receive the following year, and again in 1976.

After that first winning season, Allen explained, "An aging team is the least of my worries. If you do things right at the start of any football operation, you don't have to build and rebuild. We have a solid club in Washington. They win because they want to win." Winning, of course, has a way of unifying a team and its fans, and

the Redskins found faithful support for their new coach and his unorthodox philosophy.

In 1972, his second season, Allen gave Washingtonians their first conference title in 27 years. With an 11–3–0 record, the Redskins and the now-famous "Ramskins" defense held playoff foes Green Bay and Dallas to just three points apiece and advanced almost effortlessly to the team's first Super Bowl, before falling to the AFC champion Miami Dolphins.

In his seven years as head coach at Washington, Allen posted a record of 67–30–1, making him the winningest coach in Redskins history, at least until Joe Gibbs came along in the 1980s. George Allen took his Over-the-Hill Gang to the playoffs five times. His winning percentage (including his years with the Rams) of .684 is high enough to rank him among the top 10 coaches in NFL history.

13

The Almost Years

After the titillating 1972 trip to the Super Bowl, the talk around Washington centered on the quote attributed to the ever-positive George Allen after Super Bowl VII: "The Redskins will be back." Well, he was almost right.

Allen's teams over the next five years were always in the war but for some reason could not win a postseason battle. It was, however, a most entertaining segment in Washington Redskins lore.

Allen continued to cement his philosophy of "The Future Is Now" in 1973, even though the future and now were over for some of his old veterans, most notably 37-year-old linebacker Jack Pardee and 34-year-old cornerback Roosevelt Taylor. But Allen added All-Pro defensive back Ken Houston from the Houston Oilers; linebacker Dave Robinson, who had had an outstanding 10-year career with the Packers; tight end Alvin Reed, also from the Oilers; and the outstanding but troubled and controversial running back Duane Thomas, who had finally exceeded Tom Landry's threshold of patience in Dallas.

The quarterbacking duties in 1973 passed back and forth between Billy Kilmer, who was beset by stomach problems, and Sonny Jurgensen, who moved on a noticeably gimpy knee. Still, the Redskins moved with the force and determination of a Super Bowl contender through the year. There were only two teams in the race for the NFL East crown—the Redskins and the Cowboys.

When the two arch-rivals met for the first time that year at RFK Stadium, the Cowboys were undefeated in three games and the Redskins were in second place, having dropped a surpriser to the St. Louis Cardi-

Training camp, 1973, at Carlisle, Pennsylvania. The Skins' two premier quarterbacks of the day, Sonny Jurgensen (9) and Billy Kilmer (17) along with guard Ray Schoenke (98), enter the gates for a little summer workout. (Washington Redskins)

nals. The two teams were tied for first place, however, at the end of the day, Washington whipping Dallas, 14–7.

When they met again in the next to last game of the season down at Texas Stadium, the Redskins were alone at the top with a record of 9–3–0, but the Cowboys were just a step behind at 8–4–0. A win would clinch the division title for Washington.

But it was not to be. The Cowboys were unstoppable that day and built a 27–0 lead, which they carried into the fourth quarter. The Skins scored an inconsequential touchdown then and went back to Washington to face the Eagles.

The Redskins defeated the Eagles decisively, but the Cowboys did the same to the Cardinals in their season's finale. Both teams ended with records of 10–4–0. Within the

division, their records were also identical, 6–2–0. The next deciding factor in awarding the division title was the point differential in their two games that year, and that, by dint of the fact that the Redskins had beaten the Cowboys by only seven points while Dallas had won the other encounter by 20, gave the divisional title to the Cowboys.

Washington, however, qualified as a wild card, and therefore was headed to the playoffs for the third consecutive year under George Allen's guidance.

The home-field advantage went to the Redskins' opponents, the Minnesota Vikings, who had easily won the NFC Central with a record of 12–2–0. Coached by the glacial-faced Bud Grant and led by the elusive scrambler Fran Tarkenton, and anchored by a defensive front four consisting

The road to Super Bowl VIII starts here, George Allen said at training camp in the summer of 1973, with "Hard Work and Dedication." (Washington Redskins)

Brig Owens (23) intercepts a Roger Staubach pass in this 1973 game against the Cowboys. Washington won this bout 14–7. Owens has intercepted the most passes in Redskins history, 36. (Washington Redskins)

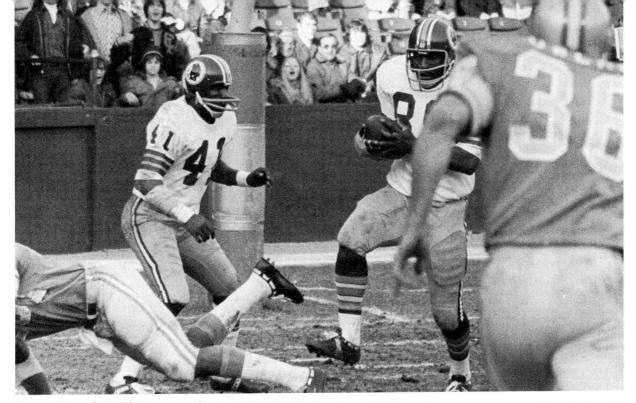

A new Over-the-Hill-Gang member in 1973, linebacker Dave Robinson intercepts a pass against the Detroit Lions. Number 41 is cornerback Mike Bass. The Skins shut out the Lions, 20–0 in Detroit. (Washington Redskins)

of Carl Eller, Alan Page, Gary Larsen, and Jim Marshall, the Vikes had become one of the truly dominating forces in the league.

It was the Redskins, though, who appeared to be the dominant force when the two teams met in chilly Bloomington, Minnesota, at least in the first half. Washington marched first, a 76-yard drive behind the passing of Billy Kilmer and the rushing of Larry Brown, but it stalled on the Minnesota seven-yard line. Curt Knight came on for what appeared to be a chip shot, but his kick went wide.

The Vikings, hardly looking like a team that had manhandled almost every opponent in the regular season, did get on the scoreboard first, with a 19-yard field goal from Fred Cox. But in the second quarter they turned around and handed the Redskins another scoring opportunity when Bobby Bryan bobbled and then dropped a Washington punt, which Bob Brunet recovered for the Skins at the Minnesota 21-yard line. Washington moved down to the three, where Larry Brown carried it in for the touchdown. At the half it was Washington 7, Minnesota 3.

The tide irrevocably turned, however, when the two teams came back onto the frozen field for the second half. After taking the kickoff, the Vikings drove 79 yards for a touchdown, 46 of them picked up when running back Oscar Reed scampered to the Washington two-yard line. A plunge by fullback Bill Brown broke the goal line plane and the Vikings moved to a 10–7 lead.

Washington fought back, however, and Curt Knight tied the score with a 52-yard field goal, which remains today the longest ever in Washington playoff history. Another Knight boot, this one a 42-yarder, in the early fourth quarter regained the lead for the Redskins.

But then Tarkenton took control. With some pinpoint passing and yards gobbled up by the runners Reed and Chuck Foreman, Minnesota moved 71 yards down the field, the climax a 28-yard touchdown pass from Tarkenton to wide receiver John Gilliam.

Defensive end Verlon Biggs (86) takes to the offense after scooping up a fumble in a 1973 game against the San Diego Chargers. The tackler is quarterback Johnny Unitas (19) in his last NFL season. Number 72 for Washington is tackle Diron Talbert. (Washington Redskins)

Billy Kilmer tried to respond in kind but instead threw the ball into the hands of Minnesota cornerback Nate Wright. Tarkenton capitalized immediately, throwing another touchdown pass to Gilliam. And the Vikes led 24–13.

Kilmer narrowed the lead moments later when he moved the Skins and finally connected for a score, a 28-yarder to Roy Jefferson. But time and another Fred Cox field goal ended Washington's hopes of back-to-back NFC titles and a trip to the Super Bowl. The final score: Minnesota 27, Washington 20.

INFLATION

Was it inflation? Or was it coach George Allen's propensity for spending the Redskin organization's money? Depends on who you listen to. Whichever, it was announced in March 1973 that ticket prices to Washington's home games were going up an average of 15 to 25%: $7 to $9, $8 up to $10, $12 up to $15. The $15 price tag tied Denver for the highest-priced ducat in the National Football League.

For financial-trivia's sake, it should be remembered that when the Skins first moved to Washington in 1937 the top price for a six-game season ticket was a mere $9.

By 1974, Redskins fans had become pleasantly accustomed to winning seasons. George Allen had obliterated the two-and-a-half-decade doldrums since Sammy Baugh had led Washington to divisional titles and NFL championship games, by taking the Skins to the playoffs three straight years and compiling an impressive regular-season record of 30–11–1.

Now, in his fourth year at the helm, he would be doing it for a different boss. Jack Kent Cooke, who had made his fortune in Canadian businesses and had been a minority stockholder in the Redskins since 1960, acquired a majority of the stock in the ball club.

Allen was also faced with the prospect of having to alter his inbred philosophy, be-cause the "now" part of the future was getting pretty old. Sonny Jurgensen had turned 40, Billy Kilmer 34, and most of the stalwart defenders were well into their 30s. So he uncharacteristically looked at some relative youngsters, the most notable of whom was quarterback Joe Theismann, who had starred at Notre Dame and had been playing in Canada since graduating in 1970. Draft rights to the young quarterback were held by Miami, so Allen traded his first-round draft pick for 1976 to the Dolphins for him. Another youthful addition was placekicker Mark Moseley. Departing, however, was ever-reliable fullback Charley Har-raway, who had been lured to the new World Football League.

The '74 season began on a roller-coaster

One of the Redskins' smallest and finest defensive backs ever, Pat Fischer (37) returns his interception of a Dan Fouts pass in a game against the San Diego Chargers in 1973. Fischer intercepted 27 passes during his 10-year career in Washington. (Washington Redskins)

track. After squeaking by the Giants in the opener, the Redskins were surprised by a decidedly underdog St. Louis Cardinals and lost 17–10. The Cards had won only four of their 14 games the year before but were suddenly blooming under new head coach Don Coryell. They proved to the Redskins and Washington fans alike that it was no fluke when they triumphed again several weeks later by a score of 23–20, racking up their seventh consecutive victory of the season. It left the Redskins with a record of 4–3–0, a distant three games behind St. Louis in the NFL East.

With Kilmer directing the Redskins' attack and Jurgensen coming on in relief throughout the season, Washington rallied, however, to win seven of its remaining eight games, while the Cardinals faltered and dropped four of their eight games. Both teams ended up with records of 10–4–0,

while the usually dominant Dallas Cowboys turned in an 8–6–0 season. The Cardinals were awarded the division crown because they had defeated the Redskins the two times they met during the regular season, and Washington had to settle for a wild-card invitation to the playoffs for the third time in Coach Allen's now four-year tenure.

Sonny Jurgensen's passing statistics—137 completions in 234 attempts, a league-high 64%, for 1,185 yards, 11 touchdowns and only five interceptions—were good enough to earn him the top ranking in the NFL for passing, which wasn't bad for a 40-year-old quarterback. Larry Brown, suffering from knee injuries, gained only 432 yards on a meager average of 2.6 yards a carry. Unsurprisingly, Charley Taylor was the most productive receiver, with 54 catches for 738 yards. And surprisingly, for a quarterback, rookie Joe Theismann returned 15 punts

Mark Moseley, square-toe and all, warms up before his first season with the Redskins in 1974. When he retired he had scored 1,206 points for Washington and kicked 263 field goals and 417 extra points. (Washington Redskins)

Over-the-Hill-Gang tackle Diron Talbert has New York Giants quarterback Craig Morton in the grasp moments before completing a picture-perfect sack. Talbert, whom Allen acquired from the Rams in 1971, stayed with the Skins through the 1980 season. (Washington Redskins)

for 157 yards. He also completed nine of 11 passes on the rare occasions when he was allowed to fill in for Kilmer and Jurgensen. Linebacker Chris Hanburger received his seventh invitation to the Pro Bowl and was joined in that classic by Charley Taylor, defensive back Ken Houston, and defensive tackle Diron Talbert.

The Redskins had to travel to Los Angeles for their postseason appearance of '74 in order to meet the Rams, easy winners in the NFL West with a record of 10–4–0. The key forces for the Rams were the rushing of Lawrence McCutcheon, who led the league with 1,109 yards gained, and a defense that boasted such proven stars as ends Jack Youngblood and Fred Dryer, tackle Merlin

Olsen, linebacker Isiah Robertson, and defensive back Dave Elmendorf.

It was an eminently forgettable day under the California sun for the Redskins, as they proved to be their own worst enemy. They turned the ball over six times to Los Angeles, three on fumbles and three on interceptions. Despite that statistic, however, Washington was clearly in the game all the way to the fourth quarter.

The Rams took the lead in the first quarter when James Harris threw four passes for a total of 60 yards in a drive that culminated in a touchdown pass to tight end Bob Klein. The Skins came back as Kilmer teamed with Charley Taylor on a 41-yard pass that set up a 35-yard field goal by Mike Bragg, who was substituting for the injured Mark Moseley. In the second period, the Redskins took the lead. Cornerback Pat Fischer nabbed a pass from Harris and returned it 40 yards to the Los Angeles 23-yard line. From there, Washington moved it to the one, where Moses Denson bucked in for the score. At the half, the Redskins led, 10–7.

The advantage was short-lived, however. In the third quarter, Larry Brown fumbled the ball over to the Rams, who tied the score with a 37-yard field goal by David Ray. Then, on the ensuing kick, Doug Cunningham fumbled the ball right back to them. The Skins managed to hold Los Angeles to a field goal, but they now trailed 13–10. Finally, in a final and decisive effort to give the game to the Rams, Sonny Jurgensen, who had replaced Kilmer, threw a pass into the hands of Los Angeles linebacker Isiah Robertson, who ran it back 59 yards for a touchdown. That was the extent of the scoring. The final score was Rams 19, Redskins 10, and for the second consecutive year Washington was eliminated from the playoffs in the first round.

Everyone was kept waiting until May of 1975 to see if Sonny Jurgensen would, a la George Blanda, continue his quarterbacking career further into his 40s. He would not. Coach Allen decided it was time for the well-liked, almost picture-perfect passer to retire.

So, after 18 years in the NFL, 11 of them with Washington, Jurgensen looked to life without a football in his hand. During his nearly two decades in the NFL, he set a slew of league passing records and was considered by many to be the best pure passer the game had ever had. Only two passers in the history of the game have career rankings higher than Jurgensen—Joe Montana and Roger Staubach. Nine years after he threw his last pass, Jurgensen would be inducted into the Pro Football Hall of Fame.

The decision to nudge Jurgensen into retirement, however, was not met with universal approval. Many sports scribes around Washington and some of the players themselves (the latter anonymously) went on record saying they thought Jurgensen should not only be retained but should hold the starting position at quarterback. It was the first of a number of controversies that Allen was to encounter over the next few years in Washington.

Larry Brown was noticeably slowed down by injuries and by the heavy load he had carried as the top gun in the Washington running game for the past six years. The defense was also weakened by injuries and age. Despite these adversities, the Redskins started off the 1975 season explosively, blowing away the New Orleans Saints, 41–3, and the Giants, 49–13.

A new star also burst onto the Washington scene, running back Mike Thomas, the Redskins' fifth-round draft choice that year out of the University of Nevada at Las Vegas. He quickly insinuated himself into the starting lineup and took over the job of chief ball-carrier.

The Skins, with Billy Kilmer shouldering almost the entire quarterbacking job now, won six of their first eight games that year and appeared headed for another postseason appearance. But they were in a hot-and-heavy race with the rejuvenated Cardinals and an always troublesome Dallas team, even though they had defeated each, the Cardinals 27–17 and the Cowboys in overtime, 30–24.

Their ambitions for the playoffs began to vanish, however, when they lost their seventh and eighth games of the season to the Cardinals and the Oakland Raiders. The Cardinals surged and locked up the NFC East, and the wild-card berth was on the line in Dallas the next to last game of the year. Both teams were 8–4–0. At day's end, Dallas

A newcomer to Washington in 1973, former Cowboy star running back Duane Thomas (47) ambles for a few yards against the 49ers. Washington defeated San Francisco at RFK, 33–9. (Washington Redskins)

was 9–4–0, Washington was 8–5–0, and their hopes of a fifth straight trip to the playoffs were dashed.

The Redskins' record of 8–6–0 was their poorest since George Allen had come to town back in 1971, and it was the first time he had not taken them to the playoffs. Of all the Skins, Mike Thomas was the most impressive. The rookie gained 919 yards rushing; only Larry Brown and Rob Goode had ever gained more in a single season for the Redskins.

Charley Taylor, now 34 years old, reached a milestone of major significance when in the last game of the season, against the Eagles, he caught his 634th pass to break the NFL career record held by Don Maynard, who had caught 633 during his days with the Giants, Jets, and Cardinals from 1958 through 1973.

George Allen promised the fans, "Your Redskins will be back. Your season will not end next year with the last game of the regular season." And, in his own inimitable way, he set about living up to his word, going after free agents because, as usual, he

did not have a first-round draft choice. One was a most propitious choice, fullback John Riggins, who had toiled with the New York Jets since 1971. Allen also signed running back Calvin Hill, who had haunted Washington defenses while starring for the Cowboys earlier in his career, and tight end Jean Fugett, another Dallas castoff.

Mike Thomas and John Riggins won the two running-back posts in the Washington backfield and Billy Kilmer maintained the quarterbacking spot, although there was now considerable controversy before and during the season about the choice. More than a few observers believed it was time for Joe Theismann to take over the job from the 36-year-old Kilmer.

The Kilmer-led Redskins got off to a good start and ended the 1976 regular season impressively. Winning their first two games at home over the Giants and Seahawks and then achieving a 20–17 overtime victory in Philadelphia against the Eagles, the Skins were tied for first place in the NFL East with the Cowboys.

It was the middle segment of the season

It was a cold, snowy day at RFK Stadium for the last game of the 1973 season, but it did not deter Roy Jefferson who cradles a Billy Kilmer pass amid the flurries. Washington defeated the Eagles that day, 38–20. (Washington Redskins)

that was the problem. In a seven-game interlude, the Redskins managed to lose to the Bears, Kansas City Chiefs, Cowboys, and Giants. With a record of 6–4–0, they were dismally behind the surging Dallas Cowboys, who had won nine of their 10 games, as well as the Cardinals, who had a record of 8–2–0.

There was a lot of dogged determination in the veteran-laden Redskins roster. Most knew their careers were coming to a close, and they rallied to Allen's exhortations that the Over-the-Hill Gang not be on the descending side of the mountain. In a crucial game in St. Louis they prevailed over the Cardinals, 16–10. The next two weeks they drubbed the Eagles, 24–0, and the Jets, 37–16. Needing a win in the last game of the season in order to secure a wild-card invitation to the playoffs, they went to Dallas to face the Cowboys, who had already clinched the division. There was an ominous overtone, however. The Redskins had never won a game at Texas Stadium, the Cowboys'

edifice that had been christened in 1971.

The aged Skins were up to the challenge, registering their first victory in Cowboy-country, a 27–14 win. With it, Washington ended the season with another 10–4–0 record, identical with that of the Cardinals. But the Redskins had defeated St. Louis the two times they met in '76, and so they earned the wild-card berth.

There were a number of highlight performances in the 1976 regular season. Mike Thomas proved to be immune from the so-called sophomore jinx and became the second runner in Redskins history to gain more than 1,000 yards in a season. His 1,103 yards were picked up on an average carry of 4.3 yards. Thomas was also the team's second-leading receiver, grabbing 28 passes for 290 yards. Tops in receptions was wide receiver Frank Grant, who caught 50 passes for 818 yards.

Mark Moseley kicked the most field goals in the league, 22, and topped the NFC in scoring 97 points. Special-teams standout

Eddie Brown led the NFL in total yards gained on punt returns, 646, which at the time was the second most in pro football history. Brown also returned kickoffs for a total of 738 yards, averaging 25 yards a return.

Brown, Mike Thomas, Ken Houston, and Chris Hanburger were voted to the Pro Bowl. It was Hanburger's *ninth* and final invitation.

Billy Kilmer, despite some midseason adversity, turned in a good year, ending up ranked sixth in the NFL, the result of completing 108 of 206 passes for 1,252 yards and 12 touchdowns. Not far behind him, ranked ninth, was Joe Theismann, who connected on 79 of 163 passes for 1,036 yards and eight touchdowns.

As they had in 1973, the Redskins had to visit Minnesota to face the Vikings, who had had little trouble conquering the NFC Central with a record of 11–2–1. In 1976, Bud Grant was still coaching the Vikes, Fran Tarkenton was still quarterbacking them, and Chuck Foreman was still their most potent ball-carrier. The defensive front four was as awesome as ever, with Carl Eller and Jim Marshall at ends and Alan Page and Doug Sutherland at tackles. The Vikes had also added a pair of fleet, sure-handed wide receivers in Ahmad Rashad and Sammy White.

It was billed by some as the "Old-Timers Game" because the Vikings had almost as many ancients now as the Redskins. However, the oldsters from the Northland, who had already been to three Super Bowls, hardly looked like they were ready for the pasture. They set the tone from the very first play of the game, when Brent McClanahan raced around end for 41 yards. Tarkenton moved the Vikes closer, then capped it with an 18-yard touchdown pass to tight end Stu Voight.

The Redskins got a 47-yard field goal from Mark Moseley in the first quarter and a 35-yarder in the third period, but while that was going on Minnesota was producing four more touchdowns to take a 35–6 lead going into the final period. For all practical purposes the game was over at that point, although the Redskins did come back with two touchdown passes from Kilmer, one for 12 yards to Frank Grant and another for three to Roy Jefferson.

It was a blowout, 35–20, and an enduring blow to George Allen, despite the fact that he was named NFC Coach of the Year. It was no longer merely being *whispered* around town that Allen could not win the big ones; it was now quite vocal. Winning seasons, yes, but he could not lead his team to victories in the playoffs, many were saying. Four of the five times he had taken them to postseason play, the Redskins had been eliminated in the first round. His regular-season record at that time, 58–25–1, was impressive to be sure, but his playoff record of 2–5–0 left much to be desired in the hearts and minds of Washington fans.

The year 1977 marked George Allen's seventh year as head coach. As he had been touted, Allen was a turnaround coach. He had brought the Redskins back into the winning column every year he had been there, and to the playoffs all but once. He did it by trading draft choices for veterans and by signing proven free agents. He all but ignored the draft; only once in his tour of duty in Washington, his first year there, did he have an early selection, a second-round choice. Every other year the team had to wait until the fourth, fifth, sixth, and once even the eighth round before it could draft a player.

It was his philosophy, and it was controversial. It had produced a team that won a lot more football games than it lost, but it had also proved to be an extraordinarily expensive way to build a winning team.

TEAM ACHIEVEMENTS, 1976

The 1976 season was a fine one—the regular season, that is. The Redskins front office catalogued it in this press release.

1976 Redskins' Outstanding Achievements

- Made playoffs for fifth time in six years
- Had sixth consecutive winning season
- Won season opener for sixth consecutive year
- Led NFL in pass-completion percentage (defense): 41.1%; NFL's lowest since 1955
- Set NFL record by recovering eight opponent fumbles in one game (vs. Cardinals, 10/28/76; record is still standing)

- Led NFL in fewest yards allowed on kickoff returns: 16.2; NFL's second-lowest total of all-time
- Led NFL with 13.2 average on punt returns
- 26 interceptions tied for second best in NFL
- Recorded 48 takeaways (second best in NFL)
- Held 10 opponents to 17 points or under
- Blocked five field goals and 1 punt
- Won five of seven games on the road
- Won four of six games on artificial turf
- Won five of seven games at RFK Stadium to up record to 33–8–1 at home over last six years

There were more than a few grumblings heard from owner Jack Kent Cooke and club president Edward Bennett Williams about the financial bottom lines over the last few seasons, and they were growing to a peak as the 1977 season rolled around. Word around town was that George Allen's spending might very well cost him his job. At the same time, there was a great deal of support for Allen among the media and fans.

The brittle relationship that had developed between Allen and his bosses, however, could not have been helped when the Skins lost their first opening game since "The Future Is Now" was launched in 1971. Washington fell to a lackluster Giants team, but rebounded the following week in its home opener by defeating the Atlanta Falcons, 10–6, and followed that up with a victory at RFK Stadium the next week over the Cardinals, 24–14.

Billy Kilmer was holding down the quarterback position, but it was tenuous. With a 3–1–0 record, the Skins went down to Texas Stadium to meet the loathsome Cowboys, who were in first place in the NFL East with a record of 4–0–0. Washington was demolished there, 34–16. Making the loss even greater, fullback John Riggins suffered a knee injury and was out for the remainder of the season. Losses in two of their next three games, to the Giants and Colts, finally precipitated a change in starting quarterbacks. It was now Joe Theismann's proverbial ballgame.

Theismann led the Redskins to three victories in their next four games, the only loss coming to the Cowboys, who were walking away with the NFL East crown. For the last two games of the season, however, Allen decided to go back to Kilmer as the starter. He regained his former effectiveness and added two more victories.

It was another winning season for Allen and his Over-the-Hill Gang, 9–5–0, but resulted in no invitation to the playoffs. The wild-card bid went to the Chicago Bears,

---

POPULARITY

From the Washington Redskins yearbook of 1977:

Redskins Set National TV Mark

The Washington Redskins winning tradition has not gone unnoticed over the past six seasons. As a matter of fact, the Redskins are perhaps the top drawing card on television coast to coast.

Since the "winning" started in 1971, the Redskins have played before over one billion people nationwide. This past season [1976], seven of the 14 Redskins games were broadcast coast to coast, with over 172 million viewers watching the action. . . .

The totals for the past six seasons show that Washington has been on national television 33 times with over 781 million viewers tuning in, plus seven playoff games with an additional 285 million viewers, for a total of 40 appearances before 1.07 billion persons.

---

who had an identical record, but got the nod because they had a better record within their division.

Injuries had hampered the Skins that year. Fullback Riggins, perennial Pro Bowler Chris Hanburger, and key defensive back Pat Fischer were relegated to injured-reserve status. Charley Taylor, now 35, was used infrequently and announced his retirement.

Mark Moseley again led the league in field goals, kicking 21 of them, and was 19 of 19 on conversions. Eddie Brown stood out again as a kick returner: 852 yards on kickoff returns, averaging 25 yards on each, and 57 punt returns for 452 yards. Mike Thomas again led the team in rushing, with 806 yards, and tight end Jean Fugett proved to be the most productive receiver, with 36 receptions for 631 yards and five touchdowns. Kilmer completed 99 of 201 passes for 1,187 yards and eight touchdowns, while Theismann had 84 of 182 caught for 1,097 yards and seven touchdowns.

After all the statistics were in and the '77 season was merely a matter of record, the Redskins suddenly surged back into the news. In early 1978, George Allen made his last big splash in Washington newspapers. As columnist Dave Brady deftly put it: "George Allen requested a visa to visit Los Angeles and was deported by Edward Bennett Williams in a coup d'état that left Washington in a swirl."

Carroll Rosenbloom, now owner of the Rams, wanted to talk to Allen about the head-coaching job out there, where he once had toiled and been fired twice by previous owner Dan Reeves. Allen, according to league custom, asked permission of his employer to talk with the Rams. Williams more than obliged, clearing Allen's way to take the job if offered by firing him.

There were a lot of words back and forth between Allen and Williams, a variety of opinions spouted by local sportswriters and media sports specialists, and a plethora of arguments among Redskins fans. But the bottom line was, George Allen was no longer Washington's head coach. In the Redskins' saga, the Allen era—controversial, exciting, frustrating, and above all, memorable—had come to an end.

SOME AFTERTHOUGHTS ON ALLEN

Edward Bennett Williams: "I gave George an unlimited expense account and he exceeded it in his first month with us."

Billy Kilmer: "George divides the world into two kinds of people—winners and quitters. He says the only losers are guys who quit. And all you have to do to win is keep putting out. . . . Some talent plus hard work equals winning."

Joe Theismann: "I don't *necessarily* play football for George Allen. I also play for my family and myself. I respect him as a great football coach and I've enjoyed playing for him—when I've had a chance to play. I don't like the fact that he favors veteran players."

Chris Hanburger: "He IS different. . . . I've never met anyone in my life who is so determined to win. As you know, people who are 'different' irritate other people. I also think you'll have to agree that most people are negative-minded, and George is a natural for these people to dislike. He's a winner, and winners antagonize negative-minded people. . . . His system is the best, his practice program is the best, his training camp is the best. . . . George is the best-organized coach I've ever been around."

A *Washington Post* editorial: "His single-minded insistence on unstinting, unquestioning reinforcement from everybody—fans, football writers, and owners alike—also prompted him to petty, self-pitying outbursts when things went wrong, as witness his embittered parting shots (he called club president Williams 'devious . . . deceitful . . . a Jekyll and Hyde). And that is why, while applauding his accomplishments and wishing him well, we look upon his parting with emotions that are mixed."

Fullback John Riggins (44), vaulting over a fallen Bear, joined the Redskins in 1976 after five fine years with the New York Jets. Riggins became the running game for Washington over the next ten years and proved to be an outstanding postseason player as well. (Washington Redskins)

THE OVER-THE-HILL GANG

Clinging to his philosophy that "The future is now," George Allen, upon becoming Washington's head coach, began wheeling and dealing in the NFL trading pits with the zest of a commodities broker. He wanted veterans, and that's what he got, 20 of them for the 1971 season.

Because, by professional football standards, most were a tad on the old side, they were quickly nicknamed the Over-the-Hill Gang. They included, in no particular order:

Boyd Dowler, age 34, a flanker. He had played for 11 years in Green Bay, most of them under Vince Lombardi.

Jack Pardee, age 35, a linebacker. He had been around since 1957, playing for the Los Angeles Rams. Allen, who had coached him there, considered him the brains of the defense.

Billy Kilmer, age 31, quarterback. He had played for the San Francisco 49ers after being drafted in 1961, then went to the New Orleans Saints in the expansion draft of 1967 and had played well on awful teams.

Richie Petitbon, age 33, a defensive back. He had played under Allen in Chicago for 10 years, including the team that won the NFL title of 1963 with strong defense. Petitbon also played for Allen for two years in Los Angeles.

The Over-the-Hill-Gang poses with their mentor, the man who acquired them all for Washington, general manager and head coach George Allen. They are, kneeling: Bob Grant (51), Sam Wyche (18), Tommy Mason (20), Boyd Dowler (86), Jack Pardee (32), Jeff Jordan (30), Speedy Duncan (45), Billy Kilmer (17); standing: Jimmie Jones (83), Mike Taylor (78), Verlon Biggs (89), John Wilbur (60), Diron Talbert (72), Coach Allen, Maxie Baughan (50), Myron Pottios (68), Ron McDole (79), Richie Pettibon (21). Missing from the picture are George Burman, Mike Hull, and Clifton McNeil. (Washington Redskins)

The fans welcomed the new and weathered faces that George Allen collected from around the league. (Washington Redskins)

Diron Talbert, age 27, a defensive tackle. He was a mere child on this team, having only four years of experience in the NFL. He had, however, played under Allen in Los Angeles. Just to prove he could play old like the rest of the team, he

continued to play for Washington for 10 years.

Myron Pottios, age 31, a linebacker. He had made two stops before settling in Washington—five years with the Pittsburgh Steelers and five with the Rams. He was yet another Allen pet, and a veteran of three Pro Bowls.

Verlon Biggs, age 28, a defensive end. He had six years with the New York Jets and a Super Bowl (III) under his belt, as well as three AFL All-Star invitations, before joining the Skins.

Sam Wyche, 26, quarterback. Allen acquired him, it was said, so he could bring the average age of his three quarterbacks down to about 33. Wyche had played for the Cincinnati Bengals as a backup for three years.

Clifton McNeil, 31, a wide receiver. He had been catching passes in the NFL since 1963 for the Cleveland Browns, San Francisco 49ers, and New York Giants. He had been invited to one Pro Bowl and, as a Brown, played in the NFL title game of 1964.

Ron McDole, 31, a defensive end. Another three-team player before joining the Skins, he came up with the St. Louis Cardinals in 1961 and then played for the Houston Oilers and the Buffalo Bills in the AFL. He spent eight seasons with Washington, making him a true antiquarian when he retired.

Speedy Duncan, 28, a defensive back and kick-return specialist. He signed with the San Diego Chargers in 1964, set a bevy of AFL kick-return records, and was a highly regarded defender in the San Diego secondary.

Tommy Mason, 32, a running back. He played six years with the Minnesota Vikings, beginning in 1961, before playing for Allen in Los Angeles and being named All Pro in 1963.

Bob Grant, 25, a linebacker. Some of his teammates looked on him as a son. He had, however, three years of experience with the Baltimore Colts, and, to keep everyone happy, tried to act old.

Mike Hull, 26, a fullback. He was another player too young to be considered over-the-hill, but Allen acquired him anyway from the Chicago Bears, where he had played occasionally since 1968.

John Wilbur, 28, a guard. He had played four years with the hated Cowboys, which normally would have precluded him from coming to Allen's Washington, but the coach had heard Wilbur was very unhappy down in Dallas, so that made it okay.

Jimmie Jones, 25, a defensive end. He was the least experienced of the newcomers, with only two years with the New York Jets before Allen bargained for him.

Jeff Jordan, 26, a running back. He came along with all the old-timers from the Rams. Having played only one year of pro ball there, the inexperienced Jordan was probably slipped into the deal by the Los Angeles front office as a practical joke on Allen.

George Burman, 28, a center. He started with the Chicago Bears in 1964, then moved to Los Angeles in 1967, having played for Allen on both teams.

Mike Taylor, 26, an offensive tackle. He had been drafted by the Pittsburgh Steelers in 1968, played two years, and then was bartered to the New Orleans Saints before Allen acquired him.

Maxie Baughan, 33, a linebacker. He had been around the league since being drafted in 1960 by the Philadelphia Eagles, who traded him to the Rams in 1966. He went to seven Pro Bowls before coming to Washington.

14

Pardee to Gibbs and Super Bowls XVII and XVIII

The modern Redskins were in reality a two-generation team, the first centered on the quarterbacking of Joe Theismann and the running of powerful John Riggins and the second the Jay Schroeder/Doug Williams-guided teams of the later 1980s. The offensive line and the defense, both of which developed into units that were among the best in the entire NFL, bridged the two offenses.

The new look got its start in 1978 under a new head coach, the 16th since the franchise moved to Washington in 1937. To replace George Allen, Washington hired a familiar face, Jack Pardee, one of the Over-the-Hill Gang who had performed nobly for the Skins and Allen earlier in the decade. The

former linebacker had ended his 15-year NFL career after the Redskins' Super Bowl season of 1972, then had signed on with the Skins as an assistant coach.

Pardee had gained head-coaching credentials first with the World Football League franchise in Washington. In 1975, he had moved on to take the head-coaching job with the Chicago Bears.

There were a number of striking similarities between Pardee and his former coach, George Allen. Pardee had illustrated a talent for turning a loser into a winner. At Chicago, he had turned a team that was 4–10–0 his first season there into a playoff-berthed 9–5–0 in 1977. Pardee was also a defensive specialist, and he liked seasoned veterans out on his field of play. And in a scenario similar to the one experienced by Allen in Washington earlier in '78, when Pardee requested permission to talk to the Redskins about the vacant head-coaching job, the Bears fired him.

The veterans on defense who Pardee had

Jack Pardee took the Redskins reins from George Allen in 1978. In three years as head coach, he had an .500 percentage, winning 24 and losing 24. (Washington Redskins)

inherited from Allen were indeed seasoned, to such a degree that their presence prompted one Washington wag to suggest that Redskin Park had more the flavor of an American Legion meeting hall than a football facility. There was 38-year-old defensive end Ron McDole and 34-year-old defensive tackle Diron Talbert. The linebacking corps included Chris Hanburger, 37; Mike Curtis, 35; and Harold McLinton, 31. Defensive backs Kenny Houston and Jake Scott were both 33. To add to that distinguished but graying group, Pardee went to the Cincinnati Bengals to acquire 36-year-old defensive end Coy Bacon and 30-year-old cornerback Lemar Parrish.

Not all oldsters on the Redskins decided to stay with the new sideline management, however. A slew of retirements were announced, among them such longtime Washington mainstays as wide receiver Charley Taylor, who left with the record of having caught more passes than anyone else in the history of the NFL (a record since broken by Charlie Joiner of the Oilers/Bengals/ Chargers), center Len Hauss, tight end Jerry Smith, and defensive backs Pat Fischer and Brig Owens.

Where Pardee noticeably differed from Allen, however, was in his choice of quarterbacks. He sent 28-year-old Joe Theismann out onto the field to start the '78 season, and relegated 38-year-old Billy Kilmer to the bench. He also geared his running game around the ferocity of fullback John Riggins.

It worked—at least through the first six games of the season. The Skins systematically disposed of the Patriots, Eagles, Cardinals, Jets, Cowboys, and Lions. As well-known sportwriter Dan Jenkins observed in an article for *Sports Illustrated,* "The Washington Redskins have not had a 6–0 record since Sammy Baugh and Andy Farkas put on Sitting Bull headdresses and leaped up in the air

Joe Theismann throws a pass in a 1978 game against the Giants. Theismann came to Washington in 1974 but did not nail down the starting quarterback job until '78. He helped beat New York in this game, 16–13. (Washington Redskins)

for a publicity photo in front of our nation's Capitol, Cordell Hull, and several Japanese envoys—which is to say the pre-John Wayne days." It was true: No Redskins team had won that many games to start a season since Ray Flaherty had coached and Baugh passed the Redskins to seven straight victories to start the 1940 football season.

What was especially pleasing in 1978 was the fact that Washington was ensconced at the top of the NFL East, two full games ahead of the arch-rival Dallas Cowboys— who the season before had crushed the Redskins in both their encounters, compiled a record of 12–2–0, and went on to win Super Bowl XII.

The Skins, however, came tumbling back to earth with a jolt. Two losses in a row to the Eagles and the Giants, along with two Dallas wins, and the lead in the NFL East was suddenly being shared. Two wins and two more losses left the Redskins with a record of 8–4–0 when they went to Dallas for a Thanksgiving Day meeting with the Cowboys, who sported an identical record. At day's end, however, the only thing the Redskins had to give thanks for was that they still had their scalps after being massacred by the Cowboys, 37–10.

All chances for a wild-card bid were frittered away as Washington dropped its last three games of the year, to the Dolphins, Falcons, and Bears. The team's final record of 8–8–0 was only good enough for third place in the NFL East, behind the Cowboys (12–4–0) and the Eagles (9–7–0).

Joe Theismann had fully secured his status as starting quarterback by the end of the season, completing 187 of 390 passes for 2,593 yards, 13 touchdowns, and a quarterback rank of eighth in the NFC. John Riggins became the third rusher in Redskins lore to churn out more than 1,000 yards in a season, joining Larry Brown and Mike Thomas on that roster, with 1,014 yards gained on average rushes of 4.1 yards.

The Redskins, still feeling "The Future Is Now" philosophy of George Allen, did not have a draft choice in the first three rounds of the 1979 draft, but in the fourth round they snared a winner in tight end Don Warren from San Diego State. They also added three outstanding young linebackers: Neal Olkewicz from Maryland, Monte Coleman out of Central Arkansas, and Rich Milot from Penn State. The rebuilding of the defense was well under way.

It was the defense, in fact, that carried the

Benny Malone (23) takes the handoff from Joe Theismann (7) and behind the blocking of John Riggins (44), heads into the line of the Atlanta Falcons. (Washington Redskins)

Redskins through most of the first half of the '79 regular season. A squeaker of a loss to Houston, 29–27, opened the season, but the Redskins rebounded with six victories in their next seven games, including a shutout of the Giants and three games in which they allowed their opponents only seven points apiece. At midseason, they were 6–2–0, a game behind the 7–1–0 Cowboys and tied with the 6–2–0 Eagles.

A surprise loss to the New Orleans Saints was followed by a not-so-surprising loss to the dynastic Pittsburgh Steelers, who were led by such stars as Terry Bradshaw, Franco Harris, Lynn Swann, John Stallworth, Mean Joe Greene, L.C. Greenwood, Mike Webster, Jack Ham, Jack Lambert, and Mel Blount, to name but a few. The loss to the Steelers was not merely a defeat but a devastation, 38–7.

After that, however, Theismann and Riggins got the Skins' offensive attack into gear. They won four of the next five games, scoring 30 points against the Cardinals, 34 to defeat the division-leading Cowboys, 38 against Green Bay, and 28 to top the Bengals. The one Sunday their offense failed to produce they lost to the Giants, 14–6.

The last game of the season brought Washington to Texas Stadium, an environment that had never been conducive to the Redskins' good fortune. They were, however, a team with their playoff destiny, as they say, in their own hands. With a record of 10–5–0, the Redskins were in a three-way tie for first place in the NFC East with the Cowboys and the Eagles.

All they had to do was win on that bitingly cold December Sunday in ever-hostile Texas.

Two of the stalwart members of the Redskins secondary at the turn of the 1980s, Lemar Parrish (24) and Mark Murphy (29). Murphy played for Washington from 1977 through 1984, and Parrish from 1978 to 1981. (Washington Redskins)

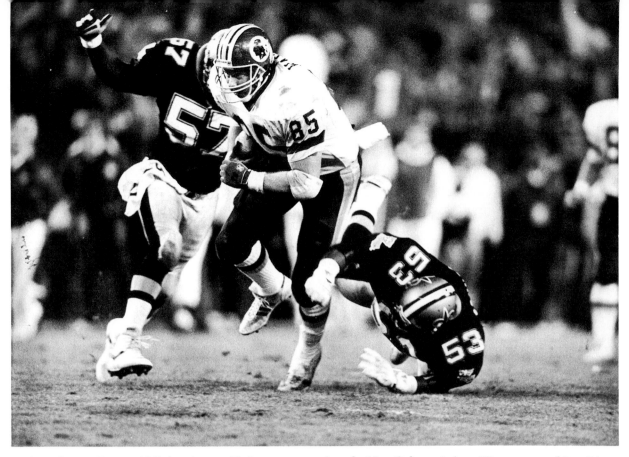

Tight end Don Warren (85) breaks a tackle in a game against the New Orleans Saints. Warren, out of San Diego State, joined the Skins in 1979 and has held the starting job through the 1989 season. (Washington Redskins)

And it certainly looked like they would. On the second play after the opening kick-off, running back Ron Springs, subbing for the injured Tony Dorsett, fumbled the ball over to the Redskins on the Dallas 34. Joe Theismann passed the Skins to the Cowboy three-yard line but was sacked on third down and goal. Mark Moseley trotted out for the field goal try, to the accompaniment of a thunderous round of booing. Cowboy fans never forget an insult, especially when it is dealt by a rival they considered as loathsome as the Redskins. The insult had been dealt a few weeks earlier in the season when the two teams met at RFK Stadium. With Washington ahead by 11 points, the game wrapped up, and only seconds remaining, Mark Moseley was sent out to further gouge the defeat into Dallas hearts by kicking a field goal. "A *flagrant* insult" was how Dallas quarterback Roger Staubach referred to it after the game.

The angry roar of the crowd, however, did not dismay Moseley and, just as he had at the end of the teams' earlier encounter, he booted it through to give the Skins a 3–0 lead.

Later in the first quarter, Dallas again tried to force the game on the Redskins. This time Robert Newhouse fumbled the ball to Washington deep in Dallas territory. This time when the Redskins were crowding the goal line, Theismann eschewed the pass and bootlegged it around end for a touchdown.

Theismann increased the lead to an intimidating 17–0 in the second quarter when he connected on a 55-yard touchdown pass to running back Benny Malone. And fans back in Washington began adjusting their schedules to accommodate the upcoming playoffs.

Roger Staubach, still smarting from Redskin flagrancy, had other ideas, however, and he led his Cowboys on a 70-yard gallop for one touchdown and then 85 yards on another drive that he capped with a TD toss to Preston Pearson. At halftime the score was Washington 17, Dallas 14.

The Cowboys corraled the lead in the third quarter when Newhouse redeemed himself with a touchdown run. As the game went into the fourth quarter, with the Redskins trailing, 21–17, an announcement over the public-address system in Texas Stadium stunned the Skins and their fans. The announcer said simply: "A final just in—the Chicago Bears 42, the St. Louis Cardinals 6."

The significance of it was the stunner. In the NFL scheme of things, for admittance to the 1979 playoffs this last day of the regular season, the Redskins, if they beat Dallas, would automatically go as the divisional champs. However, if the Redskins lost, they would still go as a wild card—*unless* the Bears, who would have an identical record, won by at least 33 points. The wild-card bid would be decided on the point differential between wins and losses during the entire season. The Skins' chances had seemed solid, because the Bears had scored a total of 33 points in only one of their 15 games that season. But somehow they had beaten the Cardinals by 36 points. Now the Redskins' only hope was to win the game which they were losing as they went into the last period of play.

On that note began one of the most hectic and exciting quarters of football in Redskins annals. Washington, behind the passing of Theismann, moved the ball into field goal range, and the booed Moseley booted his second of the day from the 14-yard line, but Washington still was a point behind.

Linebacker Monte Coleman (51) rambles with an interception against the Dallas Cowboys. The outside linebacker joined the Redskins in 1979 and remained a sustaining force in the Washington defense over the next decade. (Washington Redskins)

Then Staubach hurled a pass into the hands of Washington free safety Mark Murphy. The team steadily moved the ball until John Riggins lugged it in for the score, and suddenly the Redskins had the playoff berth back in their hands, leading 27–21.

The defense held the Cowboys and forced them to punt. Then, to the ecstasy of Redskins fans everywhere, John Riggins, on a simple draw play up the middle, broke free, headed for the sidelines and rambled 66 yards for another touchdown. It was Washington 31, Dallas 21. Moseley added a field goal and the lead was increased to 13 points.

Time was running down quickly now, but there was some cause for concern when Washington running back Clarence Harmon fumbled the ball into the arms of Dallas All-Pro tackle Randy White. Staubach, bent upon revenge, opened up, as he did so well in the waning moments of a game, and passed the Cowboys down the field, ending the drive with a 26-yarder for a touchdown to Ron Springs. The score was now 34–28.

Most spectators in Texas Stadium were looking for an onside kick, but Tom Landry left the Cowboys' fortunes in the hands of the defense. And they held, forcing Washington to punt. Dallas got the ball back on its own 25-yard line with 1:46 left in the game. Within the next minute of play, Staubach completed four consecutive passes, and Dallas was on the Redskin eight-yard line. Seconds later, eluding a horrendous Washington blitz, Staubach dropped the ball into the hands of Tony Hill at the sideline in the end zone. The extra point was good, and the Cowboys won the game 35–34. And with that last Staubach effort went the hopes of Washington for an extended 1979 season.

After the game, Roger Staubach said, "Moseley's field goal [in their first encounter during the 1979 regular season] worked for us psychologically. We were committed. I was truly committed. It carried us through."

A disillusioned and disenchanted Jack Pardee shook his head and said, "One little point takes us from division champs to the outhouse."

It was a doleful way to end an otherwise exciting and entertaining season.

The record of 10–6–0 was two games better than Pardee's first year at the helm. The Associated Press thought enough of it to name him NFL Coach of the Year, and UPI honored him as NFC Coach of the Year. The season earned Pro Bowl invitations for Mark Moseley, who kicked the most field goals of 1979 in the NFL (25) and was perfect on 39 conversion attempts, and defensive backs Ken Houston and Lemar Parrish.

Joe Theismann had produced his best season yet, completing 233 of 395 passes for 2,797 yards and 20 touchdowns, the most productive year a Redskin quarterback had turned in since Sonny Jurgensen's league-leading season of 1969. His ranking was second in the NFC to the magnificent Staubach of the Cowboys.

John Riggins rushed for 1,153 yards, a 4.4 yard-per-carry average. Wide receiver Danny Buggs caught the most passes, 46, for the most yards, 631.

Mark Moseley, disliked in Dallas but loved in Washington, assumed the title of the Redskins' all-time leading scorer, having now posted a total of 546 points in six seasons with the team, topping the 540 points scored by Charley Taylor in his illustrious career with Washington. It was the third time in four years that Moseley had led the NFL in total number of field goals, and he was the only extra-point kicker to convert 100% (39 of 39).

And so the 1970s came to a close, the team's first winning decade since the '40s. During those 10 years, Washington won 64% of its games, compiling a regular-season record of 91–52–1. It had gone to

Washington's Joe Theismann (7) lets loose with a pass in a 1980 game against the Chicago Bears. Trying to keep Bear defender Jim Osborne (68) away from Theismann is tackle Terry Hermeling (75). (Chicago Bears)

the playoffs five times and the Super Bowl once. The nine consecutive years during which the Redskins had finished .500 or better was third best in NFL history at the time, topped only by the Oakland Raiders (15 winning seasons) and the Cowboys (14).

With the advent of the 1980s, the Redskins found themselves with a first-round draft choice for the first time since 1968. They used it propitiously, drafting wide receiver Art Monk from Syracuse, who was quickly absorbed into the starting lineup. The Skins scouting system also found a free-agent center in Jeff Bostic of Clemson after the Eagles released him.

On the losing side, however, a big gap in the offensive attack was left when John Riggins, after a salary dispute, decided to sit out the season. He was replaced at fullback by Wilbur Jackson, but Riggins would be sorely missed.

Nothing seemed to go right for the Redskins at the start of the 1980 season. They lost four of their first five games, and the single win was a squeaker, 23–21 over the Giants. It was a major letdown after the previous season, when they were only a few seconds and one point away from a division title.

Things did not get a lot better as the year droned on. There were a pair of wins over the Cardinals and Saints, followed by five straight losses, three of them quite decisive: 39–14 to Minnesota, 35–21 to the Bears, and 24–0 at the hands of the Eagles. Three wins to round out the season, two of them impressive—40–17 over San Diego and 31–7 over the Cardinals—brought the Redskins only to a season's-end record of 6–10–0. It was their first losing season since 1970, and it was not well received. Before the postseason was even over, in which the Redskins were obviously not involved, head coach Jack Pardee was released.

There were a few bright spots in the otherwise dismal football year of 1979. Art Monk made first-round draft choices look like solid football logic; he was named to the NFL All-Rookie team and led the Redskins in receptions (58) and pass-reception yardage (797).

Throwing most often to Monk, Clarence Harmon, Don Warren, and Rickey Thompson, Joe Theismann turned in his most productive year yet as a Redskins quarterback. Theismann completed 262 of 454 passes (58%) for 2,962 yards and 17 touchdowns.

The Skins secondary also shone, turning in more pass interceptions than any defensive backfield in the league, a total of 34, which tied the club record set in 1964. They also held their opposition to an average of only 135.7 yards passing a game. Cornerback Lemar Parrish led the squad with seven interceptions, while cornerback Joe Lavender and safety Mark Murphy contributed six each.

Rookie Mike Nelms also proved to be a fine punt- and kickoff-return specialist, gaining 487 and 810 yards in those respective categories, which earned him a place in the Pro Bowl. The only other Redskin invited to that postseason classic was Lemar Parrish.

Overall, it was a most inauspicious way to being the 1980s. But all that was to change, as the Redskins were about to launch a campaign to become *the* team of the decade, in the dynastic tradition of the Packers of the 1960s and the Steelers of the '70s.

Christening the launch was the hiring of Joe Gibbs as head coach. Formerly the offensive coordinator of the pass-oriented San Diego Chargers, Gibbs was told to bring that offensive philosophy in his satchel when he enplaned on the West Coast to relocate in the nation's capital, where defense had reigned since George Allen had arrived via a similar route in 1971. To keynote Gibbs's

Dexter Manley (72), battling with New York Giant tackle Brad Benson, joined the Redskins in 1981 and was a mainstay in the defensive line for most of the decade. Manley holds the team record for most career sacks. (Fred Roe)

credentials in that area, the Chargers' quarterback, Dan Fouts, said on learning of Gibbs's departure, "I've learned there are two things you can't keep in this life: a secret—and a good football coach. I was sorry to see Joe go."

Gibbs proved quickly he had a trained eye for talent. In the first round of the draft he selected offensive tackle Mark May from Pittsburgh. Then he traded his second-round pick to the Baltimore Colts for experienced running back Joe Washington. As the draft wore on, he studded the Redskins roster with then-center Russ Grimm, also of Pitt, in the third round; a defensive end named Dexter Manley from Oklahoma State in the fifth round; guard Darryl Grant of Rice, who would be turned into a defensive tackle before the season was over; and tight end Clint Didier out of Portland State.

Gibbs also found a free agent from Louisville who he thought at first was a defensive lineman. When he learned that Joe Jacoby was an offensive lineman, he almost cut him from the roster. Needless to say, he changed his mind after watching Jacoby block. And finally, after ending his holdout, John Riggins returned to the Redskins backfield.

The transition to a wide-open but complex offensive attack was not immediately successful—to say the least. The Redskins were not only defeated in their first five games of the 1981 season, they were virtually walked all over:

Cowboys	26	Redskins	10
Giants	17	Redskins	7
Cardinals	40	Redskins	30
Eagles	36	Redskins	13
49ers	30	Redskins	17

With Washington in the cellar of the NFC East and off to the team's worst start since

224

1965 (the only time in history a Redskins squad lost more than its first five games in a row was the disastrous year of 1961, when the team dropped its first nine), coach Gibbs's job seemed a bit insecure.

The Redskins' first victory, against the Bears, was quickly countered with a loss to the Miami Dolphins. A come-from-behind win on a Theismann scramble enabled the Skins to eke out a 24–22 win and to post a 2–6–0 record at midseason.

The dark days were over, however; the losing was at an end. Everything began to mesh. The first team to experience it was the St. Louis Cardinals. The Cardinals came to RFK Stadium for a 42–21 drubbing behind

Middle linebacker Neal Olkewicz (52), attacking a Cleveland Brown running back, earned his way into the starting lineup in his rookie year, 1979. Signed as a free agent from the University of Maryland, he would anchor the Washington defense through the 1980s. (Washington Redskins)

the passing of Theismann and the running of Riggins, who rushed for three touchdowns that November afternoon. Next were the Lions and the Giants.

The four-game winning streak was derailed by losses to the Cowboys and Buffalo Bills, but the Skins rebounded to win their last three games of the year. They had reversed a 2–6 first-half record with a 6–2 second half. But the 8–8–0 record for the year was only good enough for fourth place in the five-team NFC East.

The strong second half of the season and the clear evidence of a potentially explosive offense, however, dominated the headlines despite the team's fourth-place finish. Coach Gibbs, whose job security at midseason seemed about as solid as that of a banana republic dictator, was going to get another chance next year.

The expanded passing attack that Gibbs incorporated into Washington's game plan enabled Joe Theismann to set a club record by completing 293 passes, a mark that still stands today, eclipsing the 288 completions by Sonny Jurgensen in 1967. The 3,568 yards he gained on those passes was second in club annals to the 3,747 Jurgensen had gained in setting the record earlier.

Joe Washington obviously fit into the new offensive scheme. He led the club in rushing with 916 yards, a 4.4-yard average, and also caught the most passes, 70, the most since the days of Charley Taylor in the mid-1960s. John Riggins added another 714 yards rushing and tied for the league lead with 13 rushing touchdowns.

Mike Nelms topped the entire NFL with a 30-yard average on kickoff returns. Art Monk gained the most yards on pass receptions, 894.

After the old labor agreement between the team owners and the players' union ended in July 1982, talk of a players' strike clouded the NFL's impending season. Still, the play-

Applying the choke hold is Washington tight end Bob Raba (86) in a 1981 preseason game against the Kansas City Chiefs, while the football stands poised and waiting. The Skins went on to post an 8–8–0 record in Coach Joe Gibbs's first season in Washington. (Washington Redskins)

ers showed up for training camps and the season moved ahead, despite the overcast skies.

There were more than clouds over the Redskins during the preseason; they were virtually enshrouded in gloom during the four-game overture. The team, so highly heralded after its resurgence during the second half of the 1981 season, lost all four, the first time that had happened since 1963 (and that 1963 team had gone on to post a regular-season record of 3–11–0).

Redskins fans, however, were delighted to find that things were not as bad as they seemed. In the opener at Veterans Stadium in Philadelphia, an explosive match that ended in overtime, the Skins posted their first win of 1982. It was a seesaw game all the way. With just a little more than a minute to play Eagles quarterback Ron Jaworski hit All-Pro wide receiver Harold Carmichael for a touchdown and Philadelphia gained a 34–31 lead. An undaunted Theismann, however, came right back and moved the Skins into Philadelphia territory. Then, with only one second remaining on the

clock, Mark Moseley came out and kicked a 48-yard field goal to tie the game. It took just less than five minutes of overtime for Washington to maneuver into Moseley's range again. This time he booted a 26-yarder, and the Redskins won, 37–34.

The next week the Redskins went down to Tampa Bay and easily dominated the Buccaneers, 21–13. Washington was alone in first place in the NFC East with a 2–0–0 record.

And then the season ended, or at least appeared to end, as the players announced they were going on strike. Fans found other things to keep them occupied on Sunday afternoons and Monday nights and the autumn moved into winter. The strike lasted seven weeks before the players finally capitulated.

The season resumed on Sunday, November 21, with a rescheduling that called for seven more games, plus a special playoff arrangement that would involve the top eight teams from each conference.

The Redskins took the field against the Giants and devoured them, then beat the

Eagles before succumbing to the Cowboys at RFK Stadium. But that proved to be the only setback of the year for Washington. With the offense functioning in perfect sync and a defense that allowed only 31 points in the last four games of the '82 season, Washington was invincible. Its 8–1–0 record was equaled only by the Los Angeles Raiders of the AFC West. And so the Redskins were back in postseason play for the first time since 1976.

Besides a volatile offensive unit and a niggardly defense, the Redskins were aided considerably by the foot of Mark Moseley, who kicked an NFL record 20 consecutive field goals in a single season and a total of 23 straight including the last three from 1981, another NFL standard at the time. As a result, he earned the honor of being named the NFL's Most Valuable Player.

Because the Redskins had the best record in the NFC, Washington fans were treated to the home-field advantage throughout the playoffs, meaning three games if the Skins continued their winning ways.

The first matchup was with the Detroit Lions, who managed to make the playoffs even though their record was a scant 4–5–0. It was, as many assumed it might be, a blowout, ignited in the first quarter by cornerback Jeris White, who picked off a Detroit pass and returned it 77 yards for a touchdown. A Moseley field goal later in the first period and then two touchdown tosses by Theismann to Alvin Garrett, playing for the injured Art Monk, in the second quarter gave Washington a 24–0 halftime lead. Theismann teamed with Garrett again in the third quarter for another touchdown. An inconsequential touchdown was ceded to the Lions a little later, but they were never in the game, and the final score was Washington 31, Detroit 7.

It had truly been Joe Theismann's day— 14 of 19 for 210 yards. And it was Alvin Garrett's as well, as he snared three touchdown passes and three other passes for 110 yards in all. John Riggins picked up 119 yards rushing.

A week later, it was another NFL Central

In the locker room with Coach Joe Gibbs. (Washington Redskins)

team that traveled to Washington to meet the Redskins. This time it was the divisional runner-up Minnesota Vikings, who had won five of their nine regular-season games and then defeated the Atlanta Falcons in the first round of the revamped playoffs for 1982.

It was much the same scenario as the week before, with the same stars shining. Washington got off to a 7–0 lead in the first quarter when Theismann threw a three-yarder to tight end Don Warren in the end zone. Following that, with Riggins tearing the Minnesota defense to shreds as he ground out yard after yard, the Skins marched to the Viking two, where Riggins then banged in for another touchdown.

Minnesota came back with a touchdown in the second period, but Washington responded with one of its own when Theismann threw 18 yards to Alvin Garrett. The score was 21–7 at the half. And it never changed. With great ball control, featuring the bruising running of Riggins, and a defense that totally shut down the Vikings, the last two quarters were scoreless.

At the final gun, John Riggins stood at midfield and bowed to the thunderous ovation of the hometown fans. He had just set a Washington playoff record and his all-time career best, gaining 185 yards rushing, with an average gain of five yards per carry. In the locker room afterwards, Coach Joe Gibbs shook his head and told the press, "Two weeks ago he [Riggins] came to me and said he was excited about the playoffs. 'Just give me the ball,' he said. I did, and he was stupendous . . . remarkable . . . phenomenal."

Theismann's stats were not shabby either—17 of 23 for 213 yards. And the mighty Redskins defense gave up only 79 yards rushing to the battered Vikes.

It set the stage for the game all Washington wanted. The Cowboys were coming to town, the only team of 1982 to have dealt

the Skins a setback. They had easily defeated Tampa Bay and Green Bay in the first two rounds of the playoffs. On the line now was the NFC title and a trip to Super Bowl XVII.

It was perhaps one of the most raucous crowds ever to fill RFK Stadium on January 22, 1983, more than 55,000 strong, and it was truly a revenge-ridden Redskins team that took the field that wintry Sunday afternoon.

Dallas won the coin toss and chose to receive. Then, behind the passing of Danny White and the running of Tony Dorsett, the Cowboys drove 75 yards. At the Washington 20, they were stopped, however, and had to settle for a field goal from Rafael Septien.

The Redskins replied in kind, mounting their own march. It was essentially the powerful plunges of John Riggins through the holes opened by Washington's superb front line, who had now come to be known as the "Hogs." After moving 65 yards to the Dallas 19-yard line, Theismann took over and tossed a 19-yard touchdown pass to wide receiver Charlie Brown.

In the second period, Dallas's Rod Hill fumbled a punt over to the Skins at the Cowboys' 11-yard line. A few plays later Riggins burst in for the score. Washington's defense was steadfast throughout the quarter—brutal, in fact. Danny White could bear witness to that. Near the end of the second period he was put out of commission by a freight train known as Dexter Manley and went to the sidelines with a concussion. At the half the Redskins had a 14–3 lead.

White's replacement, Gary Hogeboom, got the Cowboys back in the game in the third quarter with a touchdown pass to perennial All-Pro Drew Pearson. But whatever hopes Cowboys fans had of a comeback were punctured on the ensuing kickoff when Mike Nelms broke it for 76 yards to the Dallas 20-yard line. Five plays later the Redskins were at the Dallas four and all they

On the sidelines, the always cheerful cheerleaders of the Washington Redskins. (Washington Redskins)

had to do was hand the ball to Riggins and the margin was soon back to 11 points.

Hogeboom, however, countered that with an 84-yard drive that culminated in a 23-yard touchdown pass to Butch Johnson. Going into the final period of play, it was Washington 21, Dallas 17.

The Washington defense then took control in the final period to insure a victory. First, Redskins linebacker Mel Kaufman snatched a Hogeboom pass, setting up a Moseley field goal of 29 yards. Not long thereafter, Dexter Manley swatted another

Hogeboom pass into the hands of defensive tackle Darryl Grant, who lumbered 10 yards with it into the end zone. And that was it for the day's scoring. The final: Washington 31, Dallas 17. Revenge was wreaked by the rushing of Riggins, the dominance of the Hogs in front of him, the clutch passing of Theismann, and the devastating defense of the Skins.

But more importantly, Washington was going to its second Super Bowl, Super Bowl XVII, a treat Redskins fans had not savored since 1972, 10 years earlier.

TRIVIA

As the decade of the 1980s opened, the Redskins public relations office offered some statistics for the numbers-oriented fan.

Since the Redskins were founded in Boston in 1932, the team had produced in its 48 years in the NFL an overall regular-season record of 295–283–26.

Since the Redskins had moved to Washington in 1937, their posted record was 271–255–21.

Since the Redskins began playing in RFK Stadium in 1961, their record was 80–54–3.

Since 1972, the Redskins had won 77% of their games, with a 47–13–1 record.

In the then 10-year history of Monday Night Football, the Redskins had an overall record of 12–4–0, and had won all eight of their home Monday night games.

Super Bowl XVII

It may have been the shortest regular season in NFL history, but it was also the first time a conference champion had to win three playoff games to get to the league championship match. But the Redskins had done it, bringing with them a composite record of 10–1–0 to face the Miami Dolphins. Coached by Don Shula, who was no stranger to Super Bowls, having taken his Dolphins to three of them in the 1970s, Miami had rung up a 7–2–0 record before disposing of New England, San Diego, and the New York Jets in the playoffs.

All the big names from the earlier Dolphin championship teams were gone—Csonka, Griese, Kiick, Warfield, Twilley, Buoniconti, and the like. Now the team was in the hands of quarterback David Woodley, and its running game depended on the output of Andra Franklin and Tony Nathan. Its defense, which had earned the nickname "Killer Bees," was considered the best in the AFC in 1982.

The Hogs and the Killer Bees—a confrontation conceived in hell and taking place in the trenches at the Rose Bowl January 30, 1983! That is the way the matchup was hyped the week before the game (because of the strike-prolonged season and playoff schedule, only one week, instead of the normal two, separated the conference championship games from the Super Bowl).

The Redskins' game plan was a direct one. On offense, it was to establish the running game, principally behind the bulldozing power of John Riggins, and to complement it with quick, short passes from Theismann. On defense, the plan was to stop the running game and force Woodley, not considered one of the major throwing threats in the league, to pass more than he normally would.

It backfired, at least early in the first quarter. On a second-and-six situation from his own 24-yard line, Woodley dropped back, pump-faked, and then rifled the ball toward the sideline, where wide receiver Jimmy Cefalo grabbed it and outraced all

Washington defenders for a 76-yard touchdown.

The Redskins moved the ball on the ground during the first period, but they could not manage to score or even get into field position for the deadly toe of MVP Mark Moseley.

The Redskins got a break in the early part of the second quarter when defensive end Dexter Manley broke through to sack Woodley, causing a fumble that was recovered by Dave Butz on the Miami 46-yard line. The Skins reached the 14 before they were stopped, and had to settle for a Moseley field goal.

On Miami's next possession, however, Woodley moved all the way to the Washington three-yard line. There the Washington defense held and escaped with nothing more than a Uwe von Schamann field goal. Then the Hogs began to swat the Killer Bees out of the way as if they were mere annoyances, something they would continue to do the rest of the afternoon. As a result, Theismann was able to move the Redskins downfield, climaxing the drive with a four-yard touchdown pass to Alvin Garrett, and the score was tied at 10 apiece.

Unfortunately, moments later, Washington was once again behind in the game.

Front Row (left to right): DE Tony McGee, LB Quentin Lowry, KR Mike Nelms, P Jeff Hayes, RB Joe Washington, K Mark Moseley, RB Clarence Harmon, RB Otis Wonsley, WR Charlie Brown, and DT Darryl Grant. Second Row: Assistant trainer Keoki Kamau, LB Mel Kaufman, DE Dexter Manley, LB Monte Coleman, TE Rick Walker, CB LeCharls McDaniel, QB Joe Theismann, CB Joe Lavender, CB Jeris White, FS Mark Murphy, LB Rich Milot, T George Starke and trainer Bubba Tyer. Third Row: Equipment manager Jay Brunetti, assistant strength coach Jim Speros, T Donald Laster, LB Peter Cronan, LB Neal Olkewicz, FS Greg Williams, FS Curtis Jordan, C Jeff Bostic, WR Alvin Garrett, WR Virgil Seay, QB Tom Owen, RB John Riggins, assistant trainer Joe Kuczo. Fourth Row: Assistant equipment manager Stretch Williams, DT Perry Brooks, LB Larry Kubin, LB Stuart Anderson, TE Don Warren, TE Clint Didier, WR Art Monk, SS Tony Peters, CB Vernon Dean, TE Rich Caster, and QB Bob Holly. Fifth Row: DE Mat Mendenhall, T Joe Jacoby, G Russ Grimm, G Fred Dean, T Garry Puetz, DT Pat Ogrin, RB Nick Giaquinto, DE Todd Liebenstein, T Mark May, and DT Dave Butz. Back Row: Special Teams Coach Wayne Sevier, Defensive Coordinator Richie Petitbon, Receivers Coach Charley Taylor, Defensive Line Coach LaVern ''Torgy'' Torgeson, Linebackers Coach Larry Peccatiello, Head Coach Joe Gibbs, Offensive Line Coach Joe Bugel, Assistant Head Coach Dan Henning, Tight Ends Coach/Offensive Scouting Warren Simmons, Running Backs Coach Don Breaux, Administrative Assistant and Defensive Scouting Bill Hickman, and Strength Coach Dan Riley.

Miami's Fulton Walker took the kickoff at the two-yard line and streaked 98 yards for a touchdown, which still stands as the longest kickoff return in Super Bowl history. That was it for the first half, and Miami took a 17–10 lead into the locker room.

On paper it appeared the Redskins should have been the team with the winning margin at half, having soundly outgained the Dolphins, having earned more first downs, and having controlled the ball for most of the first 30 minutes of play. Joe Gibbs told the team during intermission that, if it played the same way in Act 2 *and* did not allow any big plays or costly turnovers, it would take home the Vince Lombardi Trophy.

The Redskins took to heart Gibbs's words and continued to dominate the game on offense and defense in the third quarter, but they still had difficulty scoring. All they could muster was a 20-yard field goal from Moseley, set up after Alvin Garrett had raced 44 yards on a reverse. The defense, however, completely stifled the Dolphins, allowing no points and almost no net yardage.

Miami might have added a score in the period had it not been for a fine defensive effort by Joe Theismann. Theismann? Indeed. Late in the period, deep in his own territory, Theismann threw over the middle and Dolphin defensive tackle Kim Bokamper slapped the ball up in the air. Bokamper moved under the pigskin, arms ready to cradle it, but just as he was about to grab it Theismann lunged and batted it away from him, turning a sure interception into a mere incomplete pass.

In the fourth period, the Redskins finally found the key to the Miami end zone. They entered it first when, on a fourth and one from the Dolphin 43-yard line, Gibbs decided to go for the first down. The Killer Bees swarmed in the trenches, expecting either a Riggins plunge or a Theismann sneak. Instead Theismann handed off to Riggins, who headed around left end and—after confronting only cornerback Dan McNeal, whom he virtually ran over—charged down the sidelines and in for a touchdown. It gave Washington its first lead of the day, 20–17.

The Redskins defense remained unyielding throughout the last period of play, and the offense continued to surge. Another drive, with Riggins carrying the ball most of the time, moved Washington down to the Miami six-yard line. Theismann then sealed the victory by connecting with Charlie Brown in the end zone.

The final score was Washington 27, Miami 17, but it hardly told the story of the way in which the Redskins had thoroughly dominated the game on offense and defense. The statistics, of course, revealed that, and it was quite apparent to the more than 103,000 who filled the Rose Bowl that day and the many millions more who watched it on television.

It was Washington's first Super Bowl triumph, and the franchise's first NFL title since Sammy Baugh led the Skins over the Chicago Bears back in 1942.

John Riggins, who had gained 166 yards, a Super Bowl record at the time, was a unanimous choice as the game's MVP. His total of 38 carries remains today the Super Bowl standard. Riggins also became the first player in NFL history to gain 100 or more yards in four consecutive postseason games.

The Skins offense gained more than twice the yardage of the Dolphins and chalked up 15 more first downs. There was little question at day's end that the Hogs had neutralized the sting of the Killer Bees, and that the Washington defense had destroyed both the Dolphins' running and passing games.

Joe Gibbs, whose job appeared in jeopardy a season and a half earlier, was now looking forward to a Franklin Delano Roosevelt-type tenure in Washington.

SUPER BOWL XVII

Site: Rose Bowl, Pasadena, CA
Date: January 30, 1983
Weather: 61 degrees, sunny

Attendance: 103,667
Gross receipts: $19,997,330.86
Player shares: $36,000 winner, $18,000 loser

LINEUPS

Washington Redskins	Offense	Miami Dolphins
Alvin Garrett	WR	Duriel Harris
Joe Jacoby	LT	Jon Geisler
Russ Grimm	LG	Bob Kuechenberg
Jeff Bostic	C	Dwight Stephenson
Fred Dean	RG	Jeff Toews
George Starke	RT	Eric Laasko
Don Warren	TE	Bruce Hardy
Charlie Brown	WR	Jimmy Cefalo
Joe Theismann	QB	David Woodley
Rick Walker	RB	Andra Franklin
John Riggins	FB	Tony Nathan
Mark Moseley	K	Uwe von Schamann

	Defense	
Mat Mendenhall	LE	Doug Betters
Dave Butz	LT NT	Bob Baumhower
Darryl Grant	RT RE	Kim Bokamper
Dexter Manley	RE OLB	Bob Brudzinski
Mel Kaufman	LB ILB	A.J. Duhe
Neal Olkewicz	MLB ILB	Earnie Rohne
Rich Milot	LB OLB	Larry Gordon
Jeris White	CB	Gerald Small
Vernon Dean	CB	Don McNeal
Tony Peters	S	Glenn Blackwood
Mark Murphy	S	Lyle Blackwood
Jeff Hayes	P	Tom Orosz

	Coaches	
Joe Gibbs		Don Shula

SCORING

	1st Qtr	2nd Qtr	3rd Qtr	4th Qtr	Final Score
Redskins	0	10	3	14	27
Dolphins	7	10	0	0	17

NOTES AND QUOTES FROM SUPER BOWL XVII

John Madden: "Too bad I didn't bet the ranch on my Friday prediction that the Washington Redskins would win Super Bowl XVII. . . . Riggins plain wore the Miami defense out. After a while, tackling him just wrecks a defense. He gets stronger, you get bruised. With Riggins, it's a lot like boxing. Body punches. He beats on them and beats on them, and suddenly they fall down."

Dave Butz: "I've been in the NFL for 10 years and today is the epitome of everything I've ever wanted. . . . Being Number 1, you can't get any higher. Any feeling any higher and you'd be in heaven."

Mike Downey (*Knight-Ridder Newspapers*): "It must be hard to sound tough when your football team has a cuddly nickname. Washington fans say stuff like: 'Redskins will scalp you.' Miami fans probably are stuck making threats like: 'Beware Redskins, Dolphins will push you with their noses.' "

Mickey Richards (devout fan known as Chief Redskin, dressed for the game in Indian warpaint, headdress, beads and bracelets): "I want people to know I'm a *fan*. I've been waiting 10 years for this day. I'm going to enjoy every minute of it."

Leigh Montville (*Boston Globe*): "The drunk walked next to me, going down the steps of the Rose Bowl in the final two minutes. He was wearing a full Indian headdress (ed. note: he was not Chief Redskin).

'Killer bees?' he asked.

'Killer bees?' he asked again.

'Killer wimps!' he answered as loud as he could."

Joe Gibbs: "I feel like all the people who accomplished what they want to do. I am thrilled, elated, proud and I feel good for all the people who have been pulling for the Redskins."

Jack Gibbs, Joe's father, in the Redskins locker room after the game: "That's my boy."

THE PRESIDENT HERE

As tradition now has it, the President of the United States treats the Super Bowl with the same regard as a coronation or the death of a head of state. And when its outcome has been determined, he is on the telephone to the victors. President Ronald Reagan was no exception.

When he finally got through to coach Joe Gibbs in the victorious Redskins locker room after Super Bowl XVII, he told him: "Last week I was thinking of asking John Riggins to change the spelling of his name, add an 'e' and an 'a' to it. Now I'm thinking of asking him if he'd mind if I changed the spelling of my name to put an 'i' and another 'g' in it."

After hearing that, Riggins said: "Ron is the President, but I'm the King." After a pause: "At least for tonight." After another pause: "Aw, I was just joking."

JOE GIBBS

Joe Gibbs likes strike-stressed seasons. That is not to say he likes the idea of his players, or any NFL players for that matter, going out on strike. But every time they do, he wins a Super Bowl for Washington.

In the strike-shortened season of 1982, only his second as head coach, he brought the Redskins through it with eight wins in nine games and then added three decisive victories in the playoffs before knocking off the Miami Dolphins, 27–17, in Super Bowl XVII.

With his regular squad flanking a replacement team in the discombobulated season of 1987, Gibbs guided the strikers and the scabs to a divisional title with a record of 11–4–0 (on egame was lost to the strike), through the playoffs, and into Super Bowl XX. There his marauding Redskins decimated the Denver Broncos, 42–10.

Needless to say, those two striking seasons have been the highlights of Joe Gibbs's career as head coach in Washington. Overall, however, Gibbs has, since taking over the team in 1981, become the winningest coach in Washington Redskins history. By the end of the 1989 season, his teams had won 94 games against 45 losses, breaking the mark George Allen set when his teams won 67, lost 30, and tied one game in the 1970s. His record in the playoffs stands at 11 victories and just three defeats.

Gibbs was born in Mocksville, North Carolina, on November 25, 1940, but the family moved to California a few years later. He attended Cerritos Junior College before transferring to San Diego State, where he was a rather diversified player,

moving from tight end to linebacker to guard. He began his coaching career at San Diego State in 1964, as assistant to Don Coryell.

In 1967, he was tabbed for the job of offensive-line coach at Florida State under Bill Peterson, and the teams compiled a record of 15–4–2 in the two years he was there. He went to work for John McKay at Southern Cal in 1969 as an assistant and stayed at USC for another two years, the teams winning 15 of their 20 games while he was there. After that, it was on to Arkansas to work under Frank Broyles, another two-year stint, during which the Razorbacks posted a record of 14–8–1.

In 1973, Gibbs moved to the pros. It was his former coach and mentor, Don Coryell, who made the transition possible. Coryell, now head coach of the St. Louis Cardinals, hired him to handle the offensive backfield. From that year through 1977, the Cards were 42–27–1 and took two NFC titles. In 1979, Coryell moved to San Diego to direct the Chargers, and he brought Gibbs with him. Both years that Gibbs worked with Coryell in San Diego, the Chargers triumphed in the AFC West.

After Washington had lived through more than a decade of defense-oriented football under George Allen and Jack Pardee, the front office decided it was time for somebody more concerned with honing an offensive attack. After all, the Redskins had Joe Theismann and John Riggins in the backfield and the Hogs up front. Gibbs had never held a head-coaching position before, but he was highly regarded as an offensive innovator who had tutored the pass-prolific Dan Fouts out in San Diego. The Redskins

New Washington Redskins head coach Joe Gibbs meets the press in 1981 after being hired to replace Jack Pardee. Gibbs has since gone on to win more games than any coach in Redskins history. (Washington Redskins)

brass decided to take a chance and hired him to direct Washington's destiny in the 1981 season.

After Gibbs's team lost its first five games that year, one Washington positive thinker observed, "Well, don't forget, Tom Landry lost his first five *seasons* down in Dallas and Clint Murchison didn't fire him; hell, he gave him a 10-year contract." Well, Jack Kent Cooke did not fire Gibbs either, and it proved to be just as sagacious a decision as the one made down in Texas in 1965.

After that awful start, Gibbs rallied the Redskins and the team became one of the true powerhouses of the decade. In his sophomore and junior years as chief of the Redskins, he took the Skins to back-to-back Super Bowls. In so doing, he was also named Coach of the Year by the Associated Press both years, the first time that had happened since the legendary Vince Lombardi of the Green Bay Packers was so honored in 1961 and 1962.

Under the offense-minded Gibbs, the Redskins set a National Football League

On the sideline in 1987, Joe Gibbs has a few words for his quarterback Jay Schroeder. Gibbs guided the Redskins to an 11–4–0 season that year, a division title, and an NFL championship in Super Bowl XXII. (Washington Redskins)

record for points scored in a season (541 in 1983). His philosophy: "I make up my game plan to try to confuse the opponent's defense. If you can take away what their defense has worked on, what they learned about you from studying films of your games, you can confuse them. It's kind of like a chess match."

As writer Gary Pomerantz of *The Wash-ington Post* put it, "Gibbs is a man of perception and a coach of deception." A Redskins official said, "If coaching was simply a mechanical chore, then you might see a computer terminal donning the headsets on Sunday. But it's not; on those days, the computers are silent. They don't have gut feelings. Joe Gibbs does."

COACH GIBBS BY THE NUMBERS

Year	Regular Season	Playoffs	Standing
1981	8–8–0	—	4th, NFC East
1982	8–1–0	4–0	Super Bowl champion
1983	14–2–0	2–1	NFC champion
1984	11–5–0	0–1	Division champion
1985	10–6–0	—	2nd, NFC East
1986	12–4–0	2–1	NFC runner-up
1987	11–4–0	3–0	Super Bowl champion
1988	7–9–0	—	4th, NFC East
1989	10–6–0	—	3rd, NFL East

The Super Bowl championship rings for the '82 Redskins were not even cast before innuendos in the press and among the media implied that perhaps Washington only won it because of a strike-shortened, playoff-convoluted season. After all, before the season, the team was not even considered a contender. The season itself then proved to be an anomaly. One local newspaper, while still in the wake of the championship celebration, made a point of reminding everyone that no Super Bowl champ in the previous three years had made a return visit to the season-ending classic.

At Redskin Park the negativism was ignored, and preparation for the 1983 season got under way. Once again Joe Gibbs and his scouting system drafted wisely and well. In the first round they selected cornerback Darrell Green from Texas A&I, and follow-

ing him were defensive end Charles Mann of Nevada at Reno and running back Kelvin Bryant out of North Carolina.

The preseason was a little better than the year before, with Washington defeating Cincinnati and Buffalo but falling to Atlanta and Super Bowl foe Miami. But the regular season did not begin on the note that coach Gibbs would have liked to have heard. The Cowboys, pegged to be the biggest threat in the NFL East, came to town to open the football year and set the Super Bowl champs down, 31–30.

Even in defeat, the Redskins illustrated clearly that they could indeed score points. At that particular time, however, no one knew that Washington was on its way to setting an NFL record for the most points scored in a single season.

After that initial setback, Gibbs got his

Linebacker Rich Milot puts a shoulder to the legs of a St. Louis running back in a 1983 game in which the Skins trounced the Cardinals 45–7. Milot signed with the Redskins in 1979 and stayed through the 1987 season. (Washington Redskins)

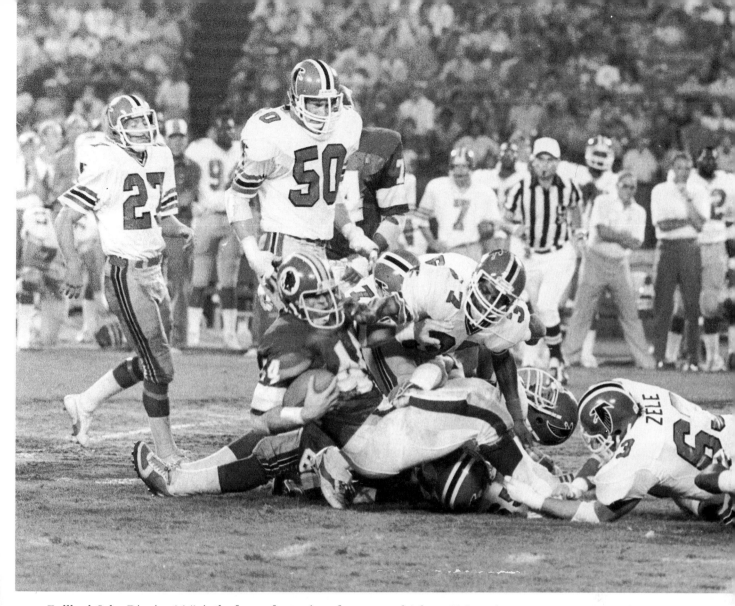

Fullback John Riggins (44) is the focus of attention of a swarm of Atlanta Falcons in a 1983 preseason meeting. (Washington Redskins)

Hogs, his running game and passing attack, and his defense on the right track. They easily knocked off the Eagles, Kansas City, and Seattle before facing the Los Angeles Raiders, who were leading the AFC West with a 4–0–0 record and were reputed to be the best that conference had to offer in '83.

It turned out to be one of the most exciting games ever staged at RFK Stadium. Behind the passing of Jim Plunkett, the Raiders built a 35–20 lead midway through the fourth quarter. And they had done it in a spectacular fashion. Plunkett had thrown four touchdown passes, one a 99-yarder to Cliff Branch that tied the NFL record for

the longest pass play in history. Greg Pruitt ran a punt back 97 yards for a touchdown, one yard shy of the all-time NFL mark.

There were seven and a half minutes left when Joe Theismann set about reversing the momentum of the game. He threw a simple screen pass to Joe Washington, who raced 67 yards with it to the Los Angeles 21-yard line. Two plays later, Theismann pitched it to Charlie Brown in the end zone for a touchdown. An onside kick was recovered by the Redskins and Theismann moved his offense to the Raider 17, where Mark Moseley kicked a field goal to bring Washington within five points of Los Angeles. The Redskins defense also rose to the occasion and held, forcing Los Angeles to punt with just under two minutes left in the game. Theismann went into the two-minute drill and completed three straight passes to Charlie Brown that brought the Redskins down to the Raiders six-yard line. On the next play, Theismann hit Joe Washington in the end zone for the game-winning touchdown. The final score: Redskins 37, Raiders 35.

The following week the Redskins demolished the Cardinals and then went to Green Bay, where they were a heavy favorite to wreak another demolition on the mediocre Packers. But the Packers proved far from

mediocre that Sunday at Lambeau Field. They jumped out in front in the first quarter when linebacker Mike Douglass scooped up a Redskins fumble and ran it 22 yards for a touchdown. Thus began one of the wildest offensive games in NFL history.

With Lynn Dickey throwing three touchdown passes for Green Bay, Theismann tossing two, and Riggins running for another pair for the Skins, among various other methods of scoring, the score was 47–45 in favor of Washington with less than a minute remaining. But then Jan Stenerud aced a 20-yard field goal for the Pack to give them the lead. Washington came back, how-

Wide receiver Alvin Garrett (89) holds on to a Joe Theismann pass in the 1983 season opener at RFK Stadium against the Cowboys. (Washington Redskins)

ever, with Theismann's now one-minute drill bringing the Redskins to the Green Bay 20-yard line. With one second remaining, Mark Moseley put foot to ball, but to the surprise and chagrin of his legion of fans missed it. And Washington suffered its second loss of the season.

In the 48–47 loss to Green Bay, two Redskins records were set: the two-team total of 1,025 yards of offense (Redskins 552, Packers 473) and the two-team total of 771 yards passing (Redskins 368, Packers 403). In addition, of 12 possessions in the second half, the two teams scored on 10 of them.

After the pyrotechnics in Green Bay, however, there was no stopping the Washington express, which was rolling nonstop toward Tampa, Florida, where Super Bowl XVIII was scheduled to take place. Amassing large scores in every game, the Redskins handily won their last nine games, including a delightful revenge over the Cowboys in the next to last game of the year, 31–10, which also clinched the division title for Washington.

When the regular season finally ended, the Skins had a record of 14–2–0, the best in the entire NFL and the most wins in the team's history.

The total of 541 points the Redskins scored that year remains the highest ever in an NFL regular season. The team averaged nearly 34 points a game.

Mark Moseley led the league in scoring with 161 points, the most ever by a kicker in a single season. The only player to score more points in a season up to that time was Green Bay's Paul Hornung, who set the NFL mark in 1960 when he tallied 176 points (15 touchdowns, 15 field goals, 41 extra points).

John Riggins set the club record for rushing yardage with 1,347, as well as number of carries, 375. Joe Theismann again topped

3,000 yards passing, his 3,714 falling only 30 short of the club standard set by Sonny Jurgensen in 1967. His 276 completions out of 459 attempts (60%) and 29 touchdowns helped to give him a ranking of number 2 in the NFC. Charlie Brown became only the third Redskin receiver to surpass 1,000 yards gained on receptions, with 1,225 (the other two were Bobby Mitchell and Charley Taylor). And, needless to say, the Hogs clearly controlled the trenches, or "trough," as it was now being called around Washington.

With the best record in the league, the Redskins again could treat their fans to home games throughout the playoffs. Their first opponents were the Los Angeles Rams, a wild-card entry who had eliminated the other wild-card team, the Cowboys, a week earlier.

The Rams, who were 9–7–0 in the regular season, had a major weapon in running back Eric Dickerson. He had led the league in rushing with 1,808 yards on an average carry of 4.6 yards, and had picked up another 404 yards on his 51 pass receptions.

Washington's game plan was obviously geared to stopping the Los Angeles running game, which in effect meant stopping Dickerson. Joe Gibbs said he would like to get some points on the board early so that the Rams would have to resort to passing to get themselves back into the game.

Washington accomplished both its goals. Dickerson was totally stopped, gaining a paltry 16 yards all afternoon on 10 carries. And the Skins were on the scoreboard early. On their first possession, they marched and John Riggins burst in for the first touchdown of the day. The next time they got the ball Theismann threw to Art Monk for a 40-yard touchdown play. On the ensuing possession Mark Moseley kicked a 42-yard field goal. The score at the end of the first quarter: Washington 17, Los Angeles 0.

In the second period, Riggins ran in two

more for touchdowns and Monk caught a 21-yarder from Theismann for still another score. The Rams managed to post seven points when Vince Ferragamo threw a TD pass to Preston Dennard, but at the half they trailed by an insurmountable margin of 38–7.

Moseley added a pair of field goals in the third quarter. Then, in the final period, Darrell Green grabbed a Ferragamo pass that bounced off Eric Dickerson's hands and streaked 72 yards for the last touchdown of the day. The defense of the Redskins was virtually impenetrable the second half. The final score, in one of the most lopsided games in NFL postseason history: Redskins 51, Rams 7.

The victory earned the Skins the right to host the team that had edged the Rams out of the NFC West title, Bill Walsh's San Francisco 49ers. Frisco had won 10 games and lost six during the regular season, and its method of attack was considerably different than that of the Rams. Walsh liked to pass, and one of the chief reasons was that he had Joe Montana at quarterback. He also had All-Pros Dwight Clark and Freddy Solomon on the receiving end, as well as rookie Roger Craig, who had proved to be a distinct threat coming out of the backfield. Clark, however, was injured and therefore unavailable for the title game.

More than 55,000 filled RFK Stadium for the NFC championship game January 8, 1984, the Redskins' 132nd consecutive sellout there. The Redskins did not come raging out of the chute as they had the week before against the Rams, but then neither did the 49ers. Both teams fumbled the ball to the other to stop scoring drives in the first period, and as the clock ran out there were only a pair of goose eggs on the scoreboard.

In the second quarter, Washington finally made its move. Theismann passed to tight end Clint Didier for a 46-yard gain. With the ball at the San Francisco four, Riggins

got the call and blasted in for a touchdown. It and Mark Moseley's conversion were the only points of the period.

The Redskins did come on with a rage at the start of the second half, however. Defensive back Darrell Green jarred the ball loose from the 49ers' Freddy Solomon, who had caught a Montana pass deep in his own territory, and then recovered it for Washington. The Skins capitalized on it when Riggins eventually bucked in from the one-yard line. Then, on their next possession, the Redskins seemed to have iced the game when Theismann tossed a 70-yard bomb to Charlie Brown. With the help of Washington's outstanding defense, the score going into the last period of play was 21–0, Washington.

The fans were not leaving the stadium to celebrate what appeared now to be imminent victory, but they were complacent, and visions of Super Bowl XVIII were dancing in a lot of their heads. The least complacent person in RFK Stadium, however, was Joe Montana. He had been stymied and stifled through three quarters of play.

With pinpoint passing, Montana moved the ball for the 49ers, and from the Washington five hit wide receiver Mike Wilson for San Francisco's first score of the day. On the 49ers' next possession, Montana dropped back from his own 24-yard line and rifled the ball to a speeding Freddy Solomon, who took it all the way downfield for another touchdown, and suddenly the 49ers were within a touchdown of the Redskins. And Montana was not through. After the 49ers forced a Washington punt, Montana conducted another successful drive, then threw his third touchdown in seven minutes, a 12-yarder to Mike Wilson. A stunned crowd became dismally aware that the ticket to the Super Bowl they thought they had in hand had been snatched away.

Now it was Theismann's turn to go to work, however. No longer could he settle

BOBBY BEATHARD

The Washington Redskins teams that appeared in three Super Bowls and five NFL postseasons in the 1980s were built on the football acumen of general manager Bobby Beathard, who was hired by team owner Jack Kent Cooke in 1978 and departed of his own volition after the 1988 season.

He had to start virtually from scratch, inheriting George Allen's slew of ancient gridsters and no draft choices until the sixth round of the 1980 draft and the fourth round of the following year's draft.

When Beathard finally got a first-round draft pick in 1980, he selected future All-Pro and NFL record-setting wide receiver Art Monk. The following year he chose offensive tackle Mark May in the first round, then traded the Skins' first-round choice for 1982 to the Los Angeles Rams and parlayed the spoils of that into 1981 selections that included guard Russ Grimm and defensive end Dexter Manley. In later rounds, he added defensive tackle Darryl Grant and tight end Clint Didier to the Redskins' roster.

The following year came Vernon Dean, another product of the previous year's swap with the Rams. And, in 1983, he chose cornerback and punt-return specialist Darrell Green in the first round.

In 1985, Beathard scored impressively by giving up his first-round choice and gaining one of the game's finer running backs, George Rogers of the New Orleans Saints, who immediately provided back-to-back 1,000-yard rushing seasons for the Redskins. And in the late rounds he selected safety Barry Wilburn and guard Raleigh McKenzie.

When the USFL collapsed before the 1986 season, Beathard made one of the biggest killings in the NFL by picking up quarterback Doug Williams, wide receivers Gary Clark and Ricky Sanders, and running back Kelvin Bryant.

Before the 1988 season, he pulled off an unlikely coup by signing All-Pro linebacker Wilber Marshall of the Chicago Bears as a free agent.

Bobby Beathard, who never played a game of professional football, began his career in the NFL as a part-time scout for the Kansas City Chiefs in 1963. In 1972, he became director of player personnel for the Miami Dolphins. During his 25-year career in NFL front offices, he has been associated with six teams that have gone to Super Bowls: Kansas City, Super Bowl IV; Miami, Super Bowls VII and VIII; and Washington, Super Bowls XVII, XVIII, and XXII.

Bobby Beathard (Washington Redskins)

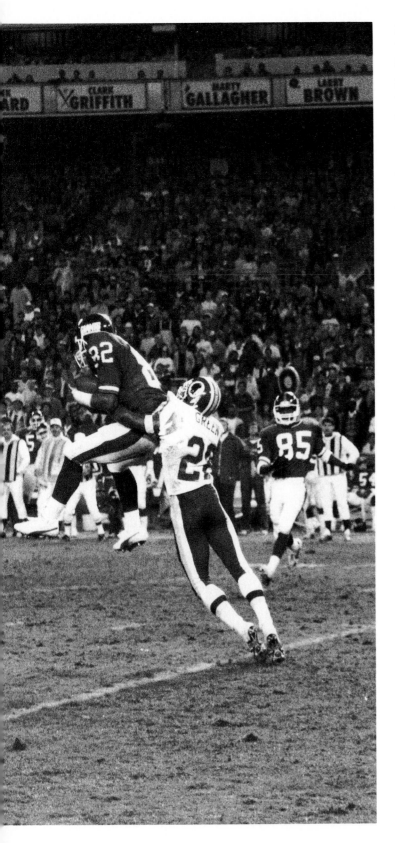

for handing the ball off in hopes of eating time off the clock. The Skins needed a score. Starting from his own 22-yard line, Theismann engineered the perfect drive, moving the ball steadily and slowly down the field. Granted, he was aided by two controversial penalties against the 49ers, a pass-interference call on a toss intended for Art Monk and a holding call against All-Pro safety Ronnie Lott. Still, Theismann used up a crucial six minutes and 12 seconds before he turned the attack over on a fourth down to the foot of Mark Moseley at the 49ers' eight-yard line.

It was a chip shot, as they say. But Moseley uncharacteristically had missed four field goal attempts earlier. The usually reliable kicker was having the worst day of his football life.

But Moseley redeemed himself, booting the ball straight through the uprights. The defense held. And the game ended with Washington on top, 24–21, and breathing a collective sigh of relief after finally thwarting one of the most exciting comebacks in NFL playoff history.

John Riggins gained more than 100 yards rushing, making it six playoff games in a row that he had broken the century mark, an NFL record. And it was the second playoff game in a row in which Charlie Brown caught passes for more than 100 yards.

So, it was on to Tampa and Super Bowl XVIII, with Joe Gibbs gleefully reminding the naysayers that a team could indeed make a return trip to the season-ending classic one January after the preceding one.

Cornerback Darrell Green (28) snares a New York Giant receiver here in a game at RFK Stadium. Green, out of Texas A & I, was a Washington first round draft choice in 1983. He was a starter from the first game of that season and has since been to three Pro Bowls. (Washington Redskins)

Super Bowl XVIII

The matchup in Tampa for the 18th Super Bowl had all the prerequisites for a wild, exciting, offensive football game. Neither Redskin nor Raider fans could forget the 37–35 thriller that Washington had won in RFK Stadium back in early October. Both teams were explosive, the Redskins having scored the most points in NFL history during their regular season and the Raiders not far behind, having scored at least 20 points in every game that year.

Under coach Tom Flores, the Raiders had produced a record of 12–4–0 and had easily triumphed in the AFC West. They had an excellent passing game anchored by the arm of Jim Plunkett, who had completed 230 of 379 passes for 2,935 yards and 20 touchdowns that year. His favorite receiver was tight end Todd Christiansen, who had pulled in 92 receptions for 1,247 yards. The Raiders also had a potential game-breaker in speedy wide receiver Cliff Branch. And, of course, they had All-Pro running back Marcus Allen, who had gained 1,014 yards rushing in '83. The defense was formidable, with linemen like Lyle Alzado and Howie Long, linebacker Ted Hendricks, and defensive back Lester Hayes.

Los Angeles had had little trouble sailing through the AFC playoffs. It whipped the once-mighty Pittsburgh Steelers, 38–10, and then squelched the Seattle Seahawks, 31–14. Marcus Allen had rushed for over 100 yards in each game, and Plunkett had passed for more than 200 in each as well.

As dominant as the Redskins had been all year, and despite the fact that they had won two more games than the Raiders, and had defeated them, the game was viewed as a toss-up by the oddsmakers. Former coach turned broadcaster John Madden was in agreement. "Last year I predicted the Redskins to upset the Dolphins. But in this game

between the Redskins and Raiders, I can't say who will win."

Well, he probably could have by halftime. The cloudy afternoon turned to pure gloom for the Redskins early in the game. Jeff Hayes was back to punt in his own end zone, but the Hogs were asleep at the trough. Derrick Jensen slithered through and slapped the ball to the turf and then fell on it for a touchdown.

The Raiders tried to be fair about the whole thing and fumbled a punt back to the Redskins, but Washington could only move to the Los Angeles 28-yard line. Mark Moseley, so good for so much of the regular season—his 33 field goals were the third most in NFL history—came on, but missed the three-pointer.

Washington went to the reliable Riggins, but the holes were not there and the Redskins were not getting anywhere. Theismann was having difficulty locating a receiver when he needed one. To make matters worse, Plunkett stung the Redskins with a toss over the middle to Cliff Branch that resulted in a 50-yard gain. Several plays later, Plunkett drilled one to Branch in the end zone, and the Raiders had a 14-point lead.

The Skins finally got a drive going midway through the second quarter, but it bogged down at the Los Angeles eight-yard line. Moseley came on and this time connected to put Washington on the scoreboard. But then the gloom got gloomier for Redskins fans. With only 12 seconds left in the half and the Skins deep in their own territory, almost everyone assumed Washington would simply run the clock out. Instead, Theismann faked a handoff and threw the ball toward the sideline to running back Joe Washington. But, Raider linebacker Jack Squirek was not fooled. He streaked in front of Washington and snatched the ball at the five-yard line, then continued on into the end zone. At the half it was 21–3, Raiders, and it had little appearance of a close game.

Washington came back in the third period with a concerted drive that ate up 70 yards and was climaxed by a one-yard plunge by Riggins into the end zone. Moseley's extra point was blocked, however. Then the Raiders countered with a 70-yard march of their own on the next possession, culminated when Marcus Allen carried it in from the five-yard line.

As the third quarter was about to close, Marcus Allen took a pitchout from Plunkett and headed around left end, saw an opening, cut back, and then broke away on a dazzling 74-yard touchdown run. It was a Super Bowl record. The score going into the fourth quarter was Los Angeles 35, Washington 9.

It was, in effect, all over at that point. A dull fourth quarter saw only one score, a 21-yard field goal for the Raiders by Chris Bahr. The final score: Raiders 38, Redskins 9, at the time the widest margin of victory in Super Bowl history.

It had been a surprise to the oddsmakers, John Madden, and especially the Redskins themselves and their loyalists. In the locker room after the game, a weary and disconsolate Joe Gibbs said: "The season is so long. You go 17, 18, 19 games without a break; it's hard on a team to go through it. We were emotionally spent. We just weren't up for it today."

The Redskins, however, had made it to back-to-back Super Bowls, joining such select company as the Green Bay Packers (I & II), Dallas Cowboys (V & VI, XII & XIII), Miami Dolphins (VII & VIII), Minnesota Vikings (VIII & IX), and Pittsburgh Steelers (IX & X, XIII & XIV).

Running back Joe Washington struggles to hold on to a Joe Theismann pass for the Redskins in a match with the Raiders in 1983. Washington played for the Skins from 1981 through 1984 and led the team in receptions in 1981, catching 70 passes that year. (Washington Redskins)

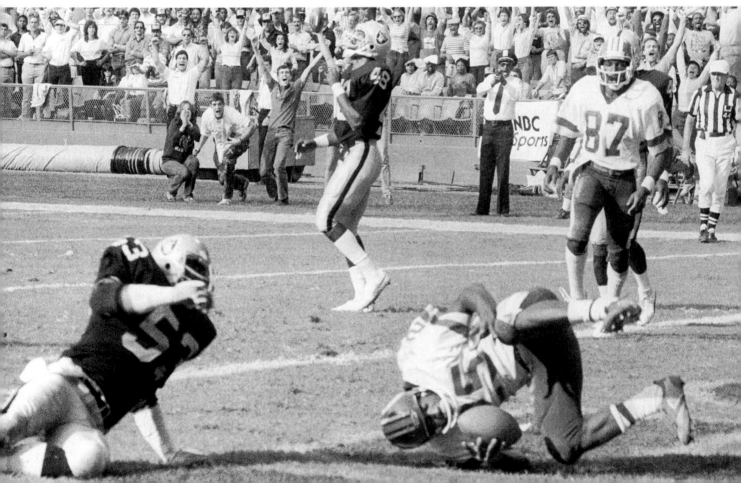

SUPER BOWL XVIII

Site: Tampa Stadium, Tampa, FL

Date: January 22, 1984

Weather: 68 degrees, cloudy

Attendance: 72,920

Gross receipts: $20,002,390.28

Player shares: $36,000 winner, $18,000 loser

LINEUPS

Redskins	Offense	Raiders
Charlie Brown	WR	Cliff Branch
Joe Jacoby	LT	Bruce Davis
Russ Grimm	LG	Charley Hannah
Jeff Bostic	C	Dave Dalby
Mark May	RG	Mickey Marvin
George Starke	RT	Henry Lawrence
Don Warren	TE	Todd Christensen
Art Monk	WR	Malcolm Barnwell
Joe Theismann	QB	Jim Plunkett
Rick Walker	RB	Marcus Allen
John Riggins	FB	Kenny King
Mark Moseley	K	Chris Bahr

Redskins	Defense		Raiders
Todd Liebenstein	LE		Howie Long
Dave Butz	LT	NT	Reggie Kinlaw
Darryl Grant	RT	RE	Lyle Alzado
Dexter Manley	RE	OLB	Ted Hendricks
Mel Kaufman	LB	ILB	Matt Millen
Neal Olkewicz	MLB	ILB	Bob Nelson
Rich Milot	LB	OLB	Rod Martin
Darrell Green	CB		Lester Hayes
Anthony Washington	CB		Mike Haynes
Ken Coffey	S		Mike Davis
Mark Murphy	S		Vann McElroy
Jeff Hayes	P		Ray Guy

	Coaches	
Joe Gibbs		Tom Flores

SCORING

	1st Qtr	2nd Qtr	3rd Qtr	4th Qtr	Final Score
Redskins	0	3	6	0	9
Raiders	7	14	14	3	38

PREDICTION

John Madden, former Raiders coach and now color commentator on CBS pro football television broadcasts, predicted that Super Bowl XVIII would be an unpredictable game.

"I compare it to Duran–Leonard [boxing bout]. Nobody knew who would win. That's what makes it such a great matchup. And there are a lot of reasons why.

"Both teams are built to play on their grass home fields, and the field at Tampa Stadium is grass.

"It'll be the Raiders defense versus the Hogs. Neither group will be intimidated.

Can you imagine Russ Grimm and John Riggins intimidated?

"Both are physical teams. There'll be no finesse out there.

"Both teams have the great running back, Marcus Allen with Los Angeles and the Redskins' Riggins. . . .

"Both teams have a great coach. Washington's Joe Gibbs is known for his offensive talents, but Tom Flores also has done an outstanding job. . . .

"It will probably come down to the number of turnovers."

Well, you can't be right all the time, John.

SHOWTIME

The Super Bowl has never been known for understatement or its lack of conspicuous consumption, pizzazz, hype, and pageantry, much less its endless parade of celebrities. As Ira Berkow wrote for *The New York Times* regarding Super Bowl XVIII: "Not since 1539, when Hernando de Soto arrived with the greatest sea armada ever assembled for the New World exploration, has Tampa Bay experienced anything like Super Bowl week.

"An estimated 80,000 people, pachyderms, and football players trooped in to participate in the numerous events of the week, many of which were centered in the small banner-strewn downtown section of this town of about 300,000.

"Frank Sinatra crooned, Jesse Jackson orated, Bob Hope joked, and belly dancers gyrated.

"Jane Fonda was here, Ted Koppel was here, but a former college lineman, Ronald Reagan was a no-show. He was receiving the 'leather-helmet' award at the National Football League alumni dinner Saturday night but called in his regrets and appreciation."

Why were they all there, or almost all? Because it was, in the vernacular of Sid Caesar, THE SHOW OF SHOWS. It lasts a week until Super Bowl Sunday finally dawns. And even then, THE SHOW still goes on: before, in, and around the game itself. This excerpt from the official program of Super Bowl XVIII gives an idea of the last act of THE SHOW—the Super Sunday crescendo.

PREGAME AND HALFTIME ENTERTAINMENT:
LOGISTICAL SPECTACULARS

Super Bowl XVIII pregame festivities will begin at Tampa Stadium 90 minutes before kickoff with highlights of the past 17 Super Bowls, which will be shown on the Diamond Vision scoreboard. . . .

One of the world's most popular recording artists, Barry Manilow, will be singing the National Anthem today. Manilow has an incredible string of 25 consecutive "Top 40" hits and 10 straight platinum albums (given for sales of one to four million). To date, he has total international sales of 50 million records. Manilow, who has won an Emmy, Grammy, and has been voted the American Music Award's Top Male Pop Vocalist, also has been selected the United Way of America's National Chairman for Youth and Voluntarism.

During the National Anthem, a color guard from MacDill Air Force Base near Tampa will be stationed on the field. As the anthem is being played, a huge (160' x 97') American flag donated by Thomas (Ski) Demski will be unfurled. The flag will stretch from the goal line to the 50-yard line.

One of the NFL's most famous figures, Bronko Nagurski, will be today's honorary coin tosser prior to kickoff. The legendary Chicago Bears fullback (who played with the Bears from 1930 to 1937 and in 1943) was elected as a charter member of the Pro Football Hall of Fame in 1963.

Walt Disney World in Orlando, Florida, promises the Super Bowl's most spectacular halftime show yet, which is titled "Super Bowl XVIII's Salute to the Superstars of the Silver Screen."

The show will feature all of the favorite Disney characters, as well as 1,200–1,400 other performers, the bulk of whom are made up of local students from the Hillsborough School District in Tampa.

Disney held auditions in October at local schools and any interested student in the district was encouraged to participate. The students who were selected began group rehearsals at 11 area high schools late in December. The individual groups rehearsed three or four times in a three-week period, and last Sunday Disney brought the groups together for a walk-through practice. On Friday, January 20, a full-scale dress rehearsal was held at Tampa's Laito High School.

Getting all the various elements and performers to the game will be a challenge for Walt Disney World. A platoon of 50–60 buses will be used to transport the performers to Tampa Stadium. The buses will arrive after kickoff in an attempt to avoid the traffic prior to the game. After the buses have arrived, all the performers will assemble outside the stadium and wait for halftime to begin. During the show, a stage crew of 200 will be on hand to help facilitate set changes.

JACK KENT COOKE

Back in 1960, when Jack Kent Cooke first bought a minority share of the Washington Redskins, George Preston Marshall was still alive and in charge, Washington was the only team in the NFL not to have a black on it, and the Redskins won only one of 12 games.

At age 18, Cooke, a native of Hamilton, Ontario, began his business career selling encyclopedias door-to-door during the Great Depression of the 1930s. From there he moved into the communications industry in Canada and became a partner in Thomson Cooke Newspapers, which eventually operated both newspapers and radio stations throughout Canada.

Sports had always been a great love in his life and he was determined to become involved. He began by buying the Toronto Maple Leaf minor league baseball team in 1951 and later an interest in the Redskins, and then became chairman of the board of California Sports, Inc., builders of the Forum arena in Los Angeles and owners of the Los Angeles Lakers of the NBA and the Los Angeles Kings of the NHL.

In 1974, Jack Kent Cooke became the majority owner of the Washington Redskins. Four years later he hired Bobby Beathard as his general manager, and a few years thereafter they both agreed that Joe Gibbs might just make the right coach for the Skins. They have since been to three Super Bowls together.

Jack Kent Cooke became a U.S. citizen in 1960. Besides the Redskins, his business interests include the Chrysler Building in New York, the *Daily News* in Los Angeles, Cooke Cable TV, and the Elemdorf Racing and Breeding Farm in Lexington, Kentucky.

Jack Kent Cooke (Washington Redskins)

JOHN KENT COOKE

John Kent Cooke has served as executive vice president of the Washington Redskins since 1981. His job, overseeing all facets of the daily operation of the franchise, covers everything from ticket sales to promotion to team logistics to relationships with the press, media, and public.

Since John Kent Cooke has been with the Redskins they have gone to three Super Bowls and won four divisional titles. The Redskins have also established one of the largest radio networks in the NFL and have developed a season-ticket waiting list of approximately 30,000.

Before joining the Skins, John Kent Cooke had served as vice president of American Cablevision Company, one of the largest privately held cable companies in the United States, and later as vice president of advertising, sales, and promotion for sports and entertainment events at the Forum arena in Inglewood, California.

Jack Kent Cooke, Jr. (Washington Redskins)

15

Between Super Bowls

"How about three Super Bowls in a row?" mused owner Jack Kent Cooke just before the start of the 1984 season. "Not even the Steelers managed that." In point of fact, only one team in history made it to three consecutive Super Bowls, the Miami Dolphins, who lost VI but won VII and VIII.

The euphoria of that thought faded quickly, however, when the Redskins were humiliated by the Dolphins in their opener at RFK Stadium, 35–17. That was followed by a 37–31 skinning at the hands of the San Francisco 49ers and their freewheeling quarterback, Joe Montana. At that point, the Skins were the only member of the five-team NFC East that had not won a game.

The Redskins rebounded after that, decisively winning their next five games in a row by a collective score of 145 to 71. The highlight was a 34–14 drubbing of the Cowboys, who were making a concerted run for the divisional title. In fact, all five teams were in the race at midseason. After the Redskins' five-game win streak ended with a loss to the Cardinals, Washington was 5–3–0 and tied with the Cowboys and Cardinals for first place, with the Giants and the Eagles a mere game behind 4–4–0.

The Skins won four of the next six games before a crucial encounter with the Cowboys down at ever-inhospitable Texas Stadium. Washington was 9–5–0, as were Dallas and the New York Giants. And the Cardinals, who were playing the Giants that same weekend, were 8–6–0.

It started off badly. The Redskins fell behind, 21–6, at the half, but, all too aware

252

John Riggins dives for a touchdown after taking a handoff from Joe Theismann (7) in 1984. It helped the Skins defeat the Giants at RFK Stadium, 30–14. Number 68 is a perennial All-Pro guard Russ Grimm. (Washington Redskins)

that any hopes they had for the playoffs hinged on the outcome of this particular game, they came back with a vengeance in the second half. With Theismann throwing and Riggins running, they turned the game into a true thriller with the perfect ending— for Washington fans, that is. It was sparked in the third period when cornerback Darrell Green picked off a Dallas pass and ran it back 32 yards for a touchdown. John Riggins was unstoppable and contributed a game total of 111 yards rushing, including the touchdown that gave the Redskins a come-from-behind victory, 30–28. It was the first time since the two teams had begun playing each other back in 1960 that the Redskins had defeated the Cowboys twice in a season.

The Cardinals beat the Giants, and now had a chance to take the divisional crown, because they were coming to Washington to meet the Redskins in the last game of the season. A victory would put them in a tie at the top with the Skins, but the title would go to St. Louis because they would have won both their games against Washington that year.

The game was even more tense than the one the week before. And it was not decided until after the two-minute warning at the end of the fourth quarter. It was then that Mark Moseley came onto the field, with the Skins losing, 27–26, to delight the hometown fans with a 37-yard field goal. The defense held, and Washington had its third straight NFC East title.

Despite the cliff-hanger of a season, it was a superb one in the statistical columns. Art

Monk set an NFL record by catching 106 passes, eclipsing the record of 101 set by Charley Hennigan of the Houston Oilers in 1964. The total of 1,372 yards he gained on those receptions was the second highest in Redskins history (Bobby Mitchell set the standard with 1,384 in 1962).

Joe Theismann had one of the best years of his career, almost as good as his record-setting season of 1981. He completed 283 of 477 passes (.593) for 3,391 yards and 24 touchdowns.

John Riggins rushed for over 1,000 yards for the fourth time in his days with the Skins. His total of 1,203 was the second highest in Washington annals, bettered only by the 1,347 he had gained the year before.

Washington was a slight favorite when it hosted the Chicago Bears, who had won the NFC Central for their first division title since 1963. Washington struck first when Mark Moseley kicked a 25-yard field goal in the first quarter. The Bears came back to tie in the second period, and then took the lead with a surprising bit of razzle-dazzle, uncharacteristic of the usual grind-it-out running game the Bears had emphasized for several decades. All-Pro running back Walter Payton took a pitchout, faked a reverse, and then instead of continuing around end, pulled up and lofted a touchdown pass to tight end Pat Dunsmore, who was standing all alone in the end zone. At the half, it was 10–3, Chicago.

The Hogs were having a tough time containing the Chicago defense. Joe Theismann spent most of the first half trying to dodge Bear rushers, and John Riggins was getting nowhere carrying the ball.

The Bears increased their lead in the third quarter when world-class speedster Willie Gault took a short sideline pass and streaked away for a 75-yard touchdown. A missed extra point left the score at 16–3. But the Redskins came back, marching to the Chicago one-yard line, where Riggins bucked in for the score.

The Bears, with their newfound passing game, again moved downfield, and two successive passes from Steve Fuller, playing for an injured Jim McMahon, to Dennis McKinnon resulted in another touchdown. Joe Theismann mounted a drive of his own and again brought the Skins to the Bear one-yard line, where again Riggins carried it in for the score. At the end of the third quarter, the score stood Chicago 23, Washington 17.

And nothing really changed in the fourth quarter. The Bears controlled the ball with their running game, and their defense was stingier than ever. The only score in the period came when Chicago punter Dave Finzer stepped out of the end zone for an intentional safety. The four-point margin eliminated Washington from postseason play, destroying all dreams of a third consecutive visit to the Super Bowl.

Joe Theismann said after the game, "The Bears defense was something else today. I'm glad to still be alive." He was, in fact, fortunate to be walking out of the playoffs under his own power. Theismann was sacked seven times. The Chicago defense also recovered two Washington fumbles and held the Skins' running attack to less than 100 yards in total.

Jack Kent Cooke decided in early 1985 that he wanted the entire ball club to himself and purchased all outstanding stock, giving him 100% ownership. He now was thinking of three Super Bowls in four years.

The Redskins, in an effort to diversify their running game and complement the power of John Riggins, traded their first-round draft choice to New Orleans for George Rogers, who had twice gained more than 1,000 yards rushing for the otherwise hapless Saints. Rogers had, in fact, gained 5,360 yards during his five years in New

Coach Joe Gibbs introduces running back George Rogers, acquired in a 1985 trade with the New Orleans Saints. Rogers would lead the team in rushing during the three years he played for Washington, including two 1,000-yard-plus seasons. (Washington Redskins)

Orleans, the third-highest total in the NFL over that span of time, behind only Walter Payton of the Bears and Tony Dorsett of the Cowboys.

Besides Rogers, the rest of the Redskins lineup looked pretty familiar in 1985. Joe Theismann and John Riggins were in the backfield. The Hogs still consisted of such talented veterans as Joe Jacoby, Mark May, Russ Grimm, R.C. Thielemann, and Jeff Bostic. Art Monk was still one of the game's most threatening receivers. Signed as a free agent to complement Monk at the other wide-receiver position was Gary Clark, a

refugee from the defunct USFL. The defense was studded with such overachievers as Dexter Manley, Charles Mann, Dave Butz, Rich Milot, Neal Olkewicz, and Darrell Green. And the team's all-time leading scorer—by far—Mark Moseley was there to apply his foot to the football.

On paper, the team looked impressive enough. On opening day, the team looked awful—even worse than it had when it opened against Miami the previous year. In 1985, the Skins began the season with demolition dealt by the Cowboys down in Texas, 44–14, the largest margin of defeat since

Psyching up before a game with the Lions in 1985. From the left, running back Otis Wonsley, wide receiver Gary Clark, quarterback Joe Theismann, running back George Rogers, and quarterback Jay Schroeder. (Washington Redskins)

Washington quarterback Joe Theismann rolls out as two voracious Chicago Bears, linebacker Otis Wilson (55) and defensive tackle Dan Hampton (99), give chase. The 1985 season proved to be Thiesmann's last in the NFL. (Chicago Bears)

they lost to the Cardinals back in 1960 by a score of 44–7.

Washington came back the next week to knock off the Houston Oilers, but then fell to the Eagles and were decimated by the Bears, 45–10, at Soldier Field in Chicago. Washington then went on to win four of their next five games before meeting up with Dallas again. This time the Redskins comported themselves better than in the opener, but still lost, 13–7.

The next game was a Monday night affair at RFK Stadium with the Giants, a team that was clearly on the rise. The New Yorkers were 7–3–0, well ahead of the 5–5–0 Skins. It turned into a game of special agony for

Washington fans in the second quarter, when Joe Theismann was sacked by All-Pro linebacker Lawrence Taylor and suffered a compound fracture of the leg, which would end his playing career. Coming on to replace him was Jay Schroeder, who had been drafted in the third round the year before out of UCLA.

It truly was a must-win situation if the Redskins were to have any chance at the postseason festivities. And it was not promising with the team in the hands of a backup quarterback who had thrown only eight passes thus far in his pro football career. His ninth was a winner, however—a 44-yarder to Art Monk and an inspiration to a team

On display, Joe Theismann's career-ending broken leg. (Washington Redskins)

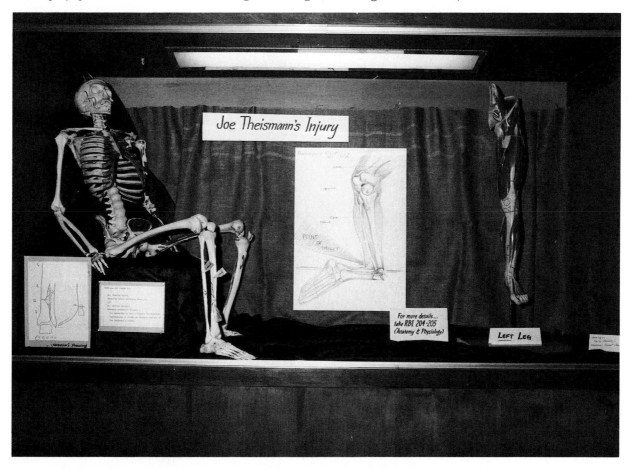

Three veteran Washington defenders converge on a Philadelphia running back, tackle Dave Butz (65), linebacker Rich Milot (57), and defensive back Vernon Dean (32). (Washington Redskins)

that had been suddenly demoralized by the horrible injury to Theismann. By evening's end, Schroeder had completed 13 of 22 passes for 221 yards, including a game-winning touchdown toss to tight end Clint Didier. The Skins triumphed 23–21 that night and remained in the running for a playoff berth.

Theismann was not the only casualty of the '85 season. John Riggins was plagued by a bad back and at 36 years old saw that his career in football was also coming to an end.

The Theismann/Riggins era was finally over. The two had fueled the Skins' offensive attack since 1978. Theismann had ably added to the great line of Washington quarterbacks, following Baugh, Jurgensen, and Kilmer into the club's record books. Riggins had gained more yards rushing than any Redskin in history. Both had led the onslaught to a pair of Super Bowls, and they had established a tradition of offensive ex-

cellence since they'd come into their own in 1978.

Their replacements, Jay Schroeder and George Rogers, did them proud, although they did not get the Skins to the playoffs, which Theismann and Riggins had done for the past three years. Behind them, Washington won four of its last five games to end the season with a 10–6–0 record. It was good enough to tie the Skins for first place in the NFC East with the Cowboys and Giants, but the tie-breaking procedure for a playoff berth excluded them. The Giants were awarded the division title, and the two NFC wild-card selections were the Cowboys and the San Francisco 49ers.

Schroeder ended the season with 112 completions for 1,458 yards and five touchdowns. In the only loss the Skins suffered with Schroeder at quarterback, against the 49ers, he set a team mark by throwing 58 passes, eight more than the record previously held by Sonny Jurgensen. His 30 completions that game were the second most in team history.

George Rogers became the fourth running back in Washington annals to rush for more than 1,000 yards, joining Larry Brown, Mike Thomas, and John Riggins. His 1,093 yards were picked up on average carries of 4.7 yards. And in the final game of the year, against the Cardinals, he became the first Washington runner to rush for more than 200 yards in a game, gaining 206 on 34 carries.

Art Monk was the second most productive receiver in the league, his 91 receptions only one short of Roger Craig of the 49ers. He picked up 1,226 yards on those catches, third best after the 1,287 by Steve Largent of the Seattle Seahawks and the 1,247 by Mike Quick of the Eagles. Gary Clark caught 72 passes for 926 yards; his five touchdowns were the most by a receiver that year. Dexter Manley tied the club record with 15 quarterback sacks (Coy Bacon had set it in 1979), and Charles Mann was only half a sack behind him with 14.5. Offensive linemen Russ Grimm and Joe Jacoby went to their third consecutive Pro Bowls and Monk to his second.

With Theismann turning his talents to broadcasting instead of quarterbacking, the Redskins needed some backup for Jay

Mark Moseley is about to add three points to the Washington scoreboard in a 1985 game against the Pittsburgh Steelers. (Washington Redskins)

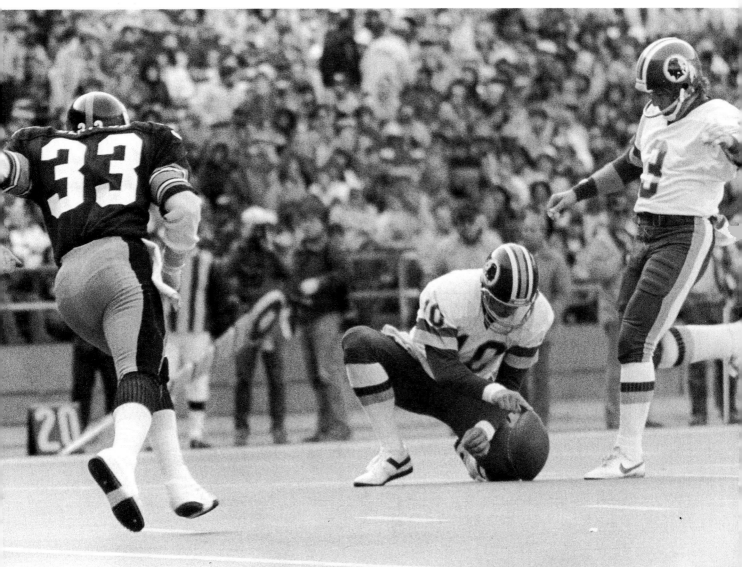

Schroeder. They acquired the rights from Tampa Bay to Doug Williams, who had quarterbacked the Buccaneers from 1978 through 1982 before defecting to the USFL, and they picked up Mark Rypien from Washington State in the sixth round of the draft.

Another player from the USFL, running back Kelvin Bryant, who had been drafted by the Redskins but chose the other league, was now returning to join George Rogers in the starting backfield for 1986.

The Redskins, after two disappointing season openers in a row, got off on the proverbial right foot in '86. They hosted the Philadelphia Eagles and destroyed them, 41–14, in a game in which Jay Schroeder passed for 289 yards and two touchdowns and George Rogers gained 104 yards rushing. A 10–6 win the following week over the Los Angeles Raiders, who had triumphed in the AFC West the previous year, and the Skins were off to their best start since 1982, the year they worked their way to Super Bowl XVII.

The following week it was the Chargers down in San Diego, with their fine passer Dan Fouts. On the strength of his arm, the Chargers marched three times for touchdowns in the first half and built a 21–10 lead. But Schroeder was not to be outdone that day. Although he only completed 16 of 36 passes, he gained 341 yards passing. Seven were hauled in by Art Monk for 174 yards and six by Gary Clark for 144 yards. Saving the best for last, Shroeder, with the Skins trailing 27–23 late in the final period, hit Clark on a 14-yard TD toss, and Washington pulled it out, 30–27.

Two more wins over Seattle and New Orleans and the 5–0–0 Redskins were sole tenants at the top of the NFC East and looking like a natural for the playoffs. The Cowboys, however, brought them back to reality the next week in Dallas, with a 30–6

drubbing that reminded everyone in Washington that the divisional race was a traditionally close one. And this was to be no exception.

After defeating the Cardinals, the Skins fell again, this time to the Giants, who were also in hot contention. It almost became a disastrous two in a row when the Vikings trundled into RFK Stadium the next week. Trailing 38–26 in the fourth quarter, Schroeder hooked up with Art Monk on a 34-yard touchdown pass, but Max Zendejas, who had taken over the kicking duties from 38-year-old Mark Moseley, missed the extra point.

Washington's defense held and the Skins took over the ball. As time was running out, Schroeder again got the Redskins going, the key play a 44-yard pass to tight end Clint Didier that left the ball on the Minnesota 2 yardline. Moments later, George Rogers banged in for the touchdown, and the score was tied. Zendejas missed the extra point again, however, and so the game went into overtime.

And again it was Schroeder. Not wanting to worry about a field goal from the erratic toe of Zendejas, he moved the Redskins downfield and capped the drive with a 38-yard touchdown pass to Gary Clark. The final score: Washington 44, Minnesota 38.

The Redskins then proceeded to win their next four in a row. They whipped Green Bay, the always-strong 49ers, the Cowboys, and the Cardinals. The Giants were surging when they came to town for the 14th game of the regular season, having won 11 games against only two losses. The Skins had an identical record.

But it truly was the year of the Giants. They would prove that beyond all reasonable doubt at the Super Bowl in Pasadena seven weeks later. One of their crucial steps in the journey to the Super Bowl was taken at RFK Stadium that December Sunday

Running back Kelvin Bryant (24) joined the Skins in 1986 after three years in the USFL. He brought with him a USFL MVP award and two USFL championship rings, as well as the hope that he would be the perfect replacement for the retired John Riggins, but injuries would plague his Redskins career. (Washington Redskins)

afternoon. With Phil Simms throwing touchdown passes to Mark Bavaro and Bobby Johnson, the Giants built a 14–7 lead at the half. Simms increased it with another score to Phil McConkey in the third period. The Redskins never got into the game, and the final score left them behind, 24–14, and in second place in the NFL East.

The Skins lost again the following week to Denver, but defeated the Eagles in the season finale. Their record of 12–4–0 was not as good as the 14–2–0 posted by the Super Bowl-bound Giants, but it was good enough to land them in the playoffs for the fourth time in the six years Joe Gibbs had been guiding their fortunes.

George Rogers posted his second 1,000-yard rushing year, a total of 1,203. Jay Schroeder wound up as the fourth-ranked

quarterback in the NFC, completing 276 of 541 passes for 4,109 yards, the latter shattering the club record of 3,747 yards passing set by Sonny Jurgensen in 1967. Gary Clark was the top Washington receiver with 74 catches for 1,265 yards and seven touchdowns. Art Monk was only a step behind with 73 for 1,068 yards and four TDs. Another team record was set with the 18 sacks collected by defensive end Dexter Manley. And seven Skins were voted onto the NFC Pro Bowl roster: Schroeder, Monk, Clark, Manley, Joe Jacoby, Russ Grimm, and Darrell Green.

The other wild-card team in the NFC that year was the Los Angeles Rams. John Robinson's Rams had been edged out of the NFC West title by a half-game by the San Francisco 49ers. They sported a record of

10–6–0, and still relied mainly on the running of Eric Dickerson, who had gained 1,821 yards rushing that year.

With a better regular-season record, the Redskins gained home-field advantage, and they entertained the hometown fans royally. Actually, it was placekicker Jess Atkinson, signed as a free agent two weeks earlier to replace the injured Max Zendejas, who was actually the focal point of the day's entertainment. Atkinson had been released by Washington in training camp earlier in the year. He had suited up for the last game of the season against the Eagles and had kicked three of three extra points, but had not been called upon to try a field goal.

That changed suddenly in the wild-card playoff game. In the first quarter, when a Washington drive stalled at the Los Angeles eight-yard line, he booted a 25-yarder to give the Skins a 3–0 lead.

Later in the same period, Jay Schroeder added some more points when he threw a 14-yard pass to Kelvin Bryant for a touchdown. Atkinson then drilled three more field goals, one in each ensuing quarter, of 20, 38, and 19 yards. A fourth-quarter touchdown by the Rams was inconsequential, and the final score was Washington 19, Los Angeles 7. Atkinson's four field goals tied the club record for the most in a playoff game (Curt Knight had kicked four against the Cowboys in the NFC title game of 1972).

The victory earned the Skins the right to visit Chicago and take on the world champion Bears, who had won the title the previous year by the largest margin (46–10) in the history of the Super Bowl.

It reminded many a senior Washington fan of those classic matchups between the two teams in the early 1940s when the Skins were quarterbacked by Sammy Baugh and the Bears by Sid Luckman.

Coached by Mike Ditka, the Bears had easily won the NFC Central Division with a record of 14–2–0, their only losses coming at the hands of the Vikings and Rams. They were a team that still depended on 32-year-old Walter Payton for much of their offensive attack. He had gained 1,333 during the regular season, the 10th time that he had gone over 1,000 yards in his 12-year pro career in Chicago. The Bears also had the best defense in the National Football League, allowing only 187 points, the lowest ever for a 16-game season. What they did not have, however, was their first-string quarterback, Jim McMahon, who was out with a shoulder injury. Coach Ditka decided to go with the diminutive Doug Flutie, who was best known for throwing a 65-yard Hail Mary pass to win the 1984 Orange Bowl for Boston College.

The Bears were still a definite favorite, despite their quarterbacking dilemma. But it was the Redskins who struck first. Jay Schroeder engineered a drive that ate up 69 yards in nine plays, 28 of which came on a touchdown toss to Art Monk. It was the only score of the first quarter.

Chicago showed its championship form in the second period. Flutie made Ditka's choice look like a wise one when he rifled the ball to speedster Willie Gault, who went 50 yards with it for a touchdown. After a Washington turnover, Kevin Butler kicked a field goal to give the Bears the lead, then added another, this one a 41-yarder, a few minutes later. Chicago had the lead, 13–7, at the half.

Something, however, happened in both locker rooms during the intermission, because when the teams came back onto the field the Bears were as stale as week-old bread and the Redskins were as fresh as a loaf just out of the oven. They regained the lead when Schroeder again connected with Monk, this one a 23-yard touchdown pass. In the fourth quarter, Washington mounted an 83-yard drive through Chicago's heralded defense, culminating in a one-yard plunge for another touchdown by George Rogers.

The rest of the period was totally controlled by Washington, and Jess Atkinson added a pair of field goals, of 35 and 25 yards, to leave the titled Bears stunned, 27–13. And so the Skins were going to the NFC championship game.

The title tilt for the 1986 season was scheduled for Giants Stadium, up in East Rutherford, New Jersey. The divisional champion Giants had annihilated the San Francisco 49ers, 49–3, the day after Wash-

ington beat the Bears. New York had defeated the Redskins in both their regular-season encounters as well, 27–20 in the Meadowlands and 24–14 down at RFK Stadium. The Giants had won their last 10 games in a row, and were looking better every game.

Coach Bill Parcells had a beautifully balanced attack. To carry the ball, he relied on a pit bull of a running back named Joe Morris, who had picked up 1,516 yards rushing during the regular season and 159 in the playoff game against the 49ers. Phil Simms was the third-rated quarterback in

Jubilant Harry Wilburn (45) celebrates one of his frequent interceptions for the Redskins. Wilburn led the NFL in interceptions with 9 in 1987, and intercepted two John Elway passes in Super Bowl XXII against the Broncos. (Washington Redskins)

OINK, OINK, THE HOGS ARE HERE

In 1982, the trenches where the Redskins' offensive line toiled became known as the trough, because that is where the hogs slopped. The hogs slopped well enough that year to be recognized as an instrumental element in the Redskins' trip to and triumph at Super Bowl XVII. These porcine creatures are aptly described in this excerpt from an article in *GameDay* magazine by sportswriter Will McDonough in 1983.

There is some beauty to the beasts who play offensive line for the Washington Redskins and proudly wear the unkempt title "Hogs."

"A Hog," says offensive coordinator Joe Bugel, who blows sweet notes when he talks about his line, "is a guy who gets down and does a dirty job without wanting to be beautiful."

Little did Bugel realize when he slapped the name on this bunch a year ago that they would become nationally famous—thanks mostly to the playoffs and Super Bowl XVII.

"In Washington, they are marketing Hog hats, Hog T-shirts, and Hog but-

tons," said right tackle George Starke, the veteran Hog. . . .

Starke, the senior member, is articulate and a man of taste.

"I've had 12 Hog designer jackets tailor-made in L.A.," he said. "I do a lot of work in L.A. during the winter [in music production] and I have some friends who designed these jackets and had them made for me."

The 12 who received the jackets are Starke; guards Russ Grimm, Fred Dean and Mark May; tackles Joe Jacoby, Don Laster and Garry Puetz; guard Ron Saul [injured reserve]; center Jeff Bostic; tight ends Don Warren and Rick Walker; and fullback John Riggins.

"We put Riggins in there because he has the personality of a Hog," Starke says, "and, besides, he hangs around with us."

"Joe Theismann? No, he's not a Hog. We'd like him to take us to dinner sometime—he owes us that. I keep on reminding him, but he hasn't done it yet.

"We go out to eat and drink together one night a week. We enjoy it. We like being with one another. . . ."

THE ORIGINAL HOGS

Jeff Bostic	Center	From Clemson	First season, 1980
Fred Dean	Guard	From Texas Southern	First season, 1972
Russ Grimm	Guard	From Pittsburgh	First season, 1981
Joe Jacoby	Tackle	From Louisville	First season, 1981
Don Laster	Tackle	From Tennessee State	First season, 1982
Mark May	Guard	From Pittsburgh	First season, 1981
Garry Puetz	Tackle	From Valparaiso	First season, 1982
John Riggins	Fullback	From Kansas	First season, 1976
Ron Saul	Guard	From Michigan State	First season, 1976
George Starke	Tackle	From Columbia	First season, 1973
Rick Walker	Tight end	From UCLA	First season, 1980
Don Warren	Tight end	From San Diego State	First season, 1979

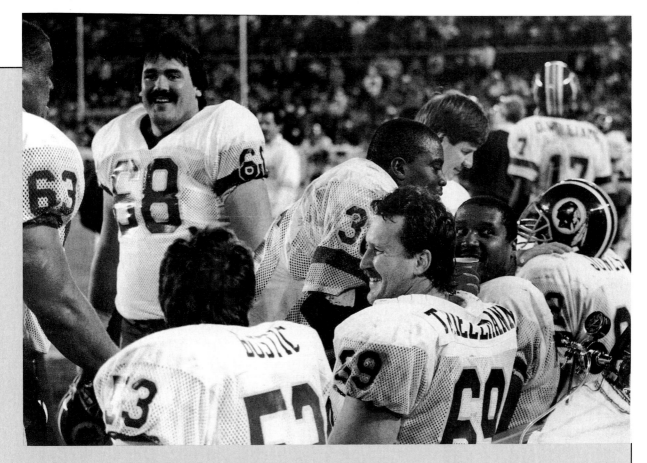

A gleeful group of Hogs slop it up on the sideline at RFK Stadium. Standing: Guard Raleigh McKenzie (63), guard Russ Grimm (68); seated: center Jeff Bostic (53), guard R. C. Thielemann (69), tackle Mark May (looking over his shoulder), and tight end Anthony Jones. (Washington Redskins)

Hog John Riggins and son. (Washington Redskins)

the NFC, having completed 259 of 468 passes for 3,487 yards and 21 touchdowns. He had an All-Pro tight end to throw to in Mark Bavaro, who led the team with 66 receptions for 1,001 yards. And the defense, which had come to be known as the "Big Blue Wrecking Crew," with linebackers like Lawrence Taylor, Harry Carson, and Carl Banks and frontmen such as Jim Burt, Leonard Marshall, and George Martin, was one of the most punishing in the entire NFL.

It was a blustery day in New Jersey when the two teams took the field to determine the NFC championship, with winds gusting over 30 miles an hour. It was such a factor that when the Giants won the coin toss they elected to go with the wind rather than receive the football.

The decision paid off. The winds hampered Jay Schroeder's passing game, and the Giants' defense shut down the Redskins' running game. While that was going on, the Giants got within range for Raul Allegre, with the wind at his back, to kick a 47-yard field goal. Later in the first quarter, Phil Simms moved the Giants downfield and then hit wide receiver Lionel Manuel on an 11-yard touchdown pass.

In the second quarter, the Redskins, now the beneficiary of the winds, tried a 51-yard field goal, but a bad snap prevented Jess Atkinson from kicking it. When the Giants took over, they marched right into the wind and down the field. From the one-yard line, Joe Morris lugged it in, and New York took a 17–0 lead into the locker room at the half.

When they came back out, the Giants played conservatively, keeping the ball on the ground and relying on their defense to stop the Skins. The defense was impregnable. The Redskin running game was totally shut down, and Jay Schroeder spent most of his time fleeing fierce blitzes and a pass rush that the Hogs could not handle. The Redskins were held scoreless in the second half, and when the stats were totaled the Redskins had gained only 40 yards rushing all day and Schroeder had completed only 20 of 50 passes and had been sacked four times.

The final score was 17–0, and the charging Giants were only one game away from the NFL championship, which they would easily win two weeks later. It was the first time the Redskins had been shut out in a postseason game since the awful 73–0 shellacking the Bears gave them back in 1940.

16

Super Bowl XXII and After

As the 1987 season approached, the talk of a players' strike was again in the air. The contract between the team owners and the NFL Players Association that had come out of the strike-shortened 1982 season had run its course, and the two factions now had to negotiate a new one. Pro football fans everywhere remembered with distaste when the players' strike lopped seven games from the regular season six years earlier, although Washington fans had the euphoric consolation of having marched through the playoffs and then winning the Super Bowl that disrupted season.

The 1987 regular season got off on schedule, however, while representatives of the owners and the union tried to bat out a contract. The Redskins had a few new faces in uniform on opening day, one of whom would play an important role in the team's

success later in the season—running back Timmy Smith, Washington's fifth-round draft choice out of Texas Tech.

Opening day at RFK Stadium was a triumphant one, but it was riddled with disasters. Jay Shroeder suffered a shoulder injury on the ninth play of the game and was replaced by Doug Williams. Then place-kicker Jess Atkinson, on his first extra-point try of the regular season, dislocated his left ankle and would not see action again that year. In addition, featured running back George Rogers and All-Pro guard Russ Grimm were sidelined with injuries. Still, the Redskins survived the day and defeated the Eagles, 34–24, helped by a pair of touchdown passes from Doug Williams to Art Monk.

The next week the lowly Atlantic Falcons, who had had losing seasons each year since

All-Pro tackle Joe Jacoby keeps a New York Jets pass rusher at bay in 1987. Jacoby signed as a free agent in 1981 and has since proven to be one of the NFL's finest offensive linemen. (Washington Redskins)

1982 and were destined to win only three games in all of 1987, hosted the Skins down at Fulton County Stadium. Ali Haji-Sheikh, a free agent who had set the NFL record for field goals in a season when he booted 35 for the Giants in 1983 but had had limited success since, was signed to replace the injured Atkinson. Atlanta seemed unimpressed by the Redskins, who had made it all the way to the NFC title game the year before, and were predicted by some to win it all in '87. And the Skins, unfortunately, took the Falcons for granted. The game went back and forth all the way. Washington had a 20–14 lead in the fourth quarter on touchdown passes from Doug Williams to Kelvin Bryant, Gary Clark, and Art Monk, but it did not last long. The Falcons sustained a drive that resulted in a four-yard touchdown run by Gerald Riggs and a conversion to give them a 21–20 victory and Washington a jolt into reality.

All of professional football received a jolt the next week when the players did indeed walk out on strike. Week three of the regular season saw all games canceled. The players put up a steadfast front, and the owners essentially ignored them and announced that the season would resume in week four with any players who chose to defy the strike plus others whom they would sign up to replace the strikers.

The Redskins fielded a brand-new team for the first replacement game, staged October 4 at RFK Stadium. Quarterbacking them was Ed Rubbert, in his first pro game after playing at Louisville. Another rookie was given the assignment of chief rusher, Lionel Vital from Nicholls State, an NCAA Class 1-AA school down in Thibodaux, Louisiana. Two more seasoned members of the offensive unit were wide receiver Anthony Allen, who'd played three years in the USFL and two with the Atlanta Falcons, and fullback Wayne Wilson, who had carried the ball for the Saints and the Vikings earlier in the decade.

The St. Louis Cardinals arrived with 10

The grand entrance, this time being made by All-Pro defensive tackle Dexter Manley in 1987. (Washington Redskins)

In the trenches. (Fred Roe)

regular players and, as a result, were a definite favorite. But with Allen gathering in three touchdown passes from Rubbert, one an 88-yard play, and another touchdown by Vital, the replacement Skins managed to triumph, 28–21.

The following week it was the replacement New York Giants, who had been massacred the week before by the replacement 49ers, 41–21. However, the world championship Giants, who were now on strike, had not fared any better, losing both games before hitting the picket line. Washington had no trouble that Sunday at the Meadowlands. Three touchdowns in the second quarter, two on short runs by Wayne Wilson and one on a 22-yard carry by Lionel Vital, were actually enough, but the novice Skins added two more in the second half, one on a 64-yard pass from Rubbert to Ted Wilson of Central Florida, and the other on a 14-yard run by Tim Jessie, a rookie from Auburn. The final score was 38–12, Washington.

The Dallas Cowboys, next on the agenda, were another heavy favorite, with veteran quarterback Danny White and a bevy of other starters snubbing the strike. But the upstarts in burgundy and gold were unimpressed. They took the lead in the first quarter on a field goal from Obed Ariri, who had had a brief kicking stint in the USFL earlier, and increased it to 10–0 in the second half when Ted Wilson took a reverse and raced around end 16 yards for a touchdown. Another Ariri field goal and the Redskins had the win, 13–7.

After three salary-less weeks of watching their replacements perform, the regulars decided the strike was not such a good idea after all and voted to return to the playing field. All but a few of the replacements went back to whatever other professions they had been practicing before their brief moments in the NFL sun.

The lost game, it was announced, would not be made up and hence the regular season would be only 15 games. The Redskins had fared well, winning all three of their replacement games, only one of three NFL teams to accomplish that. With a record of 4–1–0, they were ahead of the pack in the NFC East, with the Cowboys in second place at 3–2–0 and the Super Bowl champion Giants in a state of total collapse at 0–5–0.

When they reappeared at RFK Stadium, it did not appear that the regulars were going to be as successful as the replacements had been. With a mere 10 minutes remaining in the game against the Jets they trailed, 16–7. Jay Schroeder was back, his shoulder repaired. He finally got a drive mounted, highlighted by three passes to Kelvin Bryant, the last a two-yarder for a touchdown. Ali Haji-Sheikh's conversion brought the Skins to within two points of the Jets with about five minutes remaining. New York came back and moved the ball into field goal range, but then Dave Butz burst through and sacked New York quarterback Ken O'Brien to take them out of field goal range. After a punt, Schroeder again marched the Skins downfield, the pivotal play a 39-yard pass to wide receiver Ricky Sanders. Haji-Sheikh came on with 54 seconds left and kicked a 28-yard field goal to give Washington a 17–16 victory.

An easy win over Buffalo, 27–7, was countered by a loss up in Philadelphia to the Eagles, 31–27. The roller coaster continued the next two weeks, the Redskins triumphing over the Detroit Lions, 20–13, then losing to the Rams, 30–26. In the Detroit game, Doug Williams came off the bench to replace Schroeder, who had fallen into Coach Gibbs's disfavor. Williams threw two touchdown passes, one to Kelvin Bryant and the other to Gary Clark, to insure the win and to assure himself the starting role at quarterback the following week.

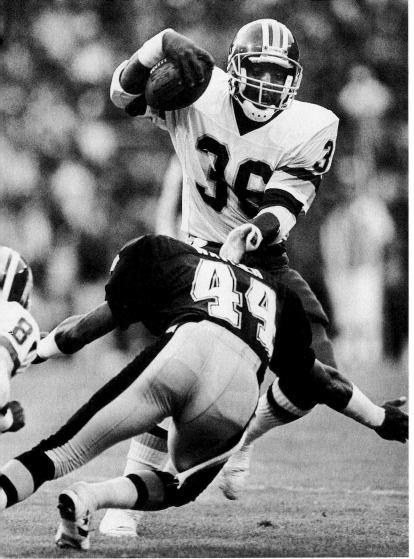

Timmy Smith picks up a few yards for the Redskins in a 1987 game at RFK Stadium. A rookie that year, Smith was picked to start in the playoffs over George Rogers and showed his appreciation by rushing for 204 yards in Super Bowl XXII. (Washington Redskins)

After the loss to the Rams, the Redskins had a record of 7–3–0. But there was little pressure from their division neighbors. The Cowboys were in second place at 5–5–0; the Eagles and Cardinals were tied for third with records of 4–6–0; and the disheveled Giants had an ignominious 3–7–0 record.

There would be no competition from any of them as the season ran through its final third. Jay Schroeder was back as starting quarterback in the confrontation with the Giants the following week, but only because Doug Williams had sprained his back in practice that week. And he managed to rouse the Redskins from a 16–0 deficit at the half to a 23–19 victory at day's end, the winning score coming on a 28-yard pass to Ricky Sanders. Behind Schroeder the following week, Washington had little trouble

with the Cardinals, thrashing them 34–17, but lost perennial All-Pro receiver Art Monk to a knee injury in the process.

In two close games, the Redskins nipped the Cowboys, 24–20, and then dropped one to the Miami Dolphins, 23–21. The last game of the season was with the Vikings up at the Metrodome in Minneapolis, and it was a repeat of the thriller the two teams staged the year before. Again Washington had to come from behind in the fourth quarter to tie the game. This time it was Doug Williams, brought in during the second half when Joe Gibbs decided to again bench Jay Schroeder. Williams found Ricky Sanders for a 46-yard touchdown pass in the third quarter, and then engineered two scoring drives in the final period, one ending with a 37-yard field goal from Ali Haji-Sheikh and the other

271

Jay Schroeder (10) hands off to Kelvin Bryant (24) behind a trio of Redskins blockers: tackle Mark May, guard R. C. Thielemann, and tight end Don Warren. Bryant led the team in rushing in 1988 with 498 yards. (Washington Redskins)

with a 51-yard touchdown pass to Sanders. The game went into overtime, just as it had the year before. And again the Redskins won the toss, received, and marched. Instead of winning it on a touchdown on their first possession this year, they did it with a Haji-Sheikh 26-yard field goal.

The Redskins' record of 11–4–0 easily took the divisional crown in a year when all four of the other NFC East teams turned in losing records. Doug Williams had earned the starting position at quarterback for the playoffs, coach Gibbs announced. Rookie running back Timmy Smith would be on the bench at the start of the playoffs, but would see a lot of action, Gibbs also said.

Once again Washington's first opponent in the playoffs was the Bears at wind-chilled Soldier Field in Chicago. The year before the Skins had upset the title-holding Bears; this year the game was rated a toss-up.

Chicago appeared to be on its way to enacting revenge for the previous year's ouster by taking a 14–0 lead in the first half. But the Redskins were far from demoralized. Williams got them moving, directing a 69-yard touchdown drive, capped when George Rogers knifed in from the three-yard line. Shortly thereafter, Williams led another march, this one climaxed by an 18-yard touchdown pass to tight end Clint Didier. At the half, the score was 14–14.

In the third quarter, Washington moved ahead in a dramatic fashion. Cornerback Darrell Green, back to return a Chicago punt, took it on his own 48-yard line, raced down the sideline, hurdled a diving Bear defender, then cut back toward the middle and took it all the way.

The 21 points that Washington logged by the end of the third quarter proved to be enough. The defense handled the rest. Key interceptions in the fourth quarter by Barry Wilburn and Dennis Woodberry and two sacks in the waning minutes by defensive end Charles Mann destroyed the Bears. All told, Bear quarterback Jim McMahon was sacked five times and intercepted three times. The final score was Washington 21, Chicago 17, and for the second consecutive year the Redskins had served as spoilers to the Bears' Super Bowl aspirations.

For the second year in a row as well, Washington would attend the NFC championship game, this one in its hometown. Facing the Skins would be the all-too-familiar Minnesota Vikings, foes in the team's last two overtime games. Minnesota had gotten into the playoffs as a wild-card team with a record of 8–7–1, but they had been less than impressive in losing three of its last four regular-season games. In the playoffs, the Vikings were decided underdogs, but decimated the rejuvenated New Orleans Saints, 44–10, and then overwhelmed the highly regarded San Francisco 49ers, 36–24.

The Vikings had shown offensive strength in their two playoff games. Wade Wilson replaced Tommy Kramer at quarterback, and with his passing and scrambling was beginning to remind Minnesotans of Fran Tarkenton, who had so entertained them with his versatility in the 1970s. Anthony Carter had developed into one of the most electrifying wide receivers in the game, and running back Darrin Nelson was a proven ground gainer.

The Washington defense, on the other hand, had been devastating through the season and the playoffs and seemed to be getting better with every game. When the Vikings came to RFK Stadium, it was the NFL's senior defensive lineman, 37-year-old Dave Butz, who rallied his fellow defenders and made the plays that stopped the otherwise surging Vikes.

Washington started the scoring in the first quarter when Doug Williams connected on a 43-yard-touchdown pass play to Kelvin Bryant. The Vikings came back to tie it at seven apiece before the half, but it was becoming clear that this game would be decided on the relative merits of the defenses of the two teams.

Washington went ahead in the third quarter when Ali Haji-Sheikh booted a 28-yard field goal. But Minnesota countered with one of its own in the fourth quarter. It was after that, that the Redskins got their first truly concerted drive of the day under way. Doug Williams, having one of his poorest days ever, had been beleaguered by the Minnesota defense, but suddenly things began to come together. He moved Washington 70 yards, culminating the drive with a seven-yard touchdown toss to Gary Clark, and the Skins were ahead, 17–10. The Vikings came right back. Wade Wilson brought them all the way to the six-yard line of the Redskins. It was fourth down, 56 seconds were remaining, and every fan in RFK Stadium was on his or her feet. Wilson dropped back and rifled the ball to running back Darrin Nelson, who was seemingly open on the goal line. But Nelson bobbled it momentarily, and then cornerback Darrell Green collided with him, sending the ball fluttering to the ground. The defense of the Redskins had prevailed.

The final score of 17–10, Washington, stood primarily because the Redskins' defenders had chased, frustrated, and feloniously assaulted the Vikings all afternoon. Wade Wilson had been sacked eight times, one short of the NFL playoff record. Two of those had been dealt by the aging Dave Butz.

The Redskins were on their way to the Super Bowl, their third appearance at that classic in the 1980s.

Super Bowl XXII

A legion of Washington fans filled every seat on flights from National and Dulles airports in late January 1988 to San Diego, site of Super Bowl XXII. Their Redskins were treating them to a third Super Bowl of the decade.

The oddsmakers, however, looked on them as three-point underdogs. The reason was a simple one, they said. Their opponent, the Denver Broncos, had John Elway at quarterback. He was considered the league's most potent weapon, commonly pulling off the big play to break open a game just when the Broncos needed it. He had three wide receivers used to streaking downfield to gather in his bombs: Vance Johnson, Ricky Nattiel, and Mark Jackson. Denver also had a fine running back in Sammy Winder, as well as All-Pros in linebacker Karl Mecklenberg and defensive end Rulon Jones. In addition, Elway had taken the same team to the Super Bowl the year before.

It was a beautiful Sunday afternoon in sunny Southern California on January 31, 1988, with a mild but cooling breeze wafting about Jack Murphy Stadium. The arena was filled to capacity, some fans sporting Indian war paint, others bright orange cowboy hats, each faction taunting the other. The pregame was over, and the players were on the field. Former Green Bay great and Hall of Famer Don Hutson handled the formalities of the honorary coin toss. Washington won and chose to receive.

With the Redskins punting after getting nowhere on their first possession, John Elway came out to take command at his own 44-yard line. He promptly demonstrated why he carried the reputation of a game-breaker. On the first play from scrimmage, he dropped back and rocketed the ball down the right sideline, where Ricky Nattiel was a step ahead of Washington cornerback Barry Wilburn. Nattiel took it in stride and streaked the rest of the way into the end zone for the first score of the day. Less than

Some pregame entertainment at Super Bowl XXII. (Washington Redskins)

Cornerback Barry Wilburn soars to intercept a John Elway pass intended for Denver wide receiver Ricky Nattiel in Super Bowl XXII. It was one of two Wilburn pulled off in that game. (Washington Redskins)

four minutes later, Elway moved the Broncos to the Redskin seven-yard line, where Rich Karlis kicked a field goal. A little later, a leg injury forced Doug Williams to leave the game; Jay Schroeder replaced him, but he could not get the Skins moving either. At the end of the first quarter, it was Denver 10, Washington 0, and it looked like the oddsmakers had been right on target.

And then there was the second quarter—the wildest 15 minutes in Super Bowl history and surely one of the most entertaining and gratifying in all of Redskins history. Williams came back to quarterback the Redskins. With a first and 10 at his own 20-yard line, Williams lofted a bomb toward the right sideline. It was snagged by Ricky Sanders, who took it all the way in for an 80-yard touchdown.

The Redskins' defense allowed the Broncos three downs and a punt. Then Williams hit tight end Don Warren for nine yards, Timmy Smith broke through the middle for 19 yards, and a few plays later Williams teamed with wide receiver Gary Clark on a 27-yard touchdown pass. The lead was now in the hands of the Skins, 14–10.

Two minutes later, Washington had the ball again. Timmy Smith took a handoff and sliced off tackle, broke to the sideline, and raced 58 yards for another touchdown.

The Washington defense allowed the Broncos another three plays and a punt. Williams then found Ricky Sanders again on the right sideline, where he was again beating the Denver defender. The result this time was a 50-yard touchdown.

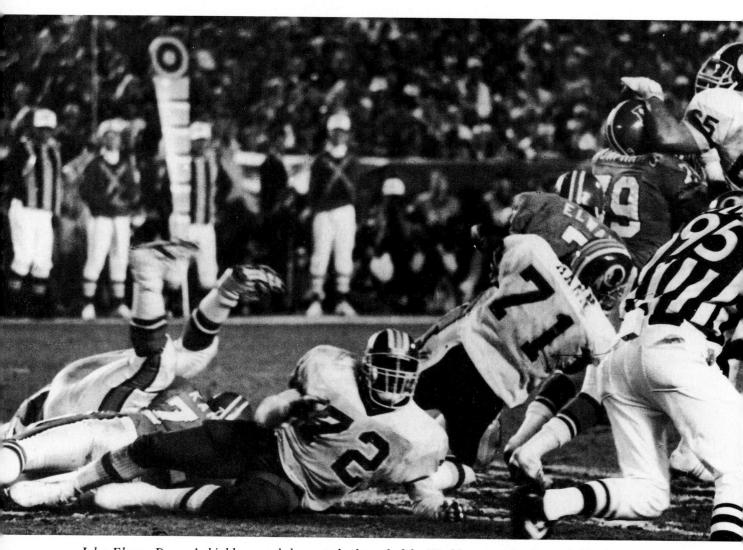

John Elway, Denver's highly regarded quarterback, sacked by Washington defensive end Charles Mann (71). On the ground is defensive end Dexter Manley (72). (Washington Redskins)

After the fourth Washington kickoff of the quarter, the Skins' defense allowed Denver only three plays, the last of which ended with an Elway pass into the hands of Washington defensive back Barry Wilburn. With the ball on the Skin 22-yard line, Timmy Smith broke off left tackle and sped 43 yards before he was finally run out of bounds. Williams completed two passes to Sanders, having his greatest day ever catching the football, then tried a different receiver, tight end Clint Didier, who caught it in the end zone. With Ali Haji-Sheikh's fifth extra point of the quarter, the Redskins led 35–10.

The quarter finally and mercifully came to an end for the Broncos, who had just suffered the ignominy of having allowed the most points ever scored in a single quarter, not just in Super Bowl annals, but in the entire history of NFL playoffs. Even the Chicago Bears, when they demolished the Redskins 73–0 in 1940, did not accumulate 35 points in a single period of play.

None of the 73,302 spectators in Jack Murphy Stadium, nor the several thousand in the press boxes, expected the Broncos to come back after such a second-quarter humiliation. And they did not. The Washington defense held them scoreless through the final two periods of play. Washington

276

Doug Williams lines up behind center Jeff Bostic in Super Bowl XXII, a sight the Denver Broncos would, in retrospect, wish they had never seen. In the second quarter, rewriting the Super Bowl record book, Williams threw four touchdown passes. (Washington Redskins)

Tight end Cling Didier (86) exults in the arms of Jeff Bostic after catching Doug Williams's fourth touchdown pass of the second quarter of Super Bowl XXII. Coming over to add his congratulations is wide receiver Ricky Sanders. (Washington Redskins)

A symbol of triumph from linebacker Monte Coleman after the Redskins destroyed the Broncos in super Bowl XXII. (Washington Redskins)

It was all over with 9:11 still to go in the fourth quarter. (Washington Redskins)

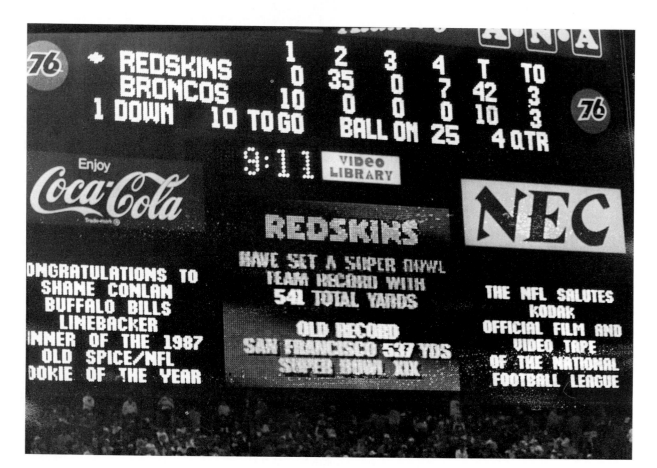

added one final score in the fourth quarter when Timmy Smith carried the ball three times for 32, seven, and four yards and a touchdown. The final score: Washington 42, Denver 10.

The record books needed a lot of updating as the jubilant Redskins left the field for the locker room and the traditional postgame celebrations. Besides the incredible second-quarter team stats, Doug Williams had passed for more yards than any player in the history of the Super Bowl, 340; Ricky Sanders had caught many of those passes for 193 yards, another Super Bowl mark;

and Timmy Smith had gained more yards rushing than any other runner since the Roman numerals had begun back in the 1960s, 204 in all. When all was said and done, the first black to quarterback a team in the Super Bowl, Doug Williams, was also recognized as the game's Most Valuable Player.

Inside the locker room, the Vince Lombardi Trophy was accepted by exuberant owner Jack Kent Cooke and exhilarated coach Joe Gibbs. It was the Washington Redskins' second NFL world championship of the decade.

SUPER BOWL XXII

Site: Jack Murphy Stadium, San Diego, CA

Date: January 31, 1988

Weather: 60 degrees, sunny

Attendance: 73,302

Gross receipts: $27,100,000

Player shares: $36,000 winner, $18,000 loser

LINEUPS

Redskins	Offense		Broncos
Ricky Sanders	WR		Vance Johnson
Joe Jacoby	LT		Dave Studdard
Raleigh McKenzie	LG		Keith Bishop
Jeff Bostic	C		Mike Freeman
R.C. Thielemann	RG		Stefan Humphries
Mark May	RT		Ken Lanier
Don Warren	TE		Clarence Kay
Gary Clark	WR		Mark Jackson
Doug Williams	QB		John Elway
Clint Didier	TE	RB	Gene Lang
Timmy Smith	RB		Sammy Winder
Ali Haji-Sheikh	K		Rich Karlis

LINEUPS (CONT)

Redskins	Defense		Broncos
Charles Mann	LE		Andre Townsend
Dave Butz	LT	NT	Greg Kragen
Darryl Grant	RT	RE	Rulon Jones
Dexter Manley	RE	OLB	Simon Fletcher
Mel Kaufman	LB	ILB	Karl Mecklenberg
Neal Olkewicz	MLB	ILB	Rickey Hunley
Monte Coleman	LB	OLB	Jim Ryan
Darrell Green	CB		Mark Haynes
Barry Wilburn	CB		Steve Wilson
Alvin Walton	S		Dennis Smith
Todd Bowles	S		Tony Lilly
Steve Cox	P		Mike Horan

Coaches

Joe Gibbs		Dan Reeves

SCORING

	1st Qtr	2nd Qtr	3rd Qtr	4th Qtr	Final Score
Redskins	0	35	0	7	42
Broncos	10	0	0	0	10

Before the start of the 1988 season, Redskins executive vice president John Kent Cooke observed that the team whose overall operations he directed from the front office had the opportunity to immortalize itself as "the team of the decade." After all, it had been to three Super Bowls and won two of them, and a fourth—or even a fifth—was not out of the question.

Those of a less positive bent were quick to remind Washington fans that none of the last three Super Bowl victors—the 49ers of XIX, the Bears of XX, the Giants of XXI—had won a single playoff game since.

Expectations were high, however, as the regular season approached. The Redskins had handily won their last three games of the preseason, and were to open before a national television audience on Monday Night Football against the Giants, a team they had beaten twice the year before.

In addition, team owner Jack Kent Cooke announced that he and his family were going to build and pay for a 78,000-seat

NOTES AND QUOTES FROM SUPER BOWL XXII

You can be right some of the time. . . . Dr. Z, Paul Zimmerman, in *Sports Illustrated*: "The brightest star going into the game is, of course, Denver quarterback John Elway. . . . [Doug] Williams is tough physically and emotionally . . . a streak thrower, and when he gets hot, few people can gobble up yards as quickly. . . . But the guess here is that Denver will win 38–31 in a shootout."

You can be very close. . . . Beano Cook of ESPN: "I predict the Redskins to win it, 41–10 [the final was 42–10]." When asked why he predicted an underdog to win by such a decisive margin, he said with a shrug, "The Redskins are the only team in Washington without too many lawyers."

Advertisers had to divvy up $1.35 million a minute for commercial time during Super Bowl XXII, the highest amount ever paid in the history of television advertising [prime evening hours on regular television ordinarily were selling for about $120,000 a half-minute]. To the advertisers' chagrin, however, the game drew only a 41.9 rating and a 62% share of all TV in use, making it the lowest-rated Super Bowl since the 1974 matching of the Minnesota Vikings and Miami Dolphins.

Doug Williams, after the 1000th time he had been reminded of his race during the media-blitz week preceding Super Bowl XXII: "Joe Gibbs and Bobby Beathard didn't bring me in to be the first black quarterback in the Super Bowl. They brought me in to be the quarterback of the Washington Redskins."

Jack Kent Cooke: "I was petrified almost to the point of immobility. I thought, 'What has happened to our Washington Redskins? Down 10–0.' Then it turns out to be better than anything in my sports career. . . . Joe Gibbs is a hell of a coach. What a job he did."

John Elway, when asked afterwards what was the single worst moment in the game for him: "The second quarter."

stadium for the Redskins. It would be an open-air stadium with natural grass. "This will be a stadium second to none, for a team second to none, and for fans second to none," Cooke said.

There were a few new faces on the '88 Redskins. Most notable was All-Pro outside linebacker Wilber Marshall, a free agent lured to the Skins from the Chicago Bears by one of the healthiest financial packages ever offered to a defensive player. Another who would see action right away was kicker Chip Lohmiller, a second-round draft choice from Minnesota.

A number of veterans had departed. Running back George Rogers, who had lost his job to Timmy Smith, was released. And quarterback Jay Schroeder, who had been demoted to serve as backup to Doug Williams, had asked to be traded and had gotten his wish when general manager Bobby Beathard struck a deal with the Los Angeles Raiders. Also waived were such familiar faces as linebacker Rich Milot, tight end Clint Didier, defensive back Vernon Dean, running back Keith Griffin, and placekicker Ali Haji-Sheikh.

In opening the 1988 regular season in the New Jersey Meadowlands, the Redskins were looking for their third consecutive victory over the Giants since the New Yorkers had knocked them out of the playoffs two years earlier. But the Skins saw a 13–3 halftime lead disappear in a rush of 24 unanswered points by the Giants in the second half. Two touchdown passes by Williams, to Kelvin Bryant and Ricky Sanders, and a 100-yard rushing effort by Timmy Smith were not enough, and the crown-bearing Skins fell, 27–20, in their '88 debut.

At home the following week, however, they alternately depressed and exhilarated the sellout crowd at RFK. Twice in the fourth quarter they dropped nine points behind, but each time they rallied. The last was enough to win the game, when Doug Williams tossed a touchdown pass to Kelvin Bryant and rookie Chip Lohmiller kicked a field goal. The final score was 30–29. Williams turned in the most productive effort of his passing career that Sunday, completing 30 of 52 passes for 430 yards, the most since Sammy Baugh set the club's single-game mark of 446 back in 1948.

A 17–10 win over the much-improved Philadelphia Eagles the next week and the Redskins looked like they were regaining their championship-season form. Coach Joe Gibbs said, "The best thing about our team right now, I think, is that I see a lot of heart. We've had hard-fought games. We have a team that is going to give a real effort."

During the next week, however, Doug Williams was rushed to the hospital after an appendicitis attack. It was indeed a blow, with the team having sent Jay Schroeder to the West Coast and the AFC. The only quarterback left was Mark Rypien, who had been on injured reserve the two previous

seasons and had thus far in his NFL career thrown only 14 passes. Rypien rose to the occasion, however, when the Skins traveled to Phoenix to face the newly relocated Cardinals. He completed 26 of 41 passes for 303 yards, including three touchdowns. Unfortunately, the rest of the team could not match Rypien's performances. The defense allowed the Cardinals 30 points that day, and the Skins lost.

When the Giants came to RFK the next week, there was a four-way tie for first place in the NFC East. Having 2–2–0 records besides the Redskins were the Giants, Cardinals, and Cowboys. When the Giants left, Washington was in second place. In a true heartbreaker, the Redskins rallied from a 24–9 deficit in the third period with two touchdown passes from Rypien, both to Ricky Sanders, which brought them to within a point of the Giants. With just over two minutes remaining, Rypien got the Skins to the New York 19-yard line, but Chip Lohmiller, who had missed what proved to be a crucial extra point earlier, missed the field goal.

Everything came together at Dallas, however. The Cowboys, who were sinking into what would turn out to be their worst season in 25 years, were pushovers. Mark Rypien continued to fill in masterfully for the recovering Doug Williams, completing 13 of 21 passes, three for touchdowns. In so doing, he increased his quarterback rating to 110.3, the highest in the NFC at the time and second in the entire NFL, behind only Boomer Esiason of the Bengals. Kelvin Bryant also turned in his first 100-yard-plus rushing day, gaining 118 on 23 carries. The final score was a sweatless 35–17 triumph for the Redskins.

Two more wins over the Cardinals and the Green Bay Packers and Washington had raised its record to 5–3–0 at the season's midpoint. The Giants were also 5–3–0 to share the divisional lead, and the Cardinals and the Eagles were only a game behind at 4–4–0.

Doug Williams was back to lead the Redskins into the second half of the season, but he had hardly been missed because of the extraordinary job turned in by Mark Rypien, who had built a quarterback rating of 114.7 by completing 70 of 116 passes (60.3%) for 1.075 yards. He had thrown 12 touchdown passes and only three interceptions.

Kelvin Bryant had truly come into his own by midseason, taking the starting running back position from Timmy Smith, and now led the team in rushing with 453 yards (a 4.8-yard average per carry) and in pass receptions with 36. Dexter Manley, as usual, led the team in quarterback sacks, with seven.

The second half of the season got off on the same dismal note as the first half had—a loss, and a shattering one at that. Down in Houston, the Oilers manhandled the Skins unmercifully, beating them 41–17. It was the fourth-worst margin of defeat for Washington since Joe Gibbs had taken over in 1981.

"I think this was a real low point for us," Gibbs said after the game. "I also think it's going to have to be a rallying point for us, because I really feel like our next seven games will be the toughest we've played since I've been here with the Redskins." The

Art Monk makes a spectacular touchdown catch in a 1988 game against the St. Louis Cardinals. Monk holds the NFL record for most receptions in a single season, set in 1984 when he caught 106 passes. (Washington Redskins)

schedule he was referring to was indeed a difficult one. Awaiting Washington were the Saints (7–1–0), the Bears (7–1–0), the 49ers (5–3–0), the Browns (5–3–0), the Eagles (4–4–0), the Cowboys (2–6–0), and the Bengals (7–1–0)—three teams heading their respective divisions and all but Dallas clearly in the running for the playoffs.

The loss to Houston did serve as a rallying point, at least for one game. Doug Williams had his best game since coming back from his appendectomy operation, throwing touchdown passes to Gary Clark and Ricky Sanders and bootlegging the ball around end for another. He was 20 of 28 for 299 yards. And, with the score tied at 24–24, he maneuvered the Skins deep into New Orleans territory, where Chip Lohmiller booted a 23-yard field goal with 47 seconds left to win the game.

The rally fizzled the following week, however. The Bears came to town revenge-minded over the ousters from the playoffs that had been doled out to them by Washington in each of the last two years. Chicago rushed to a 20–0 lead, and the Skins were never able to get back in the game. In fact, the Bears could do almost nothing wrong that day. They scored a total of 34 points and held the Redskins to 17. The Chicago defense allowed the Skins a mere 28 yards rushing all day, sacked Williams and Rypien three times, and intercepted them five times.

Things did not get any better the next week out in San Francisco. The 49ers, like the Redskins, had a record of 6–5–0 and were in a tough fight to earn a berth in the playoffs. Washington was also missing its key running back, Kelvin Bryant, who was out with a knee injury. In addition, it was a Monday night game, and the Redskins had been beaten in 10 of their last 18 appearances on Monday Night Football.

Mistakes had haunted the Redskins all season. Turnovers and costly penalties had already lost several games for Washington. "We can't keep making the number of mistakes we've been making and expect to win," Joe Gibbs warned. "Our schedule does not allow for us to make these kinds of mistakes. We have given up field position far too many times." The coach was correct. Four turnovers, two fumbles, and two interceptions resulted in 21 points for the 49ers that Monday night. And a 95-yard punt return for a touchdown by San Francisco's John Taylor demoralized the Redskins further. The final score was San Francisco 37, Washington 21.

There was still the chance of a playoff spot when the Cleveland Browns came to Washington, but the 6–6–0 Redskins trailed the Giants, Cardinals, and Eagles by a full game in the NFC East. The chance diminished considerably when the Skins blew a 13–10 lead late in the fourth quarter. With less than two minutes remaining, Cleveland's Earnest Byner burst up the middle on a draw play for the game-winning touchdown. It constituted Washington's first three-game losing streak since 1981.

The Redskins managed to keep their postseason hopes alive the following week, although just barely, when they came back in Philadelphia to knock off the Eagles. Down 19–10 with less than six minutes left in the game, Doug Williams led a drive to the Philadelphia two-yard line, then rifled a shot to tight end Terry Orr in the end zone. The defense held and Washington got the ball back. With one second on the scoreboard, Chip Lohmiller booted a 44-yard field goal, and the Redskins broke their losing streak with a 20–19 victory.

Dallas was the only team on the second half of the Redskins' 1988 schedule that was not playoff-bound. In fact, it was suffering through its worst season since entering the league in 1960, the year it lost 11 and tied one of its 12 games. The Cowboys had won only two of 14 games when they came to Washington for the next to last game of the '88 season.

But the Redskins, certainly not out of sympathy for their arch-rivals, turned the ball over five times. The result was a 24–17 loss and the Redskins were officially eliminated from playoff consideration.

Another loss the following week to the Bengals, 20–17, gave Joe Gibbs his first losing season (7–9–0) since coming to Washington.

As Gibbs put it when the disappointing season was finally over, "We played a tough schedule and lost a lot of close games. We turned the ball over far too many times on offense, and we didn't come up with nearly enough turnovers on defense."

The passing game had been good. Between the two of them, Doug Williams and Mark Rypien completed more passes (327) and gained more yardage passing (4,136) than any other quarterback in Redskins history. Three receivers had excellent years: Ricky Sanders (73 receptions for 1,148 yards), Art Monk (72 for 946 yards), and Gary Clark (59 for 892 yards).

The rushing game had left a good deal to be desired. Kelvin Bryant had been having a fine year until he was sidelined with a knee injury in the 10th game of the season. Rookie running back Jamie Morris from Michigan came on at the end of the season to handle the bulk of Washington's running game. Dexter Manley dropped opposing quarterbacks the most times (9), as he had most every year in the 1980s. Dave Butz, now 38 years old, set a club-service record, breaking the mark of 196 games played by center Len Hauss (1964–77).

The 1980s were still not over, however. Another season loomed ahead, another chance for the Skins to establish themselves as the team of the decade.

* * *

The 1989 football season began with one very familiar face missing from the Washington Redskins front office. General manager Bobby Beathard, the main architect of the Washington teams that went to three Super Bowls in the 1980s, had retired. He would, however, appear on the nation's televisions during the season, offering his insights and analyses from the broadcast booth.

The Redskins went to the 1989 college draft with a mission. Joe Gibbs was intent on recharging the team's running game. With Timmy Brown, who flashed with such dazzle in Super Bowl XXII, out of the picture and Kelvin Bryant's brittle knee an unknown and worrisome factor, the team was in desperate need of a stable and respectable ground game.

In the tradition of George Allen's "The future is now" philosophy, the Redskins began to deal. Their first round draft choice that year had been awarded to the Chicago Bears in compensation for signing free agent, all-pro linebacker Wilber Marshall the year before. Their second round choice, along with their first round choice in 1990, was then traded to the Atlanta Falcons for veteran running back Gerald Riggs. Then, they swapped running back Mike Oliphant, the Skins' third round draft choice in 1988, for the more proven Earnest Byner of the Cleveland Browns.

Riggs, a first round draft choice of the Falcons in 1982, had been Atlanta's premier running back since 1984. He led the NFC in rushing with 1,719 yards in 1985, and went to the Pro Bowl that year, and in 1986 and 1987 as well. Byner had been a mainstay in the Cleveland backfield since they drafted him in 1984. In 1985, he rushed for 1,002 yards.

The Redskins played an additional preseason game before the 1989 season because they were scheduled to meet the Buffalo Bills in the annual Hall of Fame game in

Canton, Ohio. Washington won that contest 31–6, but did it without quarterback Doug Williams who was suffering from a lower back injury.

The Redskins went on to defeat three of their next four opponents in the preseason, knocking off the Steelers, 21–14, the Dolphins, 35–21, and the Saints, 26–21. Their only loss came at the hands of the Vikings, 24–13.

The opener of the regular season pitted the winner of Super Bowl XXI, the New York Giants, against the Skins who won the following year's Super Bowl. The Giants came down to RFK Stadium for the Monday night game having beaten Washington in both their encounters of 1988, and in seven of their last ten meetings.

The Redskins were still without the services of the injured Doug Williams, and so his replacement of the year before, Mark Rypien, once again got the call. He spearheaded an offense that utilized three wide receivers—Art Monk, Gary Clark, and Ricky Sanders, and just one running back, Gerald Riggs.

The national television audience was treated to an exceptionally exciting game that Monday night between two teams with very real aspirations for the NFC East title. The Giants led 14–3 at halftime but Washington came back and finally took a 24–21 lead with less than eight minutes left in the game. Raul Allegre, however, kicked a field goal to tie it and then, on the last play of the game, kicked another, a 52-yarder, to give New York a 27–24 win.

The following week it was another serious NFC contender, the Philadelphia Eagles. In a wild offensive battle—"the strangest game anyone here has ever been associated with," according to defensive end Dexter Manley—the Redskins saw a 30–14 lead trickle away. Still, with 1 minute 16 seconds to play, Washington had the lead 37–35 and the football on the Philadelphia 19 yardline. But then Gerald Riggs fumbled the ball to Philadelphia's Al Harris who then lateralled it to defensive back Wes Hopkins. The fleet Hopkins raced 77 yards with it down the sideline, all the way to the Washington 4 yardline. Moments later Randall Cunningham pitched the game-winning touchdown to Eagles tight end Keith Jackson.

The one bright note in the otherwise disappointing game was the revitalization of the Washington running game. Gerald Riggs rushed for 221 yards on 29 carries, a career high for him and a team record.

It was a subdued Washington team that went down to Texas to play the Dallas Cowboys with whom they shared the cellar of the NFC East. The hapless Cowboys, on their way to the worst season since they went 0–11–1 in 1960 in their first year in the league, however, allowed the Skins to get back on the winning track.

Second-year running back Jamie Morris replaced an injured Gerald Riggs, who left the game with a bruised chest, and gained 100 yards on 26 carries. The defense intercepted four Dallas passes, and held the Cowboys to a mere 34 yards rushing and 190 total yards. The result was a decisive 30–7 victory over the ever-rival Cowboys.

Wins over the New Orleans Saints and the Phoenix Cardinals lifted the Redskins above the .500 mark and reminded Washington fans that they were still very much in the running for postseason action in 1989. A win against the Giants up at the Meadowlands would give the Skins a tie for first place in the NFC East. But the Giants continued to frustrate the Redskins. The Giants defeated the Redskins 20–17, dealing the Redskins their ninth loss in their last twelve encounters and knocking Washington a full two games out of first place in the divisional title race.

A victory over the Tampa Bay Buccaneers and a loss to the Los Angeles Raiders brought the Redskins to a 4–4–0 record at midseason. The Redskins were set to start the second half of the season against the Dallas Cowboys, the conference patsy with a record of 0–8–0. Doug Williams was back and he would be starting at quarterback for the Skins. Then, disaster struck. The hapless Cowboys managed to score 13 points and beat the Skins 13–3. It was demoralizing. "We're groping for answers right now," coach Joe Gibbs said after the game. "We've got to take a good look at ourselves. . . . We've got to find some way to turn this thing around."

They did the next week, defeating a favored Eagles team 10–3. They did not the week after, falling to the Super Bowl–bound Denver Broncos, 14–10.

After that, however, Washington did turn things around. They won their next five games in a row, triumphing over the Chicago Bears, Phoenix Cardinals, San Diego Chargers, Atlanta Falcons, and Seattle Seahawks.

The victory over the Chargers was Joe Gibbs's 100th victory (regular season and playoffs) as a head coach, a milestone of sorts. And the five-game win streak at the end of the season was the first time Washington had done that since the Super Bowl season of 1987.

But it was not enough to get the Redskins into the playoffs. With the surge of the Giants and Eagles in the NFC East, Washington was eliminated from postseason play in the 15th week of NFL play. Despite that disappointment, the revived Redskins team went out and decimated the Seahawks in their last game of the season 29–0.

The Skins ended the 1989 season with a record of 10–6–0. Sportswriters pointed to the surprising loss to the Cowboys as the single self-destructive game of the season. Coach Joe Gibbs did not agree. "I think back to that Philadelphia game, the loss in the second game of the season. We felt we had the game won, then the fumble, and that wacky lateral. I think about that when I think about our not making the playoffs."

There were a lot of other factors as well. Key injuries, the loss of Dexter Manley because of his suspension due to drug problems, the sudden and forced initiation of many young and inexperienced plays into the lineup.

Still, 10–6–0 was quite respectable.

Their triumverate of receivers proved to be the best in the league: Monk, Clark, and Sanders each gained more than 1,000 yards on pass receptions (1,186, 1,229, 1,138 yards respectively). It was only the second time in NFL history that three receivers on the same team broke the millenary mark (John Jefferson, Kellen Winslow, and Charlie Joiner did it for the San Diego Chargers in 1980).

Gerald Riggs, hobbled by a variety of injuries, managed to gain 834 yards rushing, with an average of 4.1 yards per carry. Earnest Byner added another 580 yards and Jamie Morris 336. Mark Rypien completed 280 of 476 passes for 3,768 yards, 22 touchdowns, and an overall NFL rating of 88.1.

Strong safety Alvin Walton led the team with 79 tackles and 56 assists as well as four interceptions. Charles Mann recorded ½ sacks more than the nine Dexter Manley had before ending his season.

It was not the end to the decade that Jack Kent Cooke, John Kent Cooke, and Joe Gibbs had wanted. Washington's claim to "Team of the Decade" fell by the wayside. But, with a young, regenerated team, prospects for the 1990s looked bright.

It had begun in 1937 in Washington with an NFL championship, a gift to the city from team founder George Preston Marshall. Over the years, such luminaries as Sammy Baugh, Wayne Millner, Bill Dudley, Gene Brito, Sonny Jurgensen, Bobby Mitchell, Charley Taylor, Billy Kilmer, Larry Brown, Chris Hanburger, Len Hauss, Ken Houston, John Riggins, Joe Theismann, the Over-the-Hill gang, and the Hogs have bejeweled the skies above Griffith and RFK stadiums.

There have been exciting games, unforgettable moments, dazzling performances, unique characters, and more than 50 years of sustained entertainment. And it is still going strong.

Hail to the Redskins.